D1649175

Measuring Library Performance
principles and techniques

Measuring Library Performance
principles and techniques

Peter Brophy

facet publishing

Published by Facet Publishing
7 Ridgmount Street, London WC1E 7AE
www.facetpublishing.co.uk

Facet Publishing is wholly owned by CILIP: the Chartered Institute of Library
and Information Professionals.

First published 2006
Reprinted 2008

British Library Cataloguing in Publication Data
A catalogue record for this book is available from the British Library.

ISBN 978-1-85604-593-3

Typeset in 11/14pt Caslon 540 BT and Geometric by Facet Publishing.
Printed and made in great Britain by MPG Books Ltd, Bodmin, Cornwall.

Contents

List of figures

List of tables

Preface

There are two competing maxims concerning performance measurement:

If you can't measure it, you can't manage it.

and

What gets measured, gets managed.

This book is an attempt to steer a course between these two, perhaps overly cynical, viewpoints. Performance measurement is vital to management. Without clear and reliable information about what is happening within an organization and in its interactions with its customers and suppliers, it is impossible to make well founded decisions to guide future development or even to monitor the effects of decisions that have been made in the past. Equally, there is always a danger that managerial attention focuses on the data that happen to be available, rather than on the rounded picture of all activities, including those which are by their nature very difficult to measure. The effect of this is that the wrong activities are prioritized and incorrect assumptions made about performance. So both dangers – attempting to manage without measuring performance and managing sub-optimally by concentrating on the information that happens to be available – need to be avoided.

Libraries have been measuring their performance for a very long time. However, whereas for many years the key measure was the size and quality of the bookstock, in more recent times attention has shifted towards the effects that the library has on the population it is intended to serve. Measures concerning stock and the provision of access to local and remote resources remain important but it is now recognized that, without a user focus, it is all too easy to lose sight of the purpose for which libraries exist and are funded. For this reason, this book is organized with its initial emphasis on the user – on satisfaction and impact – and only then on the library's processes. It is hoped that this will indicate the priority that needs to be given to these issues.

Performance measurement can never be more than a tool. Its techniques and approaches are designed to help managers to discover how well their services are performing, to identify where action is needed and to monitor what is being achieved. It may also be used to support advocacy for libraries. Whatever the intention, it must be undertaken within a broader planning framework, which sets the overall mission of the library and its strategic direction. It is supportive of that mission and strategy and must never be allowed to take on a life of its own.

This book attempts to summarize what is now a very broad subject area, to highlight current issues and initiatives and to point to areas where further development of both methodologies and practice is needed. It is hoped that it will be of interest to library practitioners, to those undertaking research in the field and to students of librarianship. Many of the first group have been among the most influential researchers and developers of performance management techniques. The final group represents the future, and those in this group will no doubt make their own contributions in due course.

I would like to acknowledge with gratitude the very many colleagues who have contributed to my understanding of this field. I hope that this book distils their wisdom adequately but of course responsibility for any errors remains mine alone. My defence is that, as Francis Bacon wrote, 'truth comes out of error more readily than out of confusion'!

A note on terminology

In this book, the following terminology is used:

- *Performance measurement*, to include 'performance assessment' and 'performance evaluation'. It is recognized that performance measurement is often an inexact science, especially when qualitative methods are used to explore human aspects of library use. Some authors prefer to speak of performance indicators to emphasize that what is 'measured' always requires interpretation.

- *Users.* A debate on the most appropriate terminology to describe those who use library services flares up from time to time. There are proponents of 'customer' (which has the advantage of emphasizing the need for customer service along the lines pursued in many service industries); 'client' (which suggests a relationship with a professional adviser, as might be offered by a lawyer or accountant); 'patron', which at one time appeared to be the favourite of library systems vendors and is still quite widely used in the USA; 'reader' (which now seems curiously old-fashioned – do those who patronize libraries no longer read as much as they used to perhaps?); and various other options. Some of those involved in electronic library developments have even suggested using the expression 'digital consumer'. 'User' is the traditional term and is retained in this volume.

Peter Brophy

Acronyms and abbreviations

ACRL	Association of College and Research Libraries
AHRC	Arts and Humanities Research Council
AIA	American Institute of Architects (USA)
ALA	American Library Association
ALT	alternative text
ANCOVA	analysis of covariance
ANOVA	analysis of variance
ARL	Association of Research Libraries (USA)
ATAG	Authoring Tools Accessibility Guidelines
BPR	business process reengineering
BSI	British Standards Institution
CALIMERA	Cultural Applications: Local Institutions Mediating Electronic Resource Access (EC funded project)
CAMILE	Concerted Action on Management Information for Libraries in Europe (EC funded project)
CAQDAS	Computer Assisted Qualitative Data Analysis Software
CBAM	Concerns Based Adoption Model
CCI	current collecting intensity (Conspectus)
CERLIM	Centre for Research in Library & Information Management, Manchester Metropolitan University (UK)
CETIS	Centre for Educational Technology Interoperability Standards (UK)
CHEA	Council for Higher Education Accreditation (USA)
CIBER	Centre for Information Behaviour and the Evaluation of Research, University College London (UK)
CIBSE	Chartered Institute of Building Services Engineers (UK)

CILIP	Chartered Institute of Library and Information Professionals (UK)
CIPFA	Chartered Institute of Public Finance and Accountancy (UK)
CMM	Capability Maturity Model
COUNTER	Counting Online Usage of Networked Electronic Resources
CRM	customer relationship management
CSS	Cascading Style Sheets
CVM	contingent valuation method
DCLG	Department for Communities and Local Government (UK)
DCMS	Department for Culture, Media and Sport (UK)
DD	document delivery
DDA	Disability Discrimination Act (UK)
DECIDE	Decision Support Models: a Decision Support System for European Academic and Public Libraries (EC funded project)
DECIMAL	Decision-making in Libraries: Decision Research for the Development of Integrated Library Systems (EC funded project)
DLA	deep log analysis
DNER	Distributed National Electronic Resource (now the JISC IE)
DRC	Disability Rights Commission (UK)
EBIP	evidence-based information practice
EBL	evidence-based librarianship
EBP	evidence-based practice
ECS	existing collection strength (Conspectus)
EDNER	Formative Evaluation of the DNER (project)
EFQM	European Foundation for Quality Management
EMOHA	East Midlands Oral History Archive (UK)
EQLIPSE	Evaluation and Quality in Library Performance: System for Europe (EC funded project)
EU	European Union
FLICC	Federal Library and Information Center Committee (US)
FLINK	Federal Library and Information Network (US)
FTE	full-time equivalent

GLO	generic learning outcome
GRP	gross regional product
HCI	human–computer interaction
HEFCE	Higher Education Funding Council for England
HELICON	Health Libraries and Information Confederation (UK)
HTML	HyperText Markup Language
ICOLC	International Coalition of Library Consortia
ICT	information and communications technologies
IE	information environment (JISC, UK)
IFLA	International Federation of Library Associations and Institutions
IIP	Investors in People
ILL	interlibrary loan
IMLS	Institute of Museum and Library Services (USA)
IMRI	Information Management Research Institute, University of Northumbria at Newcastle (UK)
IPR	intellectual property rights
ISO	International Organization for Standardization
I-SRC	I-Society Research & Consultancy Group, University of Northumbria at Newcastle (UK)
IUMPI	Information Use Management and Policy Institute (USA)
JANET	Joint Academic Network (UK)
JCR	Journal Citation Reports
JISC	Joint Information Systems Committee (UK)
LIRG	Library and Information Research Group (SIG of CILIP)
LISU	Library and Information Statistics Unit, Loughborough University (UK)
LoU	levels of use
LSC	Learning and Skills Council (UK)
MANOVA	multivariate analysis of variance
MCDM	multi-criteria decision making
MIMAS	Manchester Information and Associated Services (UK)
MINES	Measuring the Impact of Networked Electronic Services (ARL New Measures Programme)
MINSTREL	Management Information Software Tool: Research in Libraries (EC funded project)
MLA	Museums, Libraries and Archives Council (UK)

MLE	managed learning environment
NBL	narrative-based librarianship
NBP	narrative-based practice
NCES	National Center for Education Statistics (USA)
NIACE	National Institute of Adult Continuing Education (UK)
NISO	National Information Standards Organization (USA)
NOAA	National Oceanic and Atmospheric Administration (USA)
OAI-PMH	Open Archives Initiative – Protocol for Metadata Harvesting
OBE	outcome-based evaluation
OCUL	Ontario Council of University Libraries (Canada)
OPAC	Online Public Access Catalogue
PLG	Public Libraries Group (UK)
PN	The People's Network (UK)
PROBE	Post-occupancy Review Of Buildings and their Engineering
QMM	Quality Maturity Model
RATER	Reliability, Assurance, Tangibles, Empathy, Responsiveness (SERVQUAL methodology)
RCT	randomized controlled trial
RDF	Resource Description Framework
RDN	Resource Discovery Network (now Intute) (UK)
REMI	Regional Economic Models Inc. (USA)
RLG	Research Libraries Group (USA)
ROI	return on investment
RSC	Regional Support Centre (JISC, UK)
SAILS	Standardized Assessment of Information Literacy Skills (ARL New Measures Programme)
SCI	Science Citation Index
SCL	Society of Chief Librarians (public libraries, UK)
SCONUL	Society of College, National and University Libraries (formerly the Standing Conference of National and University Libraries) (UK)
SD	standard deviation
SE	standard error
SIG	special interest group
SoC	stages of concern

SPICE	Setting; Perspective; Intervention; Comparison; Evaluation (EBP methodology)
SPSS	Statistical Package for the Social Sciences
TEAL	The Effective Academic Library
TQM	total quality management
TR	technical report
UAAG	User Agents Accessibility Guidelines
UCE	University of Central England (UK)
UNESCO	United Nations Educational, Scientific and Cultural Organization
VITAL	The Value and Impact of IT Access in Public Libraries (project)
VLE	virtual learning environment
VRE	virtual research environment
W3C	World Wide Web Consortium
WAI	Web Accessibility Initiative
WCAG	Web Content Accessibility Guidelines
WLN	Western Library Network (USA)
XML	eXtensible Markup Language

1

Background

the ultimate criterion for assessing the quality of a service is its capability for meeting the user needs it is intended to serve, and . . . the value of a service must ultimately be judged in terms of the beneficial effects accruing from its use.

(Richard Orr)

■ Introduction

Performance measurement is central to library management, since without a firm grasp on what is actually being achieved it is impossible to move forward to improved service – or even to maintain the status quo. Measuring achievements against aims and objectives reveals the relevance of the service and enables managers to judge whether staff effort and resources are being used in the best possible ways. Gathering data on levels of service provides a basis for comparative assessments, either against similar organizations or against guidelines and standards. Analysing the effects the service is having on its users enables evidence of impacts and benefits to be presented, providing the ultimate justification for the service's existence.

Librarians and other information professionals have long been interested in measuring the performance of their services. Important theoretical work was undertaken in the 1940s by S. C. Bradford at the Science Museum in London (Bradford, 1948), influencing the design of the highly innovative National Lending Library for Science and Technology, later to become part of the British Library. In the 1960s Philip Morse published a groundbreaking book on library effectiveness (Morse, 1968), while in the early 1970s the concept of the 'goodness' of library services was explored by Richard Orr (Orr, 1973). He suggested that it is important to distinguish between the question 'How good is this service?', which is a matter of quality, and 'How much good does this service do?', which he characterized as a question of value. In 1977, F. W. Lancaster's *Measurement and Evaluation of Library Services* appeared, marking the entry of the topic into the mainstream of library practice (Lancaster, 1977). During the 1980s among the most influential figures in this field were Nancy Van House and Charles McClure: their work is well summarized in the influential *Measuring Academic Library Performance*, published in 1990 (Van House, Weil and McClure, 1990). In the same year José-Marie Griffiths and Don King prepared a manual on public library performance indicators for the British Library Research and Development Department (Griffiths and King, 1990).

During the 1990s considerable attention was paid to the measurement of the performance of electronic as well as traditional services. Alongside the highly innovative Electronic Libraries Programme in the UK, a study of academic libraries' services, entitled *The Effective Academic Library* (TEAL), suggested that there were five issues that needed to be assessed in order to evaluate the hybrid (i.e. physical + electronic) library:

- *integration*: the level of integration being achieved between the mission, aims and objectives of the parent institution and those of the library
- *user satisfaction*: whether the services offered were regarded as satisfactory by the users and potential users
- *delivery*: whether stated objectives regarding services were being met and whether the volume of outputs was high
- *efficiency*: outputs related to resource input – how much was being achieved per unit of resource expended?
- *economy*: cost per student.

(Higher Education Funding Council for England, 1995)

In the USA Charles McClure and John Bertot were the leading researchers in the field of electronic service performance measurement. In 2001 they published an edited collection of contributions to this field under the title *Evaluating Networked Information Services* (McClure and Bertot, 2001). The Association of Research Libraries launched a New Measures initiative in 1999, which proved both innovative and practical – spin-offs have included the LibQUAL™ Programme (see Chapter 3, 'User satisfaction') and Project COUNTER (see Chapter 6, 'Inputs'). In Europe, the EQUINOX research and development project developed a set of indicators for the electronic library (Brinkley, 1999 – see also Chapter 6, 'Inputs'). Traditional services were not neglected. An International Standard (ISO 11620) for library performance indicators was developed (see Chapter 14, 'Standards') and the International Federation of Library Associations and Institutions (IFLA) is active in this area.

In recent years interest in rigorous performance measurement has been encouraged by a number of factors. One is simply the insistence of those who provide the funding for libraries that those responsible for expenditure of what is often public money should be fully accountable. Part of that accountability is the requirement to publish performance measures. Another is the emergence of evidence-based practice (EBP), originating in the health services and emphasizing that decision making should be based on the best possible evidence rather than on a manager's experience or intuition (see Chapter 2, 'Theoretical considerations'). A further influence has been the tendency towards inter-service comparisons, such as the requirement for public libraries to demonstrate 'best practice' and continual improvement on what is in effect a competitive scale. Finally, there is a general expectation that public services will be transparent – that what they do and how well they do it should be open to public scrutiny and comment.

■ The library in society

Libraries are at heart part of a social system; they exist to serve the needs of people, to help them live, learn and develop and to act as part of the social glue which holds communities together. Many stakeholders do not make direct use of the library service but they have a legitimate interest in whether it is as good as it could be.

The people the library has to consider when it undertakes a performance evaluation may thus include:

* those who actually use the library
   — in person
   — online
   — indirectly through others

- those who would appear to be potential users, but don't currently make use of the service
- those who have strategic interests in ensuring that the library service is in place, including those who simply believe that in a civilized society a library is 'a good thing'
- librarians of other institutions who see benefit in collaborating to share costs and resources
- those who provide the resources to enable the library to function
- people not yet born who will benefit from an institution which had the foresight to preserve and conserve information-based materials.

These people may well hold differing views and values, including negative ones, about libraries. All, however, have an interest in the results of library evaluation.

Placing the spotlight on people is a useful reminder that in essence the library is, as Rowena Cullen has written, 'a social construct, and performance measurement is a consequent social construct . . . [so that] we are free to both explore the definition of "library" being imposed by any one system of measurement, and to choose which definition of "library" to employ' (Cullen, 1999). More will be said of the library in its social context in succeeding chapters.

■ Delivering library services

An initial focus on people, as individuals and in society, leads to the question of the purpose of libraries. As Curtis and Dean (2004) of the UK Audit Commission put it, there is a need 'to challenge and decide what the service is for'. Clearly, however, we are in complex territory here for, as Cullen implies, the purpose of libraries varies according to their context and multiple purposes are pursued with differing priorities. Can we say anything useful in general terms?

Perhaps the most helpful statement derives from the observation that, of all the purposes libraries pursue, the commonest is enabling people to gain access to published information. Twenty-five years ago this would have been a hotly contested claim, since the live debate at that time was between the proponents of access and the supporters of collection development. With the rapid expansion of IT-based services and the realization that providing a large number of in-depth collections was hopelessly uneconomic, the access proponents have prevailed. Of course not every library will prioritize this purpose and performance measurement must always be carried out to fit the local requirement. Some libraries would now argue that their purpose is actually to enable learning, using that term in a broad sense, and it seems likely that in the near future the ground of the debate will shift again. Nevertheless, at the present time access is the most common denominator of library service.

Thus it is the question of how well the library fulfils this purpose for each of its stakeholder groups that lies at the heart of most library performance measurement. However, we need to recognize that there are many subsidiary questions. For example:

- Is information delivered when it is needed?
- Is the format the one best suited to the user?
- Is the infrastructure in place to support use, i.e. to go beyond mere access?
- Are there important supporting services, such as literacy development, reading groups and information skills training, which need to be taken into account?

It is fundamental to performance measurement that there should be a clear understanding of the purpose of the service being assessed. If purpose is inadequately or inappropriately defined then any indicators of performance will be incapable of use as a management tool. Evaluation is concerned with the assessment of value but value is meaningless out of context. For this reason the purpose for which libraries exist and against which, ultimately, their performance needs to be assessed must always be expressed clearly in advance of evaluation.

Translating purpose into real service for real people requires planning at both the strategic and detailed levels. It should always be remembered that measuring performance is an exercise in assessing the past. It is the *use* of that data to plan an improved future which is all important. And when those plans are implemented, it is the further use of data to monitor what is actually happening that allows management to fine tune developments or even change direction entirely.

Performance measurement is therefore helpful, and indeed essential, to planning. However, there is a danger that it can itself drive performance. If, for example, libraries are told that they will be placed in a national league table based on their opening hours, then not unnaturally they will seek to extend their opening hours. If the league table is based on the number of PCs they make available for public use, they will seek to maximize the number of available PCs. Yet neither of these indicators necessarily relates to what the people being served actually want or need and neither may reflect the priorities that the users would actually express if asked. Thus it is very important that performance measures are used as no more than an *aid* to planning and service delivery, not as the driving force behind it.

■ Electronic services

Many library services are nowadays delivered by electronic means and the performance of these services is of at least equal importance to that of their traditional equivalents – if such things exist, for some IT-based services are entirely new. Databases of various kinds, e-journals, e-books, e-learning materials, digitized images, research data, audio files and other media feature large in the library's resources. In this book, as far as possible the evaluation of traditional and electronic services is treated as a whole. The reason is that the key question is always one of meeting the user's needs, while the choice of how best to deliver the service is secondary. We are still in the era of the hybrid library, where some services are better delivered physically, others electronically and yet others as a blend of the two. Library performance measurement therefore needs to take a rounded and holistic view.

■ What is being measured?

Performance measurement often concentrates attention on one of the three Es: economy, efficiency and effectiveness. These relate to the questions Richard Orr was asking in the 1970s about 'library goodness' (see above). It is important to distinguish between them.

Economy

Economy is essentially asking, 'Is this service being delivered as cheaply as possible?'. It does not ask questions about whether it is the right service or whether it is well managed. However, where there are lots of competing services, economy may become the critical criterion.

Efficiency

Efficiency is concerned with lack of waste. It asks, 'How much output is being produced per unit input?'. It is essentially about processes, for example, how many units an employee turns out per hour. If competitors are more efficient they will be able to charge lower prices and still make profits – and possibly price you out of the market. For public sector services the effects of inefficiency can be equally traumatic.

Effectiveness

Effectiveness wants to know whether the right products are being delivered. It links together fundamental aims, often the aims of external stakeholders such as government, with longer-term effects or outcomes. An important part of effectiveness assessment is the estimation of value and impact, but these are the most difficult aspects of a service to measure.

And a fourth E?

In a report published in 1996, a team of researchers at the University of Sheffield suggested that there is a need to add a fourth 'E': equity.

> Most modern statements of library purpose suggest that it is the role of the public library to provide equality of access to the wealth of information, ideas and works of imagination. We would argue that managing a public service is about managing social equity. Equity is also at the core of the objectives of both the local authorities in this study. Equity therefore needs to be assessed as part of the evaluation of the public library service. However in its recent report, *Due for Renewal* (1997), the Audit Commission refused to add equity to its three Es. The Commission is still only concerned with that which is measurable and, as a result, tends to ignore a great deal of what is important. Their report, for instance, pays little attention to factors such as the ultimate value of reading, literacy, information, and knowledge. (Proctor et al., 1996)

While some would argue that these considerations come under the heading of 'effectiveness', this forms a useful reminder of the broader personal and social impacts which libraries may achieve if they manage their resources with this in mind. We will return to these issues in Chapters 3, 'User satisfaction', and 4, 'Impact on users'.

■ The systems view

A useful way to think of the different types of performance measurement is to consider the library as a system and use the general systems view of organizations as a model. As Figure 1.1 illustrates, organizations can be thought of as using *inputs* to create *outputs* through *processes*. Outputs then have immediate *outcomes* which in turn lead to longer-term *impacts*. Performance measurement itself is concerned with measuring each of these aspects, so that management can use that knowledge to change both the application of inputs and the processes applied to them through the feedback loop. Thus knowledge of outcomes can be used to change the balance of different resources input, the processes which are applied and hence the outputs, outcomes and impacts produced.

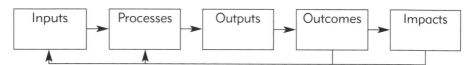

Figure 1.1 The systems view

■ Types of evaluation
Formative and summative studies

A common way of differentiating between types of evaluation is to make a distinction between *formative* and *summative* studies. The former take place alongside a development or project and are intended to help focus the development. For example, a formative evaluation of a new IT-based system might check compliance with the specification as the implementation develops and take early soundings from a sample group of users, feeding back their reactions in time for the system to be tuned to requirements. A summative evaluation, on the other hand, takes place after the end of a project and looks back at what has been achieved, including the effectiveness of the service provided and perhaps including assessment of the impacts it has had on the user community.

Longitudinal studies

Many of the studies which are undertaken to examine specific aspects of library services are one-off, single investigations, which are not directly related to previous or future assessments. However, there is also a strong tradition of *longitudinal* studies, those which enable comparisons to be made over time. The majority of these rely on statistical data. So, for example, libraries frequently assess book issues, book acquisitions, overall costs and many other factors over a time period and may produce graphs to illustrate trends. It is more unusual to find longitudinal qualitative studies although these can be extremely valuable. Why, for example, has users' book borrowing behaviour changed over the last ten years? Because such data cannot be generated automatically, qualitative longitudinal studies require long-term commitment from management or funding bodies.

With any longitudinal study, the major difficulty lies in controlling the variables. For example, it is unlikely that exactly the same users will be available for interview over a ten-year period. So are changes in behaviour due to genuine changes in what users are doing, or has the user population changed? When asking about satisfaction with services, have expectations changed and are we able to understand in what way any changes have occurred? (More will be said of satisfaction and expectations in Chapter 3, 'User satisfaction'.) Even with quantitative data there are many pitfalls – for instance, the issue statistics will be affected if there is any change in loan policy but especially if the loan period is varied during the period. With financial data, what allowance is most appropriately made for the effects of inflation? Virtually every dataset that can be produced will carry with it questions of this nature.

■ The cost of measurement

It is vital to recognize that measuring performance is an expensive business and that it is essentially non-productive. There is no *direct* benefit to the user from the effort that goes into the collection of library statistics, the undertaking of surveys and the analysis of collected data. The only benefits accrue later when management takes action based on the conclusions reached. This reflects an important insight of the quality management literature – the *cost of quality* is an overhead, which itself needs to be controlled and managed. Many organizations put systems in place to inspect products, to check on conformance to the specification, to audit compliance, to survey customer satisfaction and so on. Even though these help to achieve better services, they are not themselves productive. Hence all such costs must be kept to the minimum needed to be able to deliver products and services of the required quality.

■ Undertaking performance measurement
The evaluation plan

It is advisable to have an evaluation plan in place before actually undertaking any surveys or other activities. The plan will help to ensure that nothing is forgotten, will assist in allocating resources and will clarify thinking about each stage of the evaluation. The following topics should be covered in the plan:

1   What is to be evaluated. It is often helpful to construct a *basic results chain* which shows how impacts and outcomes are being achieved. This is in essence a matter of working backwards through the stages of the systems diagram in Figure 1.1 using basic questions to illuminate what is intended to happen. On the basis of this the evaluation questions can be specified precisely. Table 1.1 shows a framework for this exercise.

Table 1.1 Developing the evaluation plan

Question	Stage	Examples
Why?	Impacts	Why do we provide this service? What do we want to achieve by so doing?
What?	Outcomes	What signs would we expect to be able to detect that show we are producing intended outputs?
Who?		Who are we attempting to reach with those outcomes?
Where?		Where would we expect those outcomes to be found?
How?	Outputs	What outputs are we actually delivering?
	Processes	How have we arranged our internal activities so that we are producing the intended outputs that will in turn produce outcomes and impacts?
	Inputs	How are we allocating resources to the processes which will produce the desired outputs?

2   Stakeholder analysis. Who is impacted by this evaluation and what are their concerns? The net should be cast quite widely, since people with an interest will include the team undertaking the evaluation, the

subjects (such as library users), managers and perhaps funders or those with governance responsibilities.

3 Agreement on the timeframe. Will this be a brief study, perhaps of a particular aspect of service identified as needing attention? Or does it need to extend over a period so as to capture typical behaviours, including repeated interaction with the service? Or does it need bursts of activity, as might be the case with a study of learning outcomes from an information skills course, which might need to be followed up periodically by analysis of information-seeking behaviour?

4 Selection of appropriate performance indicators. What processed data, which might be in the form of textual evidence or quantitative ratios or conformance to standards, are needed in order to provide inform-ation on what is actually being achieved? A useful acronym for guiding the selection of indicators is SMART (although see also the discussion of trustworthiness below) – they should be:

- *Specific*: targeted as precisely as possible on what you want to meas-ure
- *Measurable*: it must be feasible to collect the data with which to cal-culate the indicator values
- *Achievable*: showing clearly and intuitively which direction is 'good' and which is 'bad' so that the action needed to make improvements can be identified
- *Relevant*: focused on what really matters to the service and its users
- *Timely*: the data needed will be available when required, rather than at some stage in the future when the performance measurement requirement has passed.

5 Selection of appropriate methods and the development of data collec-tion instruments. Obviously, performance measurement depends on the collection and analysis of data about the service being investi-gated. In each of the following chapters suggestions will be made about which methods and instruments are particularly relevant to dif-ferent aspects of service and different investigations. Appendix 1, 'Data collection methods', contains details of the main methods which are used in library evaluation, while Appendix 2, 'The analysis of data', outlines methods of analysing the data collected and Appendix 3, 'The presentation of results', ways of presenting the results.

An important distinction must be made between quantitative and qualitative methods:

- *Quantitative* methods are designed to find out about the *extent* of a phenomenon. For example, they reveal the average number of journal papers downloaded by a particular library's users over a specific time period.
- *Qualitative* methods are designed to explore *why* something is happening. For example, they might help us understand the purpose for which those same users downloaded journal articles, and possibly the effect on their work of having those papers available online.

6   Consideration of linking multiple methods. It is often useful to compare quantitative and qualitative data about the same service so as to gain different insights. This might be achieved by the process of *triangulation*. As the name suggests, this strategy takes the form of using three (although it could be more) independent approaches so as to view a question from different perspectives. There are different types of triangulation, including:

- *methodological triangulation*, where different methods, often including both quantitative and qualitative approaches, are used
- *observer triangulation*, where a number of different observers are used and their findings analysed separately before being compared
- *data triangulation*, which collects separate sets of data, possibly collected at different times or using different samples.

7   Selection of a sample to survey, or decision to undertake a whole population study. Sampling is also covered in Appendix 1, 'Data collection methods'. This section should detail the methods that will be used for distributing surveys, follow-up and handling queries from both those involved in carrying out the work and those being surveyed.

8   Design of pilot studies. As a general rule, each of the data collection exercises selected should include a pilot. For example, if a questionnaire is to be used a small sample of the target audience should be asked to complete it at the final draft stage. The aim is to check that the questions can be understood by respondents and that there is no ambiguity, that the distribution method works and that the data generated are capable of analysis. At a deeper level, the pilot also gives an opportunity to check that the questionnaire is generating information at the right conceptual level. For example, if you want to probe respondents' motivations, it is unhelpful if your questionnaire is simply returning monosyllabic answers or information about the mechanics of accessing the service.

9 Revision of the data collection instruments, sampling and distribution in the light of the results obtained from piloting. The plan should indicate the scope for changes to be made at this stage.

10 Data analysis procedures. The evaluation plan should provide a brief indication of the methods to be used and, where appropriate, the resources such as software packages which will be used. If training in the use of such packages will be needed, that too should be noted.

11 The presentation of results. The plan should indicate how the results will be presented, to whom and in what form. Consideration should be given to the wider dissemination of findings, perhaps to the library's users.

12 Any ethical considerations should be analysed, together with a statement of what will be done to ensure that appropriate ethical standards are observed at all times (see also below).

13 The plan should detail the resource requirements for the whole study and should state clearly and unambiguously who is responsible for what.

14 An initial statement should be made of the limitations of the intended study. This will be revised and presented as part of the reporting on the findings.

15 Finally, it is helpful if there is a statement as to who will be expected to take action on the basis of findings.

Of course, a plan as detailed as this is not needed for small studies within, say, a single branch library. Nevertheless, it is helpful if the above principles are observed and explicit decisions taken as to the length and detail of plan needed.

■ Trustworthiness

It is vital that, whatever results are produced, anyone using them should be able to have confidence that they represent what they are purported to represent. Within this requirement there are a number of considerations.

1 *Generalizability* (sometimes called 'external validity') means that the results should be indicative of the population or service being investigated as a whole rather than simply of the sample that has been investigated. Another way to look at this is to say that care must be taken not to claim that the results have wider applicability than is the

case. For example, a study of elderly users of one branch of a public library may not be generalizable to elderly users of other branches or to all users of the branch studied. However, claims to generalizability might be sustainable if the study were extended to several branches which were typical of the library authority as a whole.

2 *Appropriateness* means that the measure must be suitable for the purpose. This includes matters such as the units and scale used and compatibility with the actual service being measured. There is no point measuring the number of book issues from a purely virtual library!

3 *Validity* is the requirement that results should be accurate and that what has been measured is what was meant to be measured.

4 *Reliability* means that the survey or other instruments used are capable of producing consistent results. In other words, the exercise could be repeated (at least in theory – in practice events may have moved on) and would produce the same results again. Thus reliability is concerned with consistency. However, it is not concerned with *accuracy*. It is possible for the wrong result to be produced time after time, yet the instruments would still be 'reliable'.

An example may make the difference between validity and reliability clear. Suppose that an entrance gate counter in the library is faulty and is recording only every second person to enter the library. The fault is permanent so that the results are consistently wrong – instead of recording 400 visits a day it is recording 200. That result is 'reliable' but it is not 'valid'. If there was an intermittent fault so that the number recorded was always wrong, sometimes 300, sometimes 200, sometimes 100 and so on, then the result would be neither reliable nor valid.

A final consideration is that as far as possible results should be plainly informative. This means that they should be useful, for example to managers who are responsible for overseeing and developing the service, and they should mean what they appear to mean. This last requirement can be difficult to achieve, because performance indicators have a habit of misleading. For example, something as apparently straightforward as an overall measure of user satisfaction can be misleading in isolation, for the library may have driven away all but the most tenacious readers who would, frankly, be satisfied with anything! In most circumstances, therefore, what is needed is a set (sometimes called a 'basket') of performance measures.

▪ Ethical considerations

It is imperative that the highest ethical standards are applied to any data collection and analysis exercise which is conducted to assess library performance. Many organizations have their own internal ethical standards which must be adhered to – these are particularly strictly applied in the health service, for example. Professionally, the Chartered Institute of Library and Information Professionals (CILIP) publishes both *Ethical Principles for Library and Information Professionals* and a *Code of Professional Practice for Library and Information Professionals* (www.cilip.org.uk/profession-alguidance/professionalethics/code). The American Library Association (ALA) similarly promotes a *Code of Ethics* (www.ala.org/ala/oif/state-mentspols/codeofethics/ codeethics.htm) while the Association of Research Libraries (ARL) has a *Policy for Human Subjects* (www.arl.org/stats/privacy.html). These general principles should always be followed. There are also specific issues concerned with data collection that involves people – users and others – and the subsequent analysis of that data. These include:

- never using data about people without their knowledge and consent
- never using data collected for one purpose for a different reason, unless explicit consent is sought and granted
- never coercing people to participate in studies; for example, students should not be given the impression that non-participation in, say, a focus group will affect their course assessment
- never exposing participants to any kind of stress, for example by giving the impression that they are ignorant or unskilled
- respecting individuals' and groups' privacy at all times by avoiding intrusion and respecting confidentiality
- always allowing participants to withdraw from the study at any time, without requiring them to give a reason
- always respecting the anonymity of participants, unless explicit consent is given to reveal their identities, for instance when using a quotation
- never withholding benefits from one group for the sake of a study, for example by offering one group a new service which the librarian believes will enhance that group's experience or performance but withholding it from another.

All data collection, analysis and retention must of course take account of legal requirements, such as data protection legislation (see Chapter 4, 'Impact on users').

■ Conclusion

This book is deliberately structured to place the emphasis on effectiveness, including questions of customer satisfaction, impact and value. It does this because the most important aspect of performance measurement is the assessment of whether the fundamental purposes of a library are being met – and, as we have seen, those purposes are always related to users and potential users. The key question is what outcomes are being produced and what value generated. Thus, consideration of effectiveness needs to underpin all performance measurement – there is no point in being highly efficient if the wrong services are being delivered.

However, there is a caveat. Performance measurement is expensive and not directly productive. Thus performance measurement itself needs to be assessed, reviewed and kept to the minimum necessary for the consistent delivery of quality services. That is a challenge that subsequent chapters will try to address.

■ Resources

Key resources will be found in the resources and references sections at the end of each chapter. General resources for measuring library performance are suggested here.

- The e-mail list, lis-perf-measures@jiscmail.ac.uk has discussions on current topics in library performance measurement.
- Among organizations active in this field, IFLA is important because of the work of its Statistics and Evaluation Section (see www.ifla.org/VII/s22/index.htm). Refer to Chapter 14, 'Standards', for details of related ISO work.
- A number of toolkits are available on the web, including:
  —eVALUEd (www.evalued.uce.ac.uk/), which is primarily focused on the evaluation of electronic services in higher education, but many of its resources have wider application

—a 'companion website' to Markless and Streatfield's *Evaluating the Impact of Your Library*, at www.facetpublishing.co.uk/evaluatingimpact/index.shtml; many of the documents presented there are focused on the impact of information skills tuition

—the EFX Toolkit, which was produced as part of the evaluation of JISC services (www.cerlim.ac.uk/projects/efx/toolkit/index.html).

- A very useful set of conference proceedings has emanated from the biannual conferences organized by the I-Society Research & Consultancy Group (I-SRC) (formerly the Information Management Research Institute (IMRI)) at the University of Northumbria at Newcastle, UK. See http://northumbria.ac.uk/sd/academic/ceis/re/isrc/ for further details.
- In the USA, key activity has centred on the work of Charles McClure and John Bertot at the Information Use Management and Policy Institute (IUMPI). See www.ii.fsu.edu/index.cfm.
- For an overview of the use of performance measurement techniques in an academic library over a protracted period of time, refer to Crawford (2003).

■ References

Audit Commission (1997) *Due for Renewal: a report on the library service*, London, Audit Commission.

Bradford, S. C. (1948) *Documentation*, London, Crosby Lockwood.

Brinkley, M. (1999) The EQUINOX Project: Library Performance Measurement and Quality Management System, *Exploit Interactive* (03), www.exploit-lib.org/issue3/equinox/.

Crawford, J. (2003) Reviewing a Programme of Evaluation in an Academic Library: the case of Glasgow Caledonian University, *Performance Measurement and Metrics*, **4** (3), 113–21.

Cullen, R. (1999) Does Performance Measurement Improve Organizational Effectiveness? A postmodern analysis, *Performance Measurement and Metrics*, (sample issue), 9–30.

Curtis, D. and Dean, H. (2004) Impact and Performance Measurement in Library Services, *Performance Measurement and Metrics*, **5** (3), 90–5.

Griffiths, J.-M. and King, D. W. (1990) *Keys to Success: performance indicators for public libraries*, London, Office of Arts and Libraries.

Higher Education Funding Council for England (1995) *The Effective Academic*

Library: a framework for evaluating the performance of UK academic libraries: a consultative report to HEFC(E), SHEFC, HEFC(W) and DENI by the Joint Funding Council's Ad Hoc Group on performance indicators for libraries, Bristol, HEFCE.

Lancaster, F. W. (1977) *Measurement and Evaluation of Library Services,* Washington DC, Information Resources Press.

McClure, C. R. and Bertot, J. C. (eds) (2001) *Evaluating Networked Information Services: techniques, policy, and issues,* Medford NJ, Information Today, Inc.

Morse, P. M. (1968) *Library Effectiveness,* Boston MA, MIT Press.

Orr, R. H. (1973) Measuring the Goodness of Library Services: a general framework for considering quantitative measures, *Journal of Documentation,* **29** (3), 41–50.

Proctor, R. et al. (1996) *What Do People Do When Their Public Library Service Closes Down: an investigation into the impact of the Sheffield Libraries strike.* British Library. Research and Development Department. BLRD Report 6224, London, British Library.

Van House, N. A., Weil, B. T. and McClure, C. R. (1990) *Measuring Academic Library Performance: a practical approach,* Chicago IL, London, American Library Association.

2
Theoretical considerations

■ Introduction

All performance measurement is a form of research, involving structured investigations to try to reach a better understanding of a particular phenomenon. Because of this, it is useful to explore briefly some of the theory underpinning research studies and the gathering of evidence. This chapter offers a brief introduction to some of the key concepts. For more information the reader is directed to Robson (2002) or Sarantakos (1998).

■ Causal relationships

At the heart of all research is a belief that relationships between observed phenomena may be due to causality, and that elucidating what causes something to happen, or to be experienced, or to be felt, enables the development of knowledge. When libraries examine levels of user satisfaction, they are not simply interested in recording percentages of users with particular views but in finding out why these levels of satisfaction exist and establishing how they may be improved. Thus studies that seek to measure performance will always have an underlying aim to illuminate cause and effect. This means that such studies are never simply observational or descriptive: they seek to be incisive and analytical.

■ Theoretical perspectives 1: the positivist standpoint

Deriving originally from the work of August Comte, positivism sees scientific method as the only way to achieve new knowledge and therefore all research efforts should be clearly designed on this basis. Karl Popper, most notably in *The Logic of Scientific Discovery* published in 1934, argued that the critical issue is that of falsifiability. This in turn relies on the idea that progress is made by developing hypotheses and then by testing them to see if they are true. Popper pointed out that the truth of a hypothesis can never be demonstrated with 100% certainty since a case might exist, which has not yet occurred or been tested, which would disprove it. A single instance showing the hypothesis to be false disproves it and a new hypothesis then has to be formulated, to be disproved in its turn. So science progresses not by proving but by disproving each hypothesis.

This leads to an approach to research where the formulation of a hypothesis is the first crucial step, with research methodologies then selected to enable the hypothesis to be tested. For example, when a new drug is being brought to market, the hypothesis is that it will assist in the curing of a certain disease, the easing of pain, or whatever. (Technically, there is usually a *null hypothesis* and an *alternative hypothesis* – what is described here is the latter.) The methods adopted for testing are designed to disprove this. So the *randomized controlled trial* (RCT) is carefully designed with a test group and a control group. Individuals are selected from the overall sample and randomly assigned to one group or the other. The test group receive the drug; the control group a placebo. After the experimental phase the data are examined to see whether any differences are discernible between the groups. If no differences are found, the hypothesis is disproved, the drug discarded and the laboratory goes back to finding a new drug. If there is a difference, and assuming that it is the test group that shows positive benefits, then the hypothesis is retained *but it is not proven*. What can be said is that, on the available data, it appears that the drug is efficacious.

This kind of approach finds its way into many other fields of investigation. An information service could, for example, set up an RCT to test a new interface which it believes will be easier to use. While it would be unusual to go as far as this, the underlying theory of how experiments should be carried out is hugely influential in our field. It explains why some researchers believe that information behaviour is best studied by examining many thousands of instances of search and retrieval, rather than relying on small numbers of individual cases.

■ Theoretical perspectives 2: the relativist standpoint

While the positivist approach to science still wields enormous influence, it is widely accepted that it has a major and irreconcilable difficulty when applied to the real world. For scientific experiments to work they have to take place within a closed system, one where the various influencing factors can be controlled. So to study the effects of a new drug, great care has to be taken to remove any effects that might simply be due to age, gender, ethnicity, other drugs being taken, diet, prior medical conditions, physical circumstances and so on. The problem with this approach is that in the real world events can never be brought under that kind of control. For this reason, social scientists have adopted a number of ways of undertaking investigations and developing their understanding of the world which together can be termed *relativist* or *interpretive*. In summary, such approaches accept that reality can only be described through the eyes and understanding of the observer – which includes the researcher. To add to the complexity, all we have to describe the world is language, which itself introduces ambiguity, bias and difference. None of this denies the major achievements of scientific method and that approach's ongoing importance. However, when we seek to understand and describe complex systems, we should not expect the positivist tradition to supply all the answers.

There are a number of positions taken by those who hold relativist standpoints, although in reality what happens in most studies is that different emphases are held in tension. Nevertheless it is important to be aware of what each has to offer. In this short account there is room to describe only three relativist positions: post-positivism, critical approaches and the debate around constructivism and objectivism.

Post-positivism

The term *post-positivism* is probably the best descriptor for the position which most people working in research – scientific or otherwise – would accept in the modern world. It can be contrasted with positivism in that it recognizes that the goal of understanding reality with complete certainty through the application of scientific method is flawed, and that all we have are fallible observations from which we can draw deductions. However, the post-positivist rejects the idea that there is no external reality (*subjectivism*) and believes that research can uncover knowledge about reality, even though each individual investigator is fallible and biased.

From this standpoint, objectivity is a shared characteristic of society – it is what we do together when we make multiple observations of phenomena and criticize each other's work. Post-positivism also rejects the idea of *incommensurability*, which holds that we can never hope to understand each other's positions because of our inherent differences of language, culture, experience and so on. A valuable post-positivist approach is therefore to triangulate the findings of different investigators and debate meaning by considering different people's perspectives.

Critical approaches

The term *critical approaches* covers a variety of different views, although the dominant one is probably the feminist concept, which is based on concern about the way in which those who have power tend to dictate both what is researched and what is inferred from the outcomes of that research. As well as those taking a feminist standpoint, others who espouse critical approaches would include people concerned that the experiences and views of minorities, such as ethnic minorities or people with disabilities, are undervalued, if not ignored. This quotation makes the issue clear:

> After much critical reflection on my own work . . . during the 1980s provoked by my involvement in the disability movement, I came to the inescapable and painful conclusion that the person who had benefited most from my research on disabled people's lives was undoubtedly me. It also became apparent that there was increasing anger, hostility and suspicion amongst organisations of disabled people that much that passed for 'disability research' was nothing more than a 'rip-off'.
>
> (Oliver in Chapter 2 of Barnes and Mercer, 2003)

The underlying paradigm of critical approaches is that of *emancipatory research*, which seeks to recognize and confront social oppression in all its forms. It provides a useful and significant counter to the positivist notion that there is an unbiased and 'correct' view of the world. For libraries, it suggests that measuring library performance, including the subsequent setting and refinement of strategies to be pursued, needs to be careful to engage fully with and involve those individuals and groups who are most in danger of being marginalized.

Objectivism and constructivism

Arising from theories of learning, a contrast is commonly drawn between objectivist and constructivist pedagogies, a useful distinction and one of importance to the conduct of research studies. In a paper published some years ago, I suggested that objectivism 'views the world as an ordered structure of entities which exists and has meaning quite apart from the observer or participant. Much of science and technology has traditionally been taught on this basis: what needs to be achieved by learning is a closer and closer approach to complete (and thus "correct") understanding' (Brophy, 2001). In this analysis 'the goal of instruction is to help the learner acquire the entities and relations and the attributes of each – to build "the" correct propositional structure' (Duffy and Jonassen, 1993). In contrast, constructivist pedagogies focus on interpretation and building understanding. To quote Anne Bednar and her colleagues:

> Learning is a constructive process in which the learner is building an internal representation of knowledge, a personal interpretation of experience. This representation is constantly open to change, its structure and linkages forming the foundation to which other knowledge structures are appended. Learning is an active process in which meaning is developed on the basis of experience. This view of knowledge does not necessarily deny the existence of the real world . . . but contends that all we know of the world are human interpretations of our experience of the world. . . . learning must be situated in a rich context, reflective of real world contexts for this constructive process to occur.
> (Bednar et al., 1983)

So, on this understanding, learning is an active process in which learners place their interpretations of the 'learning event' into the context of their previous understandings and world views and are enabled both to modify their knowledge and views and to transfer their understanding to new contexts – what Michael Streibel calls 'situated cognition'. This is one of the reasons that information skills development works best when it is embedded in the tasks and activities of the participant. The learner is able to respond to the challenge of making the learning fit his or her world view, making it relevant. Clearly this cannot be achieved with an objectivist view that there is one right way to learn and one right way to view the world. But perhaps more importantly, a constructivist perspective strongly suggests that each learning event – each investigation in performance measurement terms – is cumulative, building, sometimes almost imperceptibly, on prior knowledge. It also reinforces the post-positivist understanding that by comparing, contrasting and above all listening to different viewpoints we can greatly improve the chance of building useful knowledge and perhaps even wisdom.

It is also possible to take the constructivist argument a stage further by considering the concept of social constructivism. Gergen (1994) wrote authoritatively about this, pointing out that our discourse about the world – the ways in which we think and speak about it, the ways we apprehend 'reality' – is the product of communal interchange. Because we are human beings, continually interpreting and reinterpreting our understanding of the world in a social setting, that understanding is not, and cannot be, a fixed map of 'how things are', as an objectivist stance would claim. Instead we act together, creating and recreating our understanding of the world in all its intricate and ever-changing complexity.

■ Research methods

As was described in Chapter 1, 'Background', there are two broad approaches to research, termed the *quantitative* and the *qualitative*. In fact these terms are slightly misleading as elements of quantitative analysis are frequently found in qualitative research and *vice versa*. For this reason some, Robson (2002) among them, prefer to talk of *fixed* and *flexible* designs. The former do make much use of quantitative data but one of their characteristics is that the methods to be used, and the way they will be applied, are largely fixed before the main part of the investigation is reached. With flexible designs, however, the design of the research evolves as the work progresses. There is also great emphasis in flexible designs on using *words* to describe what is happening, rather than *numbers* to gauge its extent. At the risk of oversimplification, fixed designs use an engineering model, which tends to be derived from positivist assumptions, whereas flexible designs use a social model, which in turn uses relativist suppositions. However it cannot be stressed too strongly that the terms flexible, qualitative and relativist only *tend* to go together, just as do fixed, quantitative and positivist. In reality, aspects of all these positions and approaches are intertwined in evaluations and research studies.

However, the philosophical and theoretical positions of researchers greatly influence the nature of the studies that they undertake and thus the methods which they use. The following brief descriptions outline the main methods which are used in the different traditions.

Positivist research methods
Experiments
The classic positivist research method is the experiment, in which the researcher manipulates a variable (called the *independent variable*) and observes what happens to another variable (the *dependent variable*) as a result. In fact of course, relativists also conduct experiments, so it should not be assumed that this is an exclusive approach. However, the deliberate link between experimental design and the attempt to disprove a hypothesis is a mark of positivism.

As already noted, it is usual when conducting an experiment to use a control group, not subject to the experimental manipulation, so that the effects of chance, or of placebo effects, can be discounted. More is said of this in Appendix 1, 'Data collection methods'. The big advantage of experiments is that they operate in controlled conditions so that cause and effect can be isolated.

For libraries, experimentation can be undertaken with new or revised services, although care must be taken to observe ethical considerations such as not using a control group if that disadvantages its members.

Quantitative data analysis
The positivist research tradition frequently uses available data deriving from operational activities, which might be thought of as using the real world as its experimental domain. Typically, data will be subject to statistical analysis in an attempt to find both correlations and variabilities, using techniques such as ANOVA (Analysis of Variance), ANCOVA (Analysis of Covariance) and MANOVA (Multivariate Analysis of Variance).

It would be typical of a study of this type to use large volumes of data. Indeed it has become apparent in recent years that a sub-branch of librarianship is needed to acquire, organize, describe and curate some of the huge datasets which are emerging from scientific research in such areas as astronomy and sub-atomic physics. For library service evaluation, the equivalent comes in the form of bibliometric datasets such as those produced from citation indexing and from the use of the major search engines.

Relativist research methods
Ethnography

Deriving in the main from social anthropology, *ethnography* is concerned with the study of people in their cultural context and relies on fieldwork within a particular society to provide its data. The concern is to derive *meaning* from the data collected, rather than to count occurrences of events. In this context 'society' could mean any group of people with some kind of common interest, such as a group of library users, and ethnographic approaches are now common in this context. The classic application of ethnography, epitomized by works such as Margaret Mead's *Coming of Age in Samoa*, involves becoming a participant observer within the society being studied, literally living within the society itself – this is known as *cultural immersion*. However, there are many variants of the original methodology, such as *confessional* and *reflexive* ethnologies, and the pure ethnographic concept of trying to become part of the group being studied is sometimes replaced with observation. In part this is a response to the criticism of ethnography that the participation of an external person from outside the culture inevitably affects the behaviour of members of the group being studied.

Two major types of ethnographic studies can be identified. Descriptive studies are usually called *ethnographic*. However, if a study is critical, i.e. the data are used to try to identify cause and effect relationships, it is described as *ethnological*. Whichever approach is taken, ethnography tries to take a holistic view of the world, recognizing that human behaviour in its social setting is immensely complicated and that tacit knowledge and hidden assumptions are of great importance to understanding a culture. For an accessible introduction to ethnography, the reader is referred to Agar (1996).

The term *illuminative evaluation* is sometimes used for studies, inspired by the ethnographic approach, which seek to establish what is important to participants and the factors that influence them in identifying these. In other words they attempt to identify not just what is happening but the motivations of the participants, what makes them act as they do.

By its very nature, ethnography raises many difficult ethical considerations. At the very least, subjects of ethnographic research should be aware that they are being studied and should give their consent. (See also the section on ethical considerations in Chapter 1, 'Background'.)

Case studies

The case study is another common qualitative approach and has been used extensively in libraries and information services. (For an interesting recent collection, concerned with the LibQUAL+™ methodology described in Chapter 3, 'User satisfaction', see Heath et al. (2004).) A case can refer to a particular library, to a group of library users or to a situation, such as users' interactions with a particular service in a particular setting. The case study is an investigation of what is happening in practice (i.e. it is an *empirical* investigation) within a real life context and will normally involve multiple methods of data collection. Although described here as a qualitative methodology, data collected will usually include some of a quantitative nature.

The great advantage of this approach is that it reveals detailed and contextualized data about a complex situation. However, it is important, when conducting a case study, to analyse both the case itself – what is happening – and the context of the case – where, and under what conditions, it is taking place. The reason for doing this is that others will want to be able to analyse how one case differs from another and the extent to which what is learned from the case study may be capable of wider application. It may also be that the investigator will wish to re-examine the same case at a later date, in which case contextual information is vital if differences are to be understood.

Case studies have proved very popular in the evaluation of library and information services, to the extent that it sometimes appears as if most of the evidence base is in this form! However, used judiciously, the case study can be extremely valuable especially as one source of data which can be triangulated with others. Eisenhardt (1989) provides a detailed analysis of the approach.

The case study itself will almost certainly use a variety of data collection methods, such as questionnaires, interviews and observation. These are described in Appendix 1, 'Data collection methods'.

Grounded theory

The idea behind this methodology is that the theory which explains the phenomena being observed should be allowed to emerge from the data which are collected – it is 'grounded' in that data. It explicitly rules out the idea of starting with a hypothesis and testing it. Instead, it allows the data to speak for itself.

Using a grounded theory approach characteristically involves a mixture of observation and interviewing, although it may also include quantitative or other studies. The term is also sometimes applied to the methodology of this type of study. Typically, this involves making observations and then noting down what appear to be key issues. This is repeated with other observations, interviews or whatever source of data is being used. Theory emerges from this constant development of comparisons. There is then a process of purposive sampling – looking for individuals who have different viewpoints or can shed a different light on the subject. Notes and memos are continually made and codes assigned to them and then as the theory emerges these are sorted into a meaningful order. At useful points there can be reference to the established literature. Once the process of sorting all these notes and memos has taken place, the emergent theory is written up.

Interestingly, there is a very clear link between Popper's work on falsifiability and the methods of grounded theory, in that when a theory emerges from the data there should always be an ongoing search for data which refute it. This underlines the point that, despite what appear to be fundamental differences, there are many shared beliefs among researchers of differing theoretical backgrounds.

The use of grounded theory developed in sociology and is explained in a readable introduction by one of its originators, Barney Glaser (Glaser, 1998), who also runs the Grounded Theory Institute at www.groundedtheory.com/.

■ Action research

Both positivist and relativistic approaches can be applied through *action research*, which is conducted by practitioners immersed in the delivery of the service being studied, either individually or working as a team. In the latter case the term *collaborative enquiry* is often used. It is closely related to *reflective practice* (see Chapter 9, 'Staff') and has been characterized as 'a methodology which is intended to have both action outcomes and research outcomes' (Dick, 2000).

Action research is used very widely by teachers in primary and secondary education as well as by librarians and there are good examples of both sets of professionals working together in this way. This type of research often involves an ongoing commitment, with an initial cycle of research being planned in detail followed by continuing practitioner evaluation of the issue.

■ Evidence-based practice

The recent development of evidence-based practice (EBP) in health disciplines, now finding its way into social services, business and librarianship, may provide a useful framework for considering the application of theory to library management and performance measurement. Its proponents suggest that it enables a blend of positivist and relativist approaches to be taken with evidence drawn from a variety of sources and each piece of data weighed on its merits.

Evidence-based librarianship has been defined in the following terms:

> Evidence-based Librarianship (EBL) is a means to improve the profession of librarianship by asking questions as well as finding, critically appraising and incorporating research evidence from library science (and other disciplines) into daily practice. It also involves encouraging librarians to conduct high quality qualitative and quantitative research.
>
> (Crumley and Koufogiannakis, 2002)

Andrew Booth, probably the leading proponent of this approach, prefers to speak of *evidence-based information practice* (EBIP):

> an approach to information practice that promotes the collection, interpretation and integration of valid, important and applicable user-reported, librarian-observed, and research-derived evidence. The best available evidence, moderated by user needs and preferences, is applied to improve the quality of professional judgements.
>
> (www.shef.ac.uk/scharr/sections/ir/research/ebl.html)

Within EBP there are a number of models which can be used to focus the evidence gathering and analysis task. The critical issue is to ensure that the question which needs to be answered is expressed clearly, is fully focused on what needs to be asked and is suitably structured. Booth (2003) suggests the use of the 'SPICE' model in order to ensure that the right questions are being asked:

- Setting – where is the context of the service being investigated?
- Perspective – for whom is this service being offered?
- Intervention – what is being provided?
- Comparison – what are the alternatives?
- Evaluation – how will the success of the intervention be measured?

For example, a question could be formulated along these lines:

> From the PERSPECTIVE of an elderly person confined to their own home (SETTING), is provision of books as part of the social services care package (INTERVENTION) more satisfactory to those users (EVALUATION) than the same service delivered by the library (COMPARISON)?

Critics of EBL and EBIP point to a number of issues which remain unresolved. One is that, unlike in the health services, there is a very limited published research literature on which to draw in librarianship. A second is that EBP tends to use a model of evidence which is influenced by positivist thinking, as exemplified by its use of randomized controlled trials. A third objection is that EBP undervalues the role of professional expertise. Librarians go through years of training and acquire decades of professional experience for a reason. Finally, there is the whole question of transferability. While in the health services a procedure which works in one hospital will almost certainly work in another, the same is not necessarily true of libraries.

■ Narrative-based practice

A possible counter to some of the criticisms of EBP lies in the development of *narrative-based practice* (NBP), which emerged in medicine (Greenhalgh and Hurwitz, 1998) and has been used in management and other disciplines (Brown et al., 2005). To some the use of narrative, or story, is a manifestation of knowledge management, while to others its roots lie elsewhere. Be that as it may, it is indisputable that when the goal of investigation is either increased understanding or purposive action, stories have always been powerful. Hannabuss (2000) comments on the use of narrative in organizations and the way in which members of the organization use the narrative in order to deduce more general lessons:

One of the most frequent uses of narrative in organisations [is to generalize from them]. They are unique and idiosyncratic, but they are used as a key part of sensemaking because they tell us something important about the circumstances now, and they can also be used as pointers or lessons for the future (e.g. if the company were to do this, then similar or comparable outcomes would occur). They can also be generalized from and add to the store of exemplars of successful and unsuccessful management practice which becomes the folklore of management itself.

But above all the power of stories lies in their twin ability to depict the complexity of the reality we experience and yet to communicate the essentials:

> The fascination of stories lies in their connectedness to our own lives. They appeal to experience. Further, they offer a holistic view – they consider not just the 'simple' fact, but draw in context and culture, and unashamedly offer a point of view. Some would distinguish 'story' from 'narrative', where the former is the underlying account and the latter its expression in the words of the storyteller. Others would dispute such a distinction, although recognising that the telling is as important as the tale. And linking the two, of course, is the storyteller.
>
> The question for us as librarians is whether and how the power of story can be harnessed by and for our profession.   (Brophy, 2004)

A narrative-based librarianship (NBL) would enable the challenge of reconciling the different theoretical standpoints which each of us takes, however unwittingly, to be addressed in compelling ways. Narrative does not just explain what has happened. It provides understanding of why and with what import.

■ Conclusion

Two very different underlying theories inform much of library performance measurement. The positivist framework places great emphasis on quantitative techniques and on discovering demonstrable trends from large volumes of data. The alternative, relativist model sees the library as one part of a hugely complex social system and emphasizes the qualitative approach. While for some time doubts were expressed about qualitative methods because they can appear to be less rigorous than quantitative approaches, it is now generally accepted that, provided that they are carried out appropriately, qualitative studies are perfectly appropriate and indeed essential in a wide range of fields, including library and information services. The Public Administration Select Committee of the UK House of Commons is on record as remarking that 'the danger . . . is that excessive attention is given to what can be easily measured, at the expense of what is difficult or impossible to measure quantitatively even though this may be fundamental to the service provided (for example, patient care, community policing, or the time devoted by a teacher to a child's needs)' (House of Commons, Public Administration Select Committee, 2003).

Evidence-based practice offers one possible framework for applying a judicious blend of quantitative and qualitative approaches in performance assessment. However there remain critical outstanding questions about its application to library management.

A narrative-based librarianship would help to convey the complexity of libraries operating in the real world and may prove to be a useful development to take performance measurement and associated management activity beyond the capabilities of quantitative studies.

■ Resources
- Refer to the references for key resources on research theory, especially Robson (2002) and Sarantakos (1998).
- IFLA's Library Theory and Research Section co-ordinates action at international level on theoretical approaches, including the influence of cultural norms on librarianship (www.ifla.org/VII/s24/index.htm).
- Action research is described in detail in a series of papers on the Action Research Resources website at www.scu.edu.au/schools/gcm/ar/arp/arphome.html.
- Evidence-based practice is covered in Andrew Booth and Anne Brice's *Evidence Based Practice for Information Professionals: a handbook*, London, Facet Publishing, 2004. There is a summary at www.cilip.org.uk/publications/updatemagazine/archive/archive2004/june/update0406a.htm.
- There is also a series of conferences on EBL. The most recent was held in Brisbane, Australia, in 2005 (http://conferences.alia.org.au/ebl2005/index.html).

▪ References

Agar, M. H. (1996) *The Professional Stranger: an informal introduction to ethnography*, 2nd edn, London, Academic Press.

Barnes, C. and Mercer, G. (eds) (2003) *Doing Disability Research*, Leeds, Centre for Disability Studies, University of Leeds.

Bednar, A. et al. (1983) Theory Into Practice: how do we link? In Duffy, T. and Jonassen, D. (eds), *Constructivism and the Technology of Instruction*, Hillsdale NJ, Lawrence Erlbaum Associates.

Booth, A. (2003) Bridging the Research-practice Gap? The role of evidence-based librarianship, *New Review of Information and Library Research*, **9**, 3–23.

Brophy, P. (2001) Networked Learning, *Journal of Documentation*, **57** (1), 130–56.

Brophy, P. (2004) Narrative-based Librarianship, *The Area of Information and Social Communication: Festschrift for Professor Wanda Pindlova*, Krakow, Jagiellonian University.

Brown, J. S. et al. (2005) *Storytelling in Organizations: how narrative and storytelling are transforming 21st century management*, London, Butterworth–Heinemann.

Crumley, E. and Koufogiannakis, D. (2002) Developing Evidence-based Librarianship, *Health Information and Libraries Journal*, **19** (2), 61–70.

Dick, B. (2000) A Beginner's Guide to Action Research, *Resource Papers in Action Research*, www.scu.edu.au/schools/gcm/ar/arp/guide.html.

Duffy, T. and Jonassen, D. (eds) (1993) *Constructivism and the Technology of Instruction*, Hillsdale NJ, Lawrence Erlbaum Associates.

Eisenhardt, K. M. (1989) Building Theories From Case Study Research, *Academy of Management Review*, **14** (4), 532–50.

Gergen, K. J. (1994) *Towards Transformation in Social Knowledge*, 2nd edn, London, Sage.

Glaser, B. G. (1998) *Doing Grounded Theory: issues and discussions*, Mill Valley CA, Sociology Press.

Greenhalgh, T. and Hurwitz, B. (1998) *Narrative Based Medicine: dialogue and discourse in clinical practice*, London, BMJ Books.

Hannabuss, S. (2000) Narrative Knowledge: eliciting organisational knowledge from storytelling, *Aslib Proceedings*, **52** (10), 402–13.

Heath, F. M. et al. (eds) (2004) *Libraries Act on Their LibQUAL+™ Findings: from data to action*, New York NY, Haworth Information Press.

House of Commons, Public Administration Select Committee (2003), *Fifth Report: On target? Government by measurement*, London, House of Commons, www.publications.parliament.uk/pa/cm200203/cmselect/cmpubadm/62/62.pdf.

Robson, C. (2002) *Real World Research*, 2nd edn, Oxford, Blackwell.

Sarantakos, S. (1998) *Social Research*, 2nd edn, London, Macmillan.

3
User satisfaction

■ Introduction

The days when a service organization could ignore its customers and concentrate on its internal targets are long gone. Hopefully, all libraries have moved away from the customer-as-nuisance viewpoint, what Moore (1992) characterized as the ABC (Another Bloody Customer) approach to customer service:

> all too often we are made to feel that simply by being a customer we are trespassing upon someone's leisure time; or making their life unnecessarily complicated. In some cases, usually in shops selling computers or hi-fi equipment, we are made to feel that, as customers, we fail to come up to the intellectual level of the people serving us.

Libraries now accept that they must be user-centred and show empathy with their customers. In other words, the focus of all their services needs to be on the individuals and groups who will make use of them, rather than on the library's own processes or on the materials and other resources which the library collects or to which it provides access. A small caveat needs to be added to this statement to recognize that many national and specialist libraries do focus on collection development, conservation and preservation. However, even in these cases, users of the future inform decisions on acquisition, retention and conservation priorities in the present. It follows that statements of library purpose, which as Chapter 1, 'Background', suggested need to drive performance measurement, will have a clear user focus.

The idea of focusing on users, or customers, has a long history. In librarianship it was most memorably expressed by the Indian librarian S. R. Ranganathan in his 'laws of library science', formulated 75 years ago (Ranganathan, 1931):

- books are for use
- every reader his book
- every book its reader
- save the time of the reader
- a library is a growing organism.

Interestingly, this approach preceded the adoption of similar principles in industrial and commercial organizations, which only really started to adopt customer-focused approaches in the aftermath of World War 2. A series of influential figures, known as the 'quality gurus', started to promote the idea that the quality of a product or service could only be assessed by reference to the intended user and the intended use. People like Deming, Crosby, Juran and Feigenbaum based their work on definitions of quality that emphasized that the customer's needs were paramount – for a discussion of these developments see Brophy and Coulling (1996). Arising from this work, two definitions of quality emerged – in effect they say the same thing in different ways:

- Quality is 'conformance to requirements'.
- Quality is 'fitness for purpose'.

The first states that the quality of a product or service can only be defined in terms of whether or not it meets the requirements of the customer who will purchase or use it, the second that it should be defined in terms of whether or not (or how closely) it fits the purpose that the customer has for it.

These definitions provide a very useful basis for assessing the quality of a library or information service. The questions that need to be asked are: 'Does this service fit with the requirements of the users?' and 'Does this service enable the users to fulfil their purposes in using it?'.

■ Satisfaction

An obvious way to judge the fit of a service with user requirements and purposes is to check whether users who have come into contact with the service went away satisfied. Satisfaction is generally acknowledged as a prime criterion for judging quality and a great deal of time and effort is expended on measuring it across all industries and services. Libraries are no exception and later in this chapter we will look at some of the methods which can be used to achieve this. First, however, it is important to explore the concept of satisfaction in a little more depth.

On the surface asking the users about their satisfaction with the service they are receiving is a clear way of judging performance for any user-oriented organization. Indeed, some influential writers have argued that satisfaction is the be-all and end-all of performance measurement. However, a major issue for any service provider, especially one where the 'users' are purchasing a professional service, is that they do not necessarily have a well defined view of what a 'good' service would look like. For example, in the financial services industry a customer may use a professional adviser for investment advice. If the adviser appears pleasant and willing to listen but also highly professional and knowledgeable, the client may go away feeling very satisfied with the service received. Years later it may become apparent that the advice was in fact inappropriate – as has been the case with a series of financial products over the last 25 years. So the immediate satisfaction expressed by the client was in fact misplaced. A similar situation can occur in educational institutions where students may not be in a good position to know what best practice looks like – after all few first year undergraduates have any other university experience with which to make comparisons. Similarly, do the customers of a children's library know what they should expect? And how does customer satisfaction relate to the standard of conservation undertaken in an archival collection? None of this suggest that we should avoid measuring customer satisfaction but it does suggest that we should be careful to take our customers' levels of knowledge and expertise into account.

A second issue with satisfaction measures is that they may mask more than they reveal. If the overall experience has been positive, customers may be reluctant to criticize minor failings yet these are precisely what the managers want to know about in order to take corrective action. If the overall experience has been negative, customers may neglect to mention the positive aspects. A related issue is the extent to which cultural norms affect responses to satisfaction surveys. All this suggests that we need to take great care in designing the instruments we use to measure satisfaction, so as to probe beneath immediate and overall reactions and to make allowance for our respondents' cultures.

A third issue, the adaptability of demand for services, is of particular concern to public sector organizations that operate within relatively fixed resource constraints. There is some evidence that services which are successful – attracting high levels of use – may start to drive customers away because resources become overstretched. A good example is book lending. If a library is successful in attracting heavy demand for loan items, the availability of stock diminishes. Early users may be highly satisfied, but later ones will find a much less attractive and relevant selection of stock available and are thus more likely to go away dissatisfied. However, this action in itself reduces the demand on the stock and thus users coming along later still may find that stock availability has improved. In other words, demand on the service adapts itself to levels of satisfaction. In at least one instance this led to the suggestion that, over time, satisfaction levels were in fact more or less fixed. What could be managed was the number of users, or the proportion of the user population, the library could serve at that level of satisfaction.

A further issue concerns the desirability of going beyond the achievement of satisfaction to create 'customer delight'. In the 1980s Professor Noriaki Kano devised a model of customer satisfaction which distinguishes between 'threshold' or 'basic' attributes of a service, 'performance' attributes and 'exciters' or 'delighters'. He suggested that these are useful ways to distinguish between different reactions which people display when interacting with a service. Figure 3.1 illustrates the Kano model.

The usual way of thinking about customer service is to assume that if the service is dysfunctional, then the customer will be dissatisfied and that there is a more or less linear relationship between the two, so that as functionality improves so too does customer satisfaction. Indeed, for many aspects of service, this is more or less accurate – it is shown by the dashed line in Figure 3.1. However, Kano pointed out that there are some aspects of service, labelled in the diagram 'essential features' where this relationship doesn't hold. The lower of the two curved dotted lines illustrates this. These are features which are only capable of creating dissatisfaction, because the customer takes them for granted. So, for example, the library user expects the books to be on shelves rather than in a heap on the floor. If you meet this expectation, you do not create customer satisfaction – customers remain neutral about the service. If you fail to meet this expectation, customers are dissatisfied.

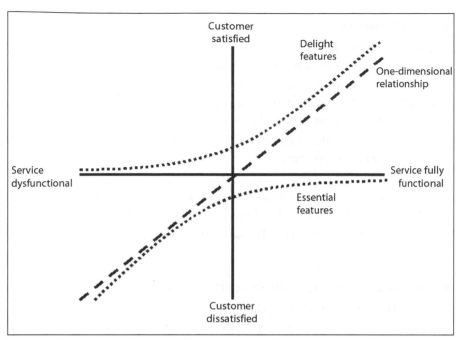

Figure 3.1 The Kano model of customer satisfaction

However, there is another group of features which can only create high levels of satisfaction and, indeed, delight. These are represented by the upper dotted curve in the diagram and consist of those aspects of service which are both welcome and unexpected. So, for example, if the library were to offer each customer a free cup of coffee (or maybe even better a free massage!) they would be impressed and their levels of satisfaction would rise. The library would hope that they would be delighted. But if this service was not offered they wouldn't express dissatisfaction, since they never expected it in the first place.

It follows that the way to move from providing mere satisfaction to delight is continuously to create good but unexpected experiences *while ensuring that essential features are always well delivered*.

A problem with this approach, however, is that over time 'delight' features tend to become 'essential'. If you offer that cup of coffee for three months and then withdraw it, the result may be customer dissatisfaction. This aspect of service has shifted into the linear model. However, this merely reflects the reality of customer service – continuous innovation is needed to stay ahead of the game.

■ User surveys

It is now common for libraries of all kinds to survey their users, not only to assess levels of satisfaction but to gauge opinions about a variety of aspects of the service being offered. User survey data are included in a number of standard data collection activities, such as the CIPFA *Public Library Statistics*. SCONUL developed a standard user survey template some years ago (see Appendix 1, 'Data collection methods') and this has been used fairly widely. An advantage of this approach is that where libraries within a sector use the same questions in a user survey there is much more chance of being able to compare results. It is also useful for libraries to have access to wording for questions which have been developed by those with experience of designing surveys, rather than having to start from scratch.

■ Attributes of customer satisfaction

The differentiation of factors that produce satisfaction or dissatisfaction which Kano pointed out is mirrored by studies that have explored how the concepts of customer satisfaction and quality service can be disaggregated into a series of different attributes. This is important, because a user may be both satisfied and dissatisfied with the library's services at one and the same time. For example, the opening times may be regarded as satisfactory but the range of stock unsatisfactory, or *vice versa*.

Within the quality management tradition, David Garvin was among the first to recognize that the classic definitions of quality and satisfaction are somewhat simplistic. He suggested that a more sophisticated approach was needed. He recognized that 'quality is a complex and multifaceted concept' and suggested that there is a series of critical dimensions or attributes that can be used as a framework for determining the overall quality of a product or service.

Garvin's view was that many of the problems of defining and recognizing quality arise because the concept can be approached from many different perspectives. He suggested that at least five views can be identified in the literature and in practice:

- the transcendental view: quality can be recognized, but cannot be defined
- the customer view: quality is fitness for the customer's purposes or conformance to the customer's requirements
- the manufacturer view: quality is conformance to specification

- the product view: quality is related to inherent characteristics of the product
- the value-based view: quality is dependent on what a customer is willing to pay for it.

(Garvin, 1984)

He went on to define a series of quality attributes, and these have been refined and built on over the intervening years since his pioneering work was first published, so that there are now many different ways of delineating quality attributes. Table 3.1 illustrates an approach developed in the context of libraries and applied to the electronic information environment in the UK (Brophy, 2004).

Table 3.1 Attributes of user satisfaction

Attribute	Definition
Performance	Concerned with confirming that a library service meets its most basic purpose, such as making key information sources available on demand.
Features	Aspects of the service which appeal to users but are beyond the essential core performance attributes, such as alerting services.
Reliability	For information services this would include availability of the service. Such problems as broken web links, lack of reliability and slowness in speed of response would be measured as part of this attribute.
Conformance	Whether the service meets the agreed standard, including conformance questions around the use of standards and protocols such as XML, RDF, Dublin Core, OAI-PMH, Z39.50, etc.
Durability	Related to the sustainability of the information or library service over a period of time.
Currency of information	How up to date the information provided is when it is retrieved.
Serviceability	The level of help available to users during, for example, information retrieval, or otherwise at the point of need. The availability and usefulness of instructions and prompts throughout an online service, perhaps with context sensitive help, could be measured in order to assess performance under this attribute.
Aesthetics and image	The appearance of the physical library and of web-based or other electronic services based on it.

Continued on next page

Table 3.1 *Continued*

Attribute	Definition
Perceived quality	The user's view of the service as a whole and the information retrieved from it, often formed in discussions with other potential users and sometimes without any actual contact with the service. It may be useful to measure perceptions both before and after a service is used for this reason.
Usability	The ease with which users can access library services. This is particularly relevant to electronic services and includes issues of accessibility (see Chapters 8, 'Outputs', and 11, 'Services for all').

■ Customer expectations

Bearing the above in mind, it is not surprising that a strong strand of research and development in this area has concerned the explicit assessment of satisfaction alongside customer expectations. The idea is that rather than trying to find an absolute measure of satisfaction, we should instead concentrate on the fit between expectations and experience – did the experience of using the service live up to customer expectations? If not, why was this so?

The leading theoreticians of this approach have been Valarie Zeithaml, A. Parasuraman and Leonard Berry who recognized that by the mid-1980s the service sector had become a huge part of the American economy, yet was failing to deliver quality (Zeithaml, Parasuraman and Berry, 1990). Zeithaml, Parasuraman and Berry set up three focus groups in each of four sectors to establish the criteria that customers themselves used when they assessed the quality of services they received. The sectors chosen for the study were retail banking, credit cards, securities brokerage and product repair and maintenance. They noted from these studies that customers find it more difficult to assess the quality of services than the quality of products. This explains the chosen methodology, which was designed to enable the members of their focus groups to discuss their expectations and experiences in depth.

After analysing the data from the focus groups, Zeithaml, Parasuraman and Berry identified ten 'dimensions' of service quality that appeared to be common across all of the services examined. These dimensions were as follows (note the similarities with and differences from the quality attributes discussed above):

1 *Tangibles*: is the service an attractive place to visit? Are the staff appropriately dressed? Do they use modern, up-to-date equipment?
2 *Reliability*: is my telephone call returned when they said it would be? Are errors made on my bank statement? Does the washing machine work (first time!) when it's been repaired?
3 *Responsiveness*: when a problem occurs, is it quickly put right? Do they arrange to repair the washing machine at a time to suit *me*?
4 *Competence*: do front-line staff give the impression of knowing what they are doing? Similarly, does a repairer appear to know how to diagnose a fault and carry out a repair with confidence?
5 *Courtesy*: are staff pleasant, even when asked difficult (or what may appear to be 'silly') questions? Does the repairer wipe his or her shoes rather than trample mud all over my hallway carpet? Do staff manage not to *appear* busy even when they are?
6 *Credibility*: does the service enjoy a good reputation – do people speak well of it? Are charges consistent with the level of service provided? Do I get a credible and worthwhile guarantee with a repair, such that I can have confidence that any problems will be put right quickly and without further expense?
7 *Security*: is it safe to use the service? For example, is my credit card safe from unauthorized use? Do I have confidence that the repair was properly carried out to an acceptable standard?
8 *Access*: if I have a problem, can I get access to a senior member of staff to help me sort out the cause? Do they answer the telephone when I ring? Is it easy to find the repair company's premises?
9 *Communication*: is the service explained clearly and the options outlined comprehensively? Do they avoid using unnecessary jargon? Do they listen to me? If something unexpected occurs and the repair company cannot keep the appointment that they've made, do they contact me in good time to rearrange it?
10 *Understanding the customer*: if I'm a regular customer, does someone on the staff recognize me? Do they try to understand my *individual* needs? Do they try to arrange the repair visit to meet my convenience rather than their own?

These dimensions were then further analysed to produce what is known as the RATER set (from the initial letters):

Reliability: the ability to perform the promised service dependably and accurately.

Assurance: knowledge and courtesy of employees and their ability to convey trust and confidence.

Tangibles: the appearance of physical facilities, equipment, personnel and communication materials.

Empathy: the caring, individualized attention the organization provides to its customers.

Responsiveness: willingness to help customers and to provide prompt service.

The RATER set formed the basis of a comprehensive methodology for assessing service quality known as SERVQUAL (Parasuraman et al., 1988). Standardized questionnaires and other instruments were developed to establish from customers:

- the relative importance of each dimension
- an assessment of performance expectations that would relate to an excellent service in the relevant field
- an assessment of the actual performance of the service being assessed.

The essence of SERVQUAL then consist of calculating 'gap scores'. If there is a positive gap between expectations and performance then there is room for improvement, and the bigger the gap the more attention is needed to that particular aspect of service. It is also possible that there are negative gaps, where the service is actually delivering more than an excellent company would. In these cases it may be that some resources should be withdrawn and re-used elsewhere, so as to achieve a more uniform level of satisfaction across the whole service.

■ LibQUAL+™

As part of its New Measures Initiative, ARL undertook a study of a SERVQUAL based methodology developed by Texas A&M University. This was one of ten studies, ranging from e-metrics (performance measures for electronic services) to the Standardized Assessment of Information Literacy Skills (SAILS) project, which ARL launched to assist librarians in tackling the challenges of service delivery at the start of the 21st century.

After a pilot project involving 12 member libraries, ARL secured a grant of just under $500,000 from the US Department of Education's Fund for the Improvement of Postsecondary Education to develop LibQUAL+™. The number of participating libraries grew rapidly, the spring 2001 participation reaching 43 different campuses. By 2006 participation had spread to over 500 libraries including a number in Canada and Europe. In the UK, a group of participating libraries has been co-ordinated by SCONUL. Background to the development of LibQUAL+™ can be found in Hernon and Whitman (2001).

LibQUAL+™ provides data collection, analysis and presentation tools. Data collection is accomplished through a web-based questionnaire delivered to students and staff in the university. The questions are grouped under three themes:

- *affect of service*: including empathy of staff, responsiveness, assurance and reliability
- *information control*: including the scope of the content made available by the library, convenience, ease of navigation, timeliness, the equipment made available and self-reliance
- *the library as place*: including utilitarian space, the building as a symbol and the library as a 'refuge'.

As implementations of LibQUAL+™ have progressed worldwide, the tools have proved flexible enough to accommodate a significant range of local variations. For example, in 2003 the SCONUL participants added five additional questions of their own, concerning:

- access to photocopying and printing facilities
- availability of main texts and readings
- provision for information skills training
- helpfulness of staff in dealing with users' IT problems
- the availability of subject specialist assistance.

In a further development, in 2004 SCONUL institutions selected their own five local questions from a range of over a hundred possibilities, thus tuning the survey to each library's particular requirements.

The essence of the LibQUAL+™ methodology lies in the assessment of the gaps between the service that the user would like to see (the 'desired' level), the service actually experienced (the 'perceived' level) and the lowest level of service that would be acceptable (the 'minimum' level). These are determined from the questionnaire returns for each dimension of service by calculating a mean score. The results are then plotted on a 'radar' chart, such as that shown in Figure 3.2.

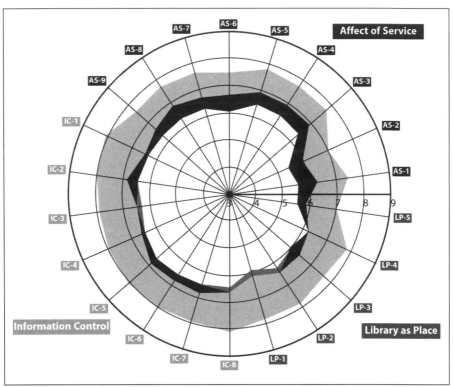

Figure 3.2 LibQUAL+™ radar chart for SCONUL libraries (reproduced by permission)

LibQUAL+™ radar charts are usually produced in colour by shading in the areas between the points that have been plotted. Red is used to indicate areas where the perceived level of service is less than the minimum – clearly these need priority attention. Green is used to indicate that for a particular dimension the perceived level of service is greater than the desired level – this suggests, as indicated earlier, that resources might be directed away from that area without loss of user satisfaction.

It is generally agreed that LibQUAL+™ has been a very successful means of enabling academic libraries to analyse the dimensions of user satisfaction, to get away from overall measures which are difficult to interpret and to focus attention on areas which are in most need of improvement. A useful summary of American libraries' experience with LibQUAL+™ was published in 2004 (Heath et al., 2004). UK libraries' use of the methodology was reported by Lock and Town (2005), who commented that while 'the survey results were as expected at the majority of participating institutions, the detailed level of results highlighted new opportunities for improvement at some institutions as the survey goes into more depth than other tools previously used'.

Despite its success, a number of questions need to be asked about the use of SERVQUAL-derived models of customer satisfaction in general and about LibQUAL+™ in particular.

1 SERVQUAL has always had a US perspective, which non-US libraries have sometimes struggled to overcome, and LibQUAL+™ is no exception to this.
2 There is a tendency to address user services as if they were designed and delivered by the individual library, as they were before the advent of IT-based services. However, in a world increasingly dominated by networked information services, designed and delivered remotely, the individual library has limited control over what the user sees, even with services for which it pays. It is often difficult to know what the users are judging when they report on their satisfaction with such services.
3 It is open to question whether undergraduate students in particular have a realistic idea of what they should expect from a university library. As Silver wrote (quoted in Crawford and Riley (2000)) it is 'not always understood that students do not enter higher education as initiated members of that culture'. First year undergraduates usually rely very heavily on set readings, so their assessment of, for example, the desired level of networked information services must be questionable. As Walters (2003) put it, 'the service orientation most likely to generate favourable user responses may not be the one that best serves the educational mission of the university . . . that is why course instructors

require their students to read 60-page primary sources rather than ten-page summaries'.

4 A major part of LibQUAL+™'s concern is with the library as place, yet this is rapidly becoming less and less important compared with the services delivered outwith the library, especially those delivered to the desktop as part of the user's educational workflow. In an academic world increasingly dominated by VLEs and VREs this emphasis is questionable.

5 LibQUAL+™ is based entirely on users' perceptions, following the fundamental tenet of Zeithaml, Parasuraman and Berry (1990) that 'only customers judge quality; all other judgements are essentially irrelevant'. This seems to suggest that there is no place for professional judgement.

6 The most serious criticism of LibQUAL+™ must be that it asks users about their experience of the *library* instead of asking them about their information access, or more general, experiences and analysing where the library fits into their activities and workflows. In this sense it is library-centric instead of user-centric.

7 The trademarking of the LibQUAL+™ name and system is an unwelcome departure in a profession which has by and large operated on the basis of open sharing of performance measurement techniques, even where it has been necessary to restrict access to the underlying data.

On a more positive note, LibQUAL+™ has certainly enabled meaningful comparisons to be made between libraries, at least at the level of overall user satisfaction. More will be said about such comparisons in Chapter 12, 'Benchmarking'.

Following on from the successful roll-out of the LibQUAL+™ methodology and system, ARL has embarked on the development of a parallel quality assessment system for digital libraries, to be called DigiQUAL™ (www.digiqual.org/digiqual/index.cfm) – again trademarked and with restricted access. This service is currently under development, but in its initial state is testing 12 'themes' of digital library service quality:

- accessibility
- navigability
- interoperability
- collection building
- resource use

- evaluating collections
- the digital library as community for users
- the digital library as community for developers
- the digital library as community for reviewers
- copyright
- the role of federations
- digital library sustainability.

(Kyrillidou and Giersch, 2005)

The background to the development of the DigiQUAL™ categories can be found in Lincoln et al. (2005).

■ Public library user satisfaction

While to date LibQUAL+™ has been largely confined to academic libraries, public libraries have been active is assessing customer satisfaction, and other aspects of the customer experience, for many years. In the UK, the leading activity is the PLUS surveys launched in 1995 by the Chartered Institute of Public Finance and Accountancy (CIPFA), which now cover over 90% of public library authorities. Separate surveys are available for adult and children's library users, and coverage has been introduced for electronic surveys (known as ePLUS). Data from these surveys are included in the annual report prepared by the Library and Information Statistics Unit at Loughborough University (LISU) (see Chapter 6, 'Inputs').

The PLUS data are used to enable public libraries to respond to the requirements of Best Value, a national framework through which all local authorities in England and Wales have been obliged to address performance across all services since 2000. Best Value indicator BV118 is concerned with satisfaction levels of library service customers. For 2006, the data required by the Department for Communities and Local Government (DCLG) were based on three indicators:

- the percentage of respondents who stated that they found a book to borrow as a proportion of all those answering the question
- the percentage of respondents who came to the library to find something out who stated that they were successful in finding it, as a proportion of all those answering the question

- the percentage of respondents who stated that 'overall' the library was 'very good' + the percentage who stated that it was 'good' as a proportion of all those answering that question.

Earlier data are publicly available on the DCLG website for local government performance (www.bvpi.gov.uk). This shows, taking the overall satisfaction levels during 2003–4 as an example, the results illustrated in Table 3.2.

Table 3.2 A selection of English public libraries' overall user satisfaction 2003–4

Authority	Very or fairly satisfied with the library service, %
Birmingham	87
Bradford	85
Buckinghamshire	94
Calderdale	94
Cambridgeshire	92
Cheshire	92
Coventry	85
Cumbria	93
Derbyshire	92
Devon	90
East Sussex	78
Kirklees	95
Lancashire	95
Leeds	91
Solihull	93
Sunderland	93
Wakefield	93

As will be seen, the results show generally very high levels of user satisfaction, although there are exceptions. A feature of the Best Value and Public Library Service Standard (PLSS) indicators is that many of them are accompanied by targets, and this seems to be a developing trend. The target is often based on previous data, for example on the top quartile performance in a previous period. For example, for children's services the target satisfaction level (as defined above) for 2006–7 was set at 90% – based on the top quartile performance from authorities completing this particular, newly introduced survey in the previous period. Whether the introduction of centrally defined targets actually results in improved performance at the local level is a matter for debate. Markless and Streatfield (2006) remark that 'the trouble with targets is that as soon as you focus on them they start to have a distorting effect'.

▪ Specific methodologies

Not every library will wish to embark on a comprehensive approach like LibQUAL+™. A variety of individual methodologies can be used to gather information on customer satisfaction in a straightforward way and most libraries carry out some kind of regular user survey. The following are particularly suitable methods (refer to Appendix 1, 'Data collection methods' for details):

- customer feedback analysis: systematically checking what users are saying about the service they receive, including queries and complaints
- questionnaires specifically designed to ask users for their opinions on services, either in general across libraries or targeted at specific services.
- focus group interviews, where a group of users is brought together to discuss their experiences of services.

Nearly all the methods used to gauge customer satisfaction involve asking the customers, but there are some indirect methods which can be useful. For example, even the fact that customers return time and again is a kind of indicator of satisfaction. While it does not tell us a lot, it does provide a very basic indication that *something* is meeting customer expectations. Checking with regular users about their motivation is an obvious performance measurement strategy, as is analysing the motivations of non-returners and non-users.

▪ Conclusion

The assessment of user satisfaction is fundamental to library performance measurement. However, simple measures of overall satisfaction probably tell the manager very little and for that reason performance assessment needs to be built on much more detailed analysis of the factors which are driving satisfaction levels for individual services. The use of quality attributes or dimensions can help to provide a rounded picture of where satisfaction levels need attention and standardized models like LibQUAL+™ with its associated tools provide a powerful means of implementing the assessment of satisfaction. At the same time, managers need to recognize that all such approaches have their limitations.

It is also useful, before leaving consideration of user satisfaction, to note that many of the analyses most commonly used attempt to quantify results. The danger of this, as discussed in Chapter 2, 'Theoretical considerations', is that numerical scores can mask the complexity of the real world of library service. It is all too easy to assume that a 'satisfactory' level of satisfaction indicates that all is well – but that may not be the case. That is why we turn next to what is a truly critical issue – is the library achieving long-term, positive impacts?

■ Resources

- User surveys are supported by the Libra package from priority Research Ltd (www.priority-research.com/), which is used by a considerable number of UK academic libraries.
- For academic libraries, SCONUL has published a briefing paper called *Measuring User Satisfaction: a practical guide for academic libraries*, and a questionnaire template for user satisfaction surveys (downloadable at www.sconul.ac.uk/activities/performance/surveys/templates.html and reproduced in Appendix 1, 'Data collection methods' as Figure A1.4). The questions address both the *satisfaction* of users and the *importance* of particular services to them.
- Public libraries PLUS resources are at www.ipfmarketresearch.net/culture/plus/default.asp, although registration is needed to access most pages.
- Many institutions are able to participate in more general user surveys conducted by their parent organization. Although this can be a double-edged sword since some autonomy is lost, it may ease the burden of survey distribution and of the analysis of results.
- LibQUAL+™ resources will be found at www.libqual.org/.

■ References

Brophy, P. (2004) The Quality of Libraries. In Hilgermann, K. and te Borkhorst, P. (eds), *Die effective Bibliothek*, München, K. G. Saur, 30–46.

Brophy, P. and Coulling, K. (1996) *Quality Management for Information and Library Managers*, Aldershot, Gower.

Crawford, J. and Riley, S. (2000) The ESEP Project at Glasgow Caledonian University and the Implications for LIS Evaluation, *Performance Measurement and Metrics*, **1** (1), 55–70.

Garvin, D. A. (1984) What Does 'Product Quality' Really Mean? *Sloan Management Review*, (Fall), 25–45.

Heath, F. M. et al. (eds) (2004) *Libraries Act on Their LibQUAL+™ Findings: from data to action*, New York NY, Haworth Information Press.

Hernon, P. and Whitman, J. R. (2001) *Delivering Satisfaction and Service Quality: a customer-based approach for libraries*, Chicago IL, American Library Association.

Kyrillidou, M. and Giersch, S. (2005) Developing the DigiQUAL Protocol for Digital Library Evaluation. In *MERLOT International Conference 2005, Nashville, Tennessee, USA, July 27, 2005*, Association of Research Libraries, www.arl.org/stats/newmeas/emetrics/MERLOT05_DigiQUAL-v6.ppt.

Lincoln, Y. S. et al. (2005) *User Perspectives Into Designs for Both Physical and Digital Libraries: new insights on commonalities/similarities and differences from the NDSL Digital Libraries and LibQUAL+(TM) data bases*, 7th ISKO Conference, Barcelona, Spain, www.libqual.org/documents/admin/ISKO.PDF.

Lock, S. and Town, J. S. (2005) LibQUAL+ in the UK and Ireland: three years' findings and experience, *SCONUL Focus*, **35**, 41–5.

Markless, S. and Streatfield, D. (2006) *Evaluating the Impact of Your Library*, London, Facet Publishing.

Moore, N. (1992) The ABC Approach to Consumer Service: quality management in a service profession. In Foreman, L., *Developing Quality in Libraries: culture and measurement for information services*, London, HMSO for the Circle of State Librarians, 7–12.

Parasuraman, A. et al. (1988) SERVQUAL: a multiple-item scale for measuring customer perceptions of service quality, *Journal of Retailing*, **64** (1), 12–40.

Ranganathan, S. R. (1931) *Five Laws of Library Science*, Madras, Madras Library Association.

Walters, W. H. (2003) Expertise and Evidence in the Assessment of Library Service Quality, *Performance Measurement and Metrics*, **4** (3), 98–102.

Zeithaml, V. A., Parasuraman, A. and Berry, L. L. (1990) *Delivering Quality Service: balancing customer perceptions and expectations*, London, Collier Macmillan.

4
Impact on users

■ Introduction

Ultimately, libraries and information services are judged by the effects of what they do. If they can demonstrate that people have become more knowledgeable or have developed new or improved skills from contact with the service, then the message to their constituencies and their funders is positive – and likely to be reinforced by the resources needed to sustain and develop those services. If there is no evidence available of any beneficial effects, then they are vulnerable to questions over their purpose and the value of maintaining them. It is not surprising that questions of *impact* therefore loom large. In this chapter the focus is on qualitative methods of assessing impact; in the next chapter the focus shifts to the question of economic impact.

It is worth noting again that terminology in this area is somewhat fluid. In particular, the term *outcomes* is sometimes used, especially in the USA, in place of *impact*. This explains why many US libraries and programmes concern themselves with outcome-based evaluation (OBE) – see, for example, the web pages of the Institute of Museum and Library Services (IMLS) at www.imls.gov/applicants/obe.shtm. Even in the UK there is ambiguity. For example, the Inspiring Learning for All website (www.inspiringlearningforall.gov.uk/), designed for supporting public libraries in their learning activities, talks of 'Tools to assess the impact of learning' on its home page, providing a link to a page which doesn't mention 'impact' at all but instead addresses the question 'What are learning outcomes?'! One of the reasons for this is that in education it is usual to talk of *outcomes* rather than *impact*: so, for example, when the Department for Education and Skills commissioned an evaluation of the University for

Industry (UfI), the resulting report was entitled: *Tracking Learning Outcomes: evaluation of the impact of the UfI*. In this book the convention of treating 'outcomes' as the more immediate effects and 'impacts' as those of the longer term is observed.

Impact assessment has become particularly important since governments introduced much more explicit policy agendas for libraries and their parent bodies. For example, throughout the world there has been high level policy concentration on matters such as lifelong learning and digital inclusion. It is not surprising, therefore, that individual libraries are called on to demonstrate that they are contributing to the achievement of strategic goals in these areas. More generally, evidence of positive impacts derives from requirements for *accountability* – libraries and information services must account for their use of public funds and for their stewardship of resources. Furthermore, where accountability used to be satisfied by measuring the efficiency of operations (perhaps using measures such as books issued per head of population) there has been a distinct shift towards effectiveness measures, including impact.

Among librarians this imperative to demonstrate impact has crystallized in a growing number of papers on the issue and is exemplified by the SCONUL/LIRG *Impact Initiative* (see www.sconul.ac.uk/activities/ performance/impact2.html). A recent book on the topic (Markless and Streatfield, 2006a) also testifies to the interest in the subject:

> All types of libraries and information services traditionally collect a range of performance information that can tell you as managers something about the *efficiency* of your services – sometimes flippantly described as 'busy-ness statistics'. What is now required is better information about the *effectiveness* of services, or the impact of services on users. [Original emphasis]

■ What is 'impact'?

Impact can be defined in different ways, but in the context of library services it may be most helpful to think of it as any *effect* of a service, product or other 'event' on an individual or group. It may:

- be positive or negative
- be what was intended or something entirely different

- result in changed
  - attitudes
  - behaviours
  - outputs (i.e. what an individual or group produces during or after interaction with the service)
- be short or long term
- be critical or trivial.

It is worth exploring these issues in a little more detail.

Positive or negative?

It is natural to 'accentuate the positive' (as the Johnny Mercer/Harold Arlen song had it!) and it is noticeable that many studies focus on identifying the positive benefits which arise from a service. To give one example, the rhetoric surrounding the successful People's Network implementation at first focused almost entirely on the undoubted success of this nationwide initiative to get PCs and internet access into every public library branch. It was only later that the drawbacks, such as the loss of space for bookstock, started to hit the headlines but little evidence was available on the extent of this impact. This example suggests that care is needed to take a holistic view on the effects a new or revised service is creating, in order to come to a rounded view of the positive and negative impacts.

Intentional or unintentional impact?

Again, one of the common features of impact studies is that they seek to assess whether intended impacts have been achieved. At the time of writing, there is a controversy in the UK media over whether secondary schools are promoting vocational qualifications at the expense of core subjects such as English and Mathematics in order to advance in published league tables. The intention of the government in publishing these tables was clearly not to discourage literacy but some argue that that is precisely their impact. This is an example of the old adage, 'what gets measured gets done'!

What is changed?

Because of the cost and time needed to conduct long-term qualitative investigations, impact studies very often rely on what people *say* about a service; what may be more important is whether – as a result of the service – people change the way they act. What may be even more important is whether as a result of the service they are able to do something – say produce a report or start a business – which they would not have been able to do before. In other words, impact studies may focus on improved perception yet it may be more important to track changed behaviours and new skills.

How long does impact last?

A question that is often neglected is whether an impact lasts over a protracted period. This is a particular issue for anyone developing new information systems since short-term impact may be overtaken by the next innovation. The challenge is to sustain a significant impact even when the service is no longer novel but has been integrated into workflows. Google is probably one of the best examples of this kind of achievement, since it has overcome the 'new innovation' phase to become the natural point of reference for many people's queries. Almost certainly long-term impact will only normally be achieved through constant innovation, something of which, again, Google is very aware.

Is impact critical or trivial?

There are many different effects that a service can have, and the fact that it achieves these does not of itself mean that they would be regarded as worthwhile by the user – even if they were positive in nature. There is always a danger that a cosmetic change to a service – such as the redesign of the website – can produce initial positive responses but that its actual impact turns out to be limited, perhaps as people become used to the new style or look. At the same time it is perfectly possible for small changes to have significant or even critical impact – as for example when a photocopier is placed on an adjustable-height table and suddenly becomes accessible to a user in a wheelchair.

■ Collecting data on impact

A variety of methods can be used to collect data on the impact of services (see below and Appendix 1, 'Data collection methods') but because what is being investigated is what has happened to individual people, there are ethical and legal issues to consider. The ethical issues were covered briefly in Chapter 1, 'Background'. It is important also to bear in mind the provisions of data protection legislation. In particular, this means that data about individuals must only be used for the purpose for which they were collected and must not be retained longer than is necessary for that purpose. In the UK, the legislation sets out eight principles which must be followed and similar principles are in force in other countries. Personal information must be:

- fairly and lawfully processed
- processed for limited purposes
- adequate, relevant and not excessive
- accurate and up to date
- not kept longer than necessary
- processed in accordance with the individual's rights
- secure
- not transferred to countries outside the European Economic Area, unless there is adequate protection.

These considerations form a minimum framework for personal data when investigating impact or indeed other aspects of library performance.

■ Assessing impact
The Concerns Based Adoption Model

One of the characteristics of impact measurement is that it is almost always longitudinal. What is being assessed is how people have changed over time and what the significant factors have been in bringing about this change. In order to provide a structured framework it is useful to be able to categorize the different stages through which people may pass as they change under the influence of, in our case, library services. One starting point for developing this kind of approach is what has become known as the Concerns Based Adoption Model (CBAM). Originating with work in teacher education in the 1960s and 1970s (Fuller, 1969; Hall et al., 1975),

CBAM is mainly concerned with the adoption of innovations, although it can be applied more widely. It provides foci on Stages of Concern (SoC) and Levels of Use (LoU).

SoC is concerned with the ways in which participants in, say, a new project or innovative way of working respond to the challenge of engagement. Some 'participants', for example, may be totally unaware of what is going on, others may show interest but no change in behaviour while yet others may change their whole way of working. Similar reactions may be found in a customer interacting with a service. The SoC concept helps to elucidate the way in which engagement changes and develops over time. Bonamy et al. (2004) describe an example of the model applied to e-learning innovation and development.

LoU suggests that instead of regarding stakeholders as users or non-users it is more helpful to think in terms of different levels of engagement – so, for example, one 'non-user' may have decided to have nothing to do with the innovation while another may be actively preparing to make use of it. Yet another may quickly change from non-use to become a frequent user.

The original application of this model to library and information services was in a part of a project, the Formative Evaluation of the Distributed National Electronic Resource (EDNER), which was designed to evaluate the UK Joint Information Systems Committee (JISC) Information Environment (see Kemp and Goodyear, 2003; Brophy et al., 2004b). Subsequently, we have been able to develop the model further to help differentiate between levels of impact in a number of studies.

In the EDNER work, there were a number of studies seeking to determine how much impact different projects were achieving among the higher and further education communities. We interviewed a wide range of academic staff in different institutions. For example, when asked about the impact of internet access from home or office, or on the move, typical comments were:

The amount of information is both an advantage and a disadvantage. You can find some wonderful stuff, but have to wade through lots and lots to find it.

Instant information on anything I need, and also the fact that I can download it and therefore use it in class directly . . .

I use the internet because I'm lazy (laughs), because I don't want to have to get up and go to the library and you know if you find the article on the internet you can just print it straight off instead of having to search through journal issues and photocopy them.

I can search in my underwear!

(Brophy et al., 2004a)

Clearly all these are impacts, but equally they show significant differences. Although we were able to group similar comments and thus produce some quantified data, this did not in itself allow us to characterize levels of impact. At that stage it was recognized that more work was needed.

The opportunity to develop this model further came with work undertaken during the early stages of The People's Network (PN) implementation, which involved the installation of public access PCs in all public libraries. In this work, there was similarly a need to consider how impacts might best be assessed and characterized. This was a typical example of a large implementation, which would impact on many different stakeholders and where their reactions and behaviours would undoubtedly differ markedly. In a paper commissioned for the PN website (Brophy, 2002) the author suggested that it would be helpful to think in terms of a Levels of Impact (LoI) model. This has subsequently been developed to that shown in Table 4.1 below, with a numeric code given to each level.

Table 4.1 Levels of Impact (LoI)

–2	Hostility	Users may be so disappointed with the service that they decide that it is a total waste of money. Perhaps the result is a letter of condemnation to an influential third party such as a councillor or senior manager.
–1	Dismissive	The user is not actively hostile but simply feels that the service is not worthwhile. It is a waste of personal effort to get involved, even if no attempt is made to undermine the service. There is a barrier to future engagement.
0	None	The user has neither positive nor negative feelings or views about the service. It is almost as if it didn't exist.
1	Awareness raised	Here the service has just about had a positive impact but simply in terms of the user being made aware of something of which they were not aware beforehand. They know the service exists, do not dismiss it out of hand and might turn to it in the future if they feel a need. They might also mention it, or possibly even recommend it positively, to friends and colleagues.

Continued on next page

Table 4.1 *Continued*

2	Better informed	As a result of coming into contact with the service the user has better information than before. This information may have been memorized or recorded for future use and is clearly of relevance.
3	Improved knowledge	The information obtained has been considered and the user is now more knowledgeable about the subject. This level equates to the lowest level of learning impact.
4	Changed perception and/or ability	The knowledge gained has resulted in a change to the way that the user looks at a subject. Real learning has taken place and/or a new skill acquired.
5	Changed world view	Here the users have been transformed by the service. Their view of the world has shifted significantly and constructive learning has taken place which will have long-term effects. Transferable skills have been acquired.
6	Changed action	The new world view has led to the users acting in a way they would not have done before. Learning has turned into action, so that the encounter with the service has changed not just those users but – in some way – the broader world.

The Levels of Impact approach proved helpful in initial evaluations of The People's Network (Brophy, 2003, 2004) where it informed analysis of qualitative data collected by local authority staff, in particular the analysis of comments from users. These were small-scale studies and relied on data contributed by local authorities' own staff. However, while undoubtedly 'accentuating the positive', some of the comments made by users clearly indicated that some people at least had been impacted to at least LoI level 4. For example:

He had no idea how to operate a computer and he was clutching a piece of paper with email addresses on it. It transpired that he had been born in 1911, he had been away for 3 days and wanted to send an email to his granddaughter to let her know of his whereabouts. Needless to say he required a great deal of assistance in setting up a Hotmail account so that he could receive replies from her at the library. He had no idea how to operate the mouse and needed help with suggestions for passwords etc., but he was a willing learner and amazingly patient and accepting of this new technology which enabled him to communicate with his relatives.   (Brophy, 2003)

Phil worked for several years as a country park ranger. His job mainly involved manual work but he wanted to progress into managing a park himself. He realized that he would need computer skills in order to develop his employment potential and decided to take the first step by attending the taster sessions at Wellingborough library. Phil attended Introduction to Computers and Introduction to the Internet sessions. He has since got a job as the manager of a heritage site in Essex.   (Brophy, 2004)

Academic library impact

While academic libraries have long been interested in their impact, a new focus for activity was created as a result of a joint SCONUL/LIRG Workshop held in Scarborough in December 2002. This event resulted in the launching of an Impact Implementation Initiative, which was in essence an action research programme undertaken by practitioners with advice from evaluation experts. The latter had many years experience of conducting library evaluation, and had published two influential volumes entitled *The Effective College Library* (Streatfield et al., 1997) and *The Really Effective College Library* (Markless et al., 2000). Deriving from that work, they further developed an 'impact process model', which in essence helped practitioners examine their own interventions in the learning and teaching process – 'a process to help people to decide together what they mean by impact and how impact can be evaluated for their innovation' (Markless and Streatfield, 2006a). Initial results from this programme of work have been encouraging (Markless and Streatfield, 2005, 2006b).

Public library impact

A very useful piece of work, funded by the Laser Foundation, followed up the widely perceived need to find ways to demonstrate the impact and value of UK public libraries across the whole range of their activities. Undertaken by PricewaterhouseCoopers the study published its final report in July 2005 (PricewaterhouseCoopers LLP, 2005). The suggestion in this report was that in each area identified for investigation both quantitative and qualitative evidence should be collected. For example, when measuring the impact of the public library on older people in the home the following indicators could be used:

- the numbers of older people accessing services for homebound users (in terms of numbers of visits to homebound users, frequency of visits and issues) – a quantitative measure
- Results of interviews with these users of the service, asking questions such as: 'Does the service from the library improve your life in any way?' and 'Do you feel that this service better enables you to live independently?' – in other words qualitative evidence.

Of course, care is needed to pose such questions in a neutral way so that both negative and positive comments are gathered. It is also useful if non-users are surveyed to find out what differences there are in their experiences. Impact measures have now been introduced for UK public libraries, using largely surrogate indicators (see page 66).

■ The impact of electronic services

Although the general approaches to measuring impact outlined above are fully applicable to both traditional and electronic services, some features of the latter require special consideration. A number of research and development projects have explored these issues; a selection of the more important of these is described in this section.

Staying with UK public libraries, a project entitled The Value and Impact of IT Access in Public Libraries (VITAL) was undertaken by staff at CERLIM between 1999 and 2001 (Eve and Brophy, 2001). This explored different methodologies which can be used. One finding was that

> in assessing the value of library services there has been something of a trend towards the recording of 'rich pictures' of use. These are individual accounts of the value and impact of interaction between a user (or sometimes group of users) and a library service. They are indicative and must be used carefully, for no one interaction can tell the whole story of a library's service performance. Nevertheless, when used as *part* of the story and when their evidence is triangulated with other evidence, they form a valuable input.   [original emphasis]

The main methods used by VITAL were:

- development of a profile providing the background and context of the library being studied i.e. the collection of baseline qualitative and quantitative data about the demographics of each library authority as well as the provision and, where possible, use of ICT services
- a printed questionnaire, distributed to library users
- a questionnaire to non-users, either asked face-to-face or over the telephone
- a series of semi-structured interviews with existing ICT users.

It will be seen that the design of this study made very deliberate use of triangulation (see Chapter 1, 'Background') so that findings from one method could be compared and contrasted with those from the others before conclusions were drawn. By testing the methodology across three very different public library authorities (one very rural; one very urban; one with significant towns and in the commuter belt) the VITAL team was able to develop a robust set of tools.

In contrast to VITAL, the Measuring the Impact of Networked Electronic Services (MINES) programme (www.arl.org/stats/newmeas/mines.html), part of the ARL's New Measures toolkit, uses a web-based survey form and collects data on who is using specific resources, where they are located at the point of use and their purpose in making use of these services. MINES for Libraries™ (as with other acronyms it has invented, ARL has trademarked this term) was field tested in a number of the Ontario Council of University Libraries' (OCUL) 20 member libraries in connection with their collaborative Scholars Portal during 2004–5 (Kyrillidou et al., 2005). The web survey was programmed to appear on users' workstation screens when they conducted a search during a two hour period once a month. Although this enabled interesting data on the reasons for use to be collected, it did not really address the effects of that usage. However, it is likely that this methodology will be further developed as part of the continuing New Measures Initiative.

The other major US development in library impact (or outcomes) assessment is centred round the Information Use Management and Policy Institute (IUMPI) at Florida State University, and particularly the work of Charles McClure and John Bertot. They have commented that in work they undertook to investigate the use of e-metrics (Fraser and McClure, 2002):

To a large degree, the E-metrics study found that academic libraries are not well prepared to demonstrate the extent to which they contribute to the organization's accomplishment of institutional outcomes. Moreover, libraries are looking at outcomes at the library level when, in fact, they reside within an institutional context.   (Bertot and McClure, 2003)

It is this institutional context which has provided much of the added complexity of electronic library performance measurement in general, and of impact assessment in particular. Bertot and McClure continue, in the same paper:

. . . outcomes assessments, as well as other types of library assessment, have yet to address factors and issues arising from the networked environment that seriously complicate valid assessment approaches. Indeed, little of the outcomes assessment work to date considers the evaluation of network-based services or resources – and how those services/resources differ from traditional library services or resources. And yet, libraries are increasing the network-based services and resources that they provide.

The eVALUEd project (www.evalued.uce.ac.uk/) at the University of Central England (UCE) is a UK-based attempt to address these questions and has published a toolkit of techniques (www.evalued.uce.ac.uk/tools_ archive/index.htm). A section of this website is devoted to impact measurement (www.evalued.uce.ac.uk/evaluating/impact/index.htm) and includes three sections:

- impact on learning and teaching
- impact on graduate skills
- impact on research.

The eVALUEd site contains suggestions for suitable methods for exploring impact, derived from the team's work on the HEFCE-funded e-measures project, as well as a number of case studies. For example, there is a detailed account of focus groups run at UCE with library staff and with students; for the latter, one of the questions asked was, 'Do you think that e-resources have improved the standard of your work?'. The answers the students gave included:

- generally yes
- can search the Internet to find topics you may not know much about
- increased access to core reading – access to print material is a problem when lots of students are after the same book
- sharing resources between Faculties is possible
- wider range of options for background research
- lecturers easy to contact because of email
- yes – wider background reading and more information available, therefore getting a broader perspective
- the downside is that more information = more work.

(www.evalued.uce.ac.uk/resources/docs/UWE.htm)

This is interesting on a number of levels and particularly because it illustrates how widely students interpret the term 'e-resources'. They certainly do not think of this as 'electronic resources supplied by the library', instead including both search engines (which other research suggests is likely to be Google) and e-mail. Libraries need to be aware that the services they offer are viewed by users, and particularly by IT-savvy students, as simply one part of a complex landscape of information and communication tools.

■ Surrogate measures of impact

It is often only feasible to assess impact by using surrogate measures – in other words indicators that suggest that it is likely that impact has occurred, without explicitly measuring that impact. An example of this approach can be found in the standard set of impact measures for public libraries recently been introduced by the UK government, developed in part through the Laser study referred to above. These measures are intended to sit alongside the *Public Library Service Standards*, which were issued in 2004 (see Chapter 14, 'Standards'). The impact measures introduced for 2005–6 are listed below (taken from www.mla.gov.uk/resources/assets//F/fff_faqs20050825_9034.doc):

Economic vitality
- Adult learning session attendee hours per capita per 10,000 population
Healthier communities
- Level of adult non fiction and children's non fiction reference and lending

stock of health related books as a percentage of the total reference and
lending stock of adult non fiction and children's non fiction books
- Number of issues per item of health related adult non fiction and children's
non fiction books

Quality of life
- Number of people receiving an 'At Home' Library Service
- Percentage of users of the service classing the choice of materials received
as very good or good

Raising standards across schools
- Number of packs delivered to children as a percentage of the eligible pop-
ulation at:
  — stage 1   new births to 9 months
  — stage 2   18–30 months
  — stage 3   36–48 months
- Number of new library members 0–4 years per year
- Cost of providing a Bookstart service per new member 0–4 years
- Percentage of eligible population 4–12 years who start the summer reading
challenge
- Percentage of boys participating in the scheme as a ratio of the percentage
of boys in the population
- Percentage of starters who complete the summer reading challenge
- Cost per head of starter
- Percentage of starters who also join the library

Safer and stronger communities
- Percentage take up of available ICT time in libraries.

It is immediately apparent that nearly all of these are surrogate impact
measures – they do not attempt to measure impact directly but use indicators that are suggestive of actual impact. For example, the first measure,
'Adult learning session attendee hours per capita per 10,000 population',
is intended to be indicative of 'economic vitality'. An assumption is being
made that the more adults that attend learning sessions in the library, the
more vibrant the local economy will become. At best, therefore, these are
very indirect measures of actual impacts. However, the use of this measure has been justified in the following way:

Research done by the National Institute of Adult Continuing Education
(NIACE) in 2000 found clear evidence that people involved in adult learning

identified real benefits in terms of better employment opportunities. This was identified as an increase in confidence, improved skills and self esteem among respondents. This is supported by research carried out by the Centre for the Economics of Education which concluded that . . . both literacy and numeracy are important determinants of economic outcomes.
   (www.mla.gov.uk/resources/assets//F/fff_sp_econvit_20050309_doc_4296.doc)

This is an important element in any use of surrogate measures – there should be some evidence of a causal link between what is actually meas-ured and the impact being claimed. Often the link is very indirect and frequently inferences are being drawn where there are gaps which need to be filled by additional evidence. Thus the NIACE research referred to was actually a report entitled *The Impact of Learning on Health* (Aldridge et al., 2000). In this case there is therefore a clear need for further evidence of the causal link, and a note added to the MLA justification provides this: 'It is accepted that the research quoted is now dated and that this is an area which could benefit from new research' (*op. cit.*).

The whole area of surrogate measures does need a lot of further research, since it is crucial that all the evidence is put in place along the chain from the trend being assessed to the actual impacts claimed. Librarians need to exercise great care, therefore, in making claims based on such measures until all this evidence has been assembled.

■ Impact on learning

Most libraries, and certainly those in the public and educational sectors, acknowledge that one of their primary purposes is to enable and encour-age learning. Indeed, it is useful to remember that the support of learning was the stated purpose of Antonio Panizzi when he developed the British Museum Library, later to form the core of the UK's national library. He said: 'I want a poor student to have the same means of indulging his learned curiosity, of following his rational pursuits, of consulting the same authorities, of fathoming the most intricate inquiry as the richest man in the kingdoms' (Miller, 1967).

This concern to develop libraries which are supportive of learning can be seen in publications and position papers published down the interven-ing years and remains among the most critical objectives today. One of the most important questions to arise is therefore how impacts on learning can best be assessed. A recent report for the Museums, Libraries and Archives Council (MLA) suggested that 'a key area for further research is to identify and develop mechanisms for libraries to measure and evaluate their informal adult learning services' (Ashcroft et al., 2005). This is clearly an enormous question and one which continues to attract huge interest among educationalists, so it is not to be expected that librarians will yet have found definitive answers. However, some useful work has been done to try to demonstrate libraries' significance in this respect.

The MLA's Inspiring Learning for All framework (www. inspiringlearningforall.gov.uk/) includes a series of tools for assessing learning outcomes (but note the comment on terminology on page 54 – there is some ambiguity between what is meant by 'outcomes' and 'impact' in this work). There are five generic learning outcomes (GLOs), which 'offer museums, libraries and archives a way of identifying and talking about the learning outcomes which their users experience'. These are:

- GLO1: Increase in knowledge and understanding
- GLO2: Increase in skills
- GLO3: Change in attitudes and values
- GLO4: Evidence of enjoyment, inspiration, creativity
- GLO5: Evidence of activity, modified behaviour, progression.

Each of the generic learning outcomes is explained in some detail in a document which can be downloaded from the website (www. inspiringlearningforall.gov.uk/uploads/More about the GLO's.doc). Douglas (2004) has given an example of the application of this framework to the 2003 Summer Reading Challenge, showing that:

- 95% of the children wanted to read lots more books
- 45% read a book they wouldn't have wanted to before
- 65% would tell their friends to read a book they'd enjoyed
- 92% of the books were new to the Summer Reading Challenge children
- 68% said they liked to write or draw or play games about a book
- 59% said they found out something from a book they didn't know before.

As the Inspiring Learning for All website points out, public libraries, museums and archives differ significantly from educational libraries in that in the former 'learning . . . takes place in informal settings, where people may not have consciously set out to "learn" something, and where their learning takes surprising and often unexpected directions'. This poses particular challenges for evaluators who are trying to assess performance.

■ Enhancing student performance

The question of whether library use, apart from taught programmes, leads to improved student performance is a critical one. In the USA, the Association of College and Research Libraries (ACRL) stated the issues clearly in a Task Force report published in 1998:

> Outcomes, as viewed by the task force, are *the ways in which library users are changed as a result of their contact with the library's resources and programs.* The task force considers simple satisfaction a facile outcome, however, too often unrelated to more substantial outcomes that hew more closely to the missions of libraries and of the institutions they serve. The important outcomes of an academic library program involve the answers to questions like these:
>
> Is the academic performance of students improved through their contact with the library?
> By using the library, do students improve their chances of having a successful career?
> Are undergraduates who used the library more likely to succeed in graduate school?
>
> Questions like these are difficult to answer. . . . The task force posits, however, that it is changes in library users such as the ones addressed in these questions that comprise the outcomes with which academic librarians should be concerned.
>
> (Association of College and Research Libraries, 1998,
> in Hernon and Dugan, 2002)

A number of studies have been carried out to try and answer this type of question. Barkey (1965) found evidence that students who scored well academically also tended to borrow a greater than average number of books from the library. Yet another study found that 'an academic library's services were negatively related to undergraduates' library use for undergraduates attending research universities and comprehensive colleges and universities' (Whitmire, 2002). However, the same study reported that 'money spent on academic library resources produces great self reported critical thinking for undergraduates attending research universities'. The establishment of robust evidence for a direct link between use of a library and better performance in formal education is perhaps the holy grail of librarianship – it has not yet been found!

■ Information literacy

In recent years librarians have been concentrating a great deal of effort on 'information skills' and 'information literacy', although the latter terminology has tended to be restricted to the academic sector. Their concern is that users of libraries should be able to develop the skill set needed to become confident consumers and producers of information, and that this should encompass both traditional and electronic resources.

Information skills and information literacy programmes need to be seen in the context of broader institutional, local, regional and national frameworks. Thus for the university library the critical issue is how the running of an information literacy programme contributes to the achievement of university objectives, most notably through enabling student learning or, to be more precise, enabling specific course and module learning outcomes to be achieved. For a public library, which may offer information skills tuition to disadvantaged groups in the community, alignment with the objectives of government policy initiatives through bodies like the Learning and Skills Council (LSC) will be critical. It is now almost axiomatic that information literacy tuition needs to be integrated or embedded into the mainstream of learning, so as to demonstrate its relevance to the students at the point they have reached. Standalone information literacy activity has been found to be poorly attended and ineffective. This adds to the complexity of evaluation, because it is rare to be able to isolate the other factors which have accompanied the library's programme and influenced outcomes and impact. Nevertheless, educationalists have long experience of student assessment, seeking to identify the effects of different interventions. For this reason it is important that library-administered programmes are accompanied by some kind of student assessment, which enables the fit between desirable learning outcomes and attainment to be measured.

The detailed treatment of educational assessment, and how it can be applied to information literacy programmes, goes well beyond the scope of this book, but the following issues should be considered:

- It is impossible to assess learning unless there are clear and measurable learning objectives, expressed as desirable learning outcomes, in place.
- Assessment regimes are an integral part of structured learning events and need to be planned in from the start, not added on as an afterthought.
- There is ample evidence that students tend to be motivated by what will be assessed and in many cases focus only on what is needed to pass an assessment. Again this has to be factored in to overall planning.
- Particular issues are raised by assessment of online learning, including authentication of who is taking the test.

The development of generic learning outcomes, as described above, is an example of how outcomes-focused evaluation can be undertaken in libraries.

There is a growing body of evidence about the effectiveness of different information skills programmes (see, for example, Society of College, National and University Libraries, 2004) and increasing expertise in assessing key issues such as integration into the curriculum. SCONUL has defined the critical success factors for information literacy programmes as:

- competent library staff
- sufficient organisational resources
- identifiable student outcomes
- effective multi-dimensional partnerships
- institutional strategic framework
- sustained pedagogic quality.

(Town, 2001)

■ Conclusion

The assessment of the impacts that libraries have on people's lives is the most complex and most difficult evaluation that can be carried out in measuring library performance. A wide range of methodologies needs to be used to gather both qualitative and quantitative data, so as to be able to paint an accurate and rounded picture of the difference that the library makes. This is an area that is likely to see considerable research and development in the near future, since the questions of impact loom large across every sector. In the meantime a considerable number of tools have been designed and made available to assist in this type of library performance measurement.

■ Resources

- A useful bibliography on library impact and outcomes is maintained by Roswitha Poll at the Universitäts- und Landesbibliothek Münster, Germany. See www.ulb.uni-muenster.de/projekte/outcome/downloads/ bibliography-impact+outcome.pdf.
- An overview of impact measurement in libraries, museums and archives was undertaken by a team at Robert Gordon University in Aberdeen in 2002 and remains a useful baseline (Wavell et al., 2002).
- The SCONUL/LIRG Impact Initiative has produced a number of resources. Refer to www.sconul.ac.uk/activities/performance/impact2. html for further information.
- In addition to the VITAL project final report (see Eve and Brophy (2001)) a Workbook is available at www.cerlim.ac.uk/projects/ vital/workbook.doc.
- The ARL New Measures toolkit can be accessed at www.arl.org/stats/ newmeas/index.html. It includes:
  — Assessing ILL/DD Services
  — COUNTER
  — DigiQUAL™
  — E-metrics
  — Higher Education Outcomes Research Review
  — Investigation of Cost Drivers
  — Learning Outcomes
  — LibQUAL™
  — MINES
  — SAILS.
- ARL is also developing a gateway to its various performance measurement tools (see www.statsqual.org/).

- The eVALUEd website includes a tool for creating your own impact evaluation instruments. See www.evalued.uce.ac.uk/custom_tools/index.htm.
- A demonstrating impact toolkit developed by WebJunction (a librarians' co-operative in the USA) is available at http://webjunction.org/do/DisplayContent?id=1193.

■ References

Aldridge, F. et al. (2000) *The Impact of Learning on Health*, Leicester, NIACE.

Ashcroft, L. et al. (2005) *Provision for Adult Learners in Public Libraries in England*, London, Museums, Libraries and Archives Council.

Association of College and Research Libraries. Task Force on Academic Library Assessment (1998) *Report*, Chicago IL, American Library Association, www.ala.org/acrl/outcome.html.

Barkey, P. (1965) Patterns of Student Use of a College Library, *College and Research Libraries*, **26**, 115–18.

Bertot, J. C. and McClure, C. R. (2003) Outcomes Assessment in the Networked Environment: research questions, issues, considerations, and moving forward, *Library Trends*, **51** (4), 590–613.

Bonamy, J. et al. (2004) *The Evaluative Research of Complex Projects in e-Learning: the case of the EQUEL (e-Quality in e-Learning) Project*, Networked Learning Conference, Lancaster, UK, www.shef.ac.uk/nlc2004/Proceedings/Individual_Papers/Bonamy_et_al.htm.

Brophy, P. (2002) *The Evaluation of Public Library Services: measuring impact*, (Issues Papers No. 1), London, Museums, Libraries and Archives Council, www.mla.gov.uk/documents/pn_impact-issue-paper.pdf.

Brophy, P. (2003) *The People's Network: a turning point for public libraries*, London, Museums, Libraries and Archives Council, www.mla.gov.uk/documents/pnreport.pdf.

Brophy, P. (2004) *The People's Network: moving forward*, London, Museums, Libraries and Archives Council, www.mla.gov.uk/documents/id1414rep.pdf.

Brophy, P. et al. (2004a) *EDNER: Formative Evaluation of the Distributed National Electronic Resource: stakeholder consultation and analysis: information usage in higher education*, (Deliverable MDA 3a, EDNER Project), Manchester, CERLIM, www.cerlim.ac.uk/edner/dissem/a3a.doc.

Brophy, P. et al. (2004b) *EDNER+: final report*, Manchester, CERLIM, www.cerlim.ac.uk/projects/iee/reports/final_report.doc.

Douglas, J. (2004) Inspiring Learning for All, *Library + Information Update*, **3** (4), 36–7.

Eve, J. and Brophy, P. (2001) *The Value and Impact of End-User IT Services in Public Libraries*, Library and Information Commission Research Report 102, CERLIM, Manchester Metropolitan University, www.cerlim.ac.uk/projects/vital/abs-pref.php.

Fraser, B. and McClure, C. R. (2002) Toward a Framework for Assessing Library and Institutional Outcomes, *Portal: libraries and the academy*, **2** (4), 505–28.

Fuller, F. F. (1969) Concerns of Teachers: a developmental conceptualization, *American Educational Research Journal*, **6** (2), 207–26.

Hall, G. et al. (1975) Levels of Use of Innovation: a framework for analyzing innovation adoption, *Journal of Teacher Education*, **26** (1), 52–6.

Hernon, P. and Dugan, R. E. (2002) *An Action Plan for Outcomes Assessment in Your Library*, Chicago IL, American Library Association.

Kemp, B. and Goodyear, P. (2003) *Surveys of Impact. EDNER: Formative Evaluation of the Distributed National Electronic Resource: Deliverable W-P C-2*, Lancaster, Lancaster University.

Kyrillidou, M. et al. (2005) *MINES for Libraries: Measuring the Impact of Networked Electronic Services and the Ontario Council of University Libraries' Scholars Portal: final report*, Washington DC, Association of Research Libraries.

Markless, S. and Streatfield, D. (2005) Facilitating the Impact Implementation Programme, *Library and Information Research*, **29** (91, special issue devoted to the Impact Implementation Programme), 10–19.

Markless, S. and Streatfield, D. (2006a) *Evaluating the Impact of Your Library*, London, Facet Publishing.

Markless, S. and Streatfield, D. (2006b) Gathering and Applying Evidence of the Impact of UK University Libraries on Student Learning and Research: a facilitated action research approach, *International Journal of Information Management*, **26** (1), 3–15.

Markless, S. et al. (2000) *The Really Effective College Library*, Twickenham, Information Management Associates for the Library and Information Commission.

Miller, E. (1967) *Prince of Librarians: the life and times of Antonio Panizzi of the British Museum*, London, Deutsch.

PricewaterhouseCoopers LLP (2005) *Libraries Impact Project*, LASER Foundation, www.bl.uk/about/cooperation/pdf/laserfinal6.pdf.

Society of College, National and University Libraries (2004) *Learning Outcomes and Information Literacy*, London, SCONUL.

Streatfield, D. et al. (1997) *The Effective College Library*, Bristol, Further Education Development Agency.

Town, S. (2001) Performance Measurement of Information Skills Education: what's important? Report and findings of a workshop held at the SCONUL AGM and Conference, Glasgow, April 2001, *SCONUL Newsletter*, (22), 21–3.

Wavell, C. et al. (2002) *Impact Evaluation of Museums, Archives and Libraries: available evidence project*, Aberdeen, Robert Gordon University, www.rgu.ac.uk/files/imreport.pdf.

Whitmire, E. (2002) Academic Library Performance Measures and Undergraduates' Library Use and Educational Outcomes, *Library and Information Research*, **24** (2), 107–28.

5
Social and economic impact

■ Introduction

Direct impact on individuals, and on the specific groups which the library serves, has been discussed in the last chapter. However, alongside that kind of impact measurement, there has been growing interest among librarians in recent years in trying to assess the broader social and economic impacts of their services. In other words, what does the library mean in terms of the development and sustenance of communities and societies? What does the existence of a library add to the economic performance of a city, region or nation?

■ Social impact

Studies of social impact start from the observations that all organizations have effects on the societies within which they operate, that they have responsibilities to those societies and that the extent of their impact needs to be monitored and assessed. The concepts of social responsibility and social impact were brought into sharp focus by the events of 3 December 1984 at Bhopal in India:

> Shortly after midnight poison gas leaked from a factory in Bhopal, India, owned by Union Carbide Corporation. There was no warning, none of the plant's safety systems were working. In the city people were sleeping. They woke in darkness to the sound of screams with the gases burning their eyes, noses and mouths. They began retching and coughing up froth streaked with blood. Whole neighbourhoods fled in panic, some were trampled, others convulsed and fell dead. . . . Within hours thousands of dead bodies lay in the streets.
>
> (www.bhopal.net/index1.html)

Subsequently the factory's owner, the Union Carbide Corporation, a subsidiary of the Dow Chemical Company, had to pay $470 million in a legal settlement. The company's website states: 'Since the time of the incident, the chemical industry has worked to voluntarily develop and implement strict safety and environmental standards to help ensure that an incident of this type never occurs again' (www.bhopal.com/).

Partly as a result of incidents like this, it is now accepted that good governance requires that all organizations monitor and take positive action on their impacts on society, with responsibilities going far beyond mopping up after adverse effects have been noticed. It is also worth noting that, while in the UK and USA shareholders still remain dominant, in many other countries a much broader view of corporate stakeholding is taken.

This change has not only affected the private sector. Both public and private enterprises now accept that they have social obligations, including responsibility for their impact on and contribution to the environments in which they operate. But there is also a third part of the economy, known as the 'social enterprise' sector. It encompasses a wide variety of organizations and initiatives and adds another dimension to this issue:

> It ranges from – at one end of a long continuum – small, local initiatives such as village halls, local markets, pre-school playgroups run by volunteers but often with some part-time paid work – playing a definite role in local economies, to – at the other end – substantial, highly commercial, competitive and successful businesses such as Govan Workspace in Glasgow, Coin Street Community Builders with its Oxo Tower on London's south bank, Greenwich Leisure (£50m turnover, 50 leisure centres in London, 3500 employees), Ealing Community Transport, the Big Issue and even the Eden Project in . . . Cornwall.
>
> (Pearce, 2005)

These are examples which illustrate the concept of *social capital*, a term coined in the 1970s by the French sociologist Pierre Bourdieu although its precise definition remains a matter for debate. However, it encapsulates the observation that people build value through the social networks in which they participate. Although initially sociologists focused on the ways in which it emerges and is sustained among individuals and groups, there is now considerable interest in the role that organizations play in the development of social capital.

Clearly, modern societies operate through a complex network of organizational types. Some are privately owned and funded, some publicly owned and resourced through taxation and some owned by communities, paying their way through a variety of mechanisms, including local fund-raising and grants from government and commercial interests. All of these organizations have impacts on society and on the development of social capital.

An important consideration for libraries and information services is that they operate at the intersection between the public, private and social sectors. Some libraries are very much focused on public services with largely public funding; others are almost entirely based within the private sector. Few, as yet, are social enterprises, although it is noticeable that a number of public library authorities are turning to local groups and volunteers to keep rural branches operating. For example, Buckinghamshire County Council resolved in January 2006 to close eight branch libraries but 'to invite proposals by 31 May 2006 from parish councils and other local community organizations that wish to take on the responsibility of directly providing long term, sustainable library services to their community, at no cost to the County Council' (www.buckscc.gov.uk/bcc/get//assets/docs/cab_20060123_item6.pdf).

The impact of library closures, or significant service reductions, on communities is not much studied although the University of Sheffield undertook a revealing investigation of the impacts of temporary closures of public libraries caused by a local authority strike in 1995 (Proctor et al., 1996). Any library performance measurement worthy of the name should be examining such impacts.

Social inclusion

A major concern for all libraries, but particularly those serving the public, is that of *social inclusion*. Although it may appear that public libraries, by their nature, espouse the principles of social inclusion, being open to all, in fact things are not so simple. Different services and different styles of delivery appeal to different groups, so that strategic and management priorities greatly affect service perceptions and usage. For example, a 2003 study of public libraries in the UK found that 'whilst white groups will predominantly use libraries to borrow or return books, other communities make greater use of the facilities to search for information, sit, study, read newspapers and to borrow CDs and videos' (PLB Consulting Ltd, 2003).

The *Public Libraries, Ethnic Diversity and Citizenship* study (Roach and Morrison, 1998) found that the 'public library service has not yet managed to engage freely with ethnically diverse communities', and that its structure 'is restrictive in terms of service access and denies ethnic minorities a stake in the public library system'. In a later, major report for Resource: the Council for Museums, Archives and Libraries it was suggested that efforts to modernize public libraries were having limited impact on social exclusion and that a more fundamental change, and commitment to social justice, was needed (Muddiman et al., 2000). Such findings emphasize that when seeking evidence of impact it is important to link studies and findings to the library's purpose and to all its stakeholder groups, as described in Chapter 1, 'Background'.

In response to these concerns, an organization called The Network (with the strap line 'Tackling social exclusion in libraries, museums, archives and galleries') has been established (see www.seapn.org.uk/index.html). Among the useful resources made available on this website are a series of working papers by leading authors in this field such as John Vincent, John Pateman and Dave Muddiman, which provide valuable background for any evaluation of social inclusion.

Social accounting and audit

The methodology known as 'social accounting and audit' has been used extensively in examining the social impact of many different kinds of organization. It has been described as

> a process which provides a flexible framework for an organisation . . .
>
> • to account fully for its social, environmental and economic impact and report on its performance
> • to acquire the information essential for planning future action and improving performance
> • to establish channels of accountability to its key stakeholders.
>
> (Pearce and Kay, 2005)

Social accounting tends to be used to describe the social impacts of private sector organizations. The main application of social audit in the library and information sector has been by Bob Usherwood and his team at the University of Sheffield. In a report for the British Library in 1998, they described the application of the methodology to two public libraries. One was in a primarily rural area (Somerset) while the other was urban (Newcastle upon Tyne).

The first step in the process was to identify all the stakeholders of the libraries, although the researchers report that 'with hindsight and increased resources we would widen the range of stakeholders in any future work', suggesting that considerable effort is needed to identify, contact and talk to the full range of interested parties (Linley and Usherwood, 1998; Usherwood and Linley, 1999).

The main research method used in this work was individual interviewing of members of the library staff and elected councillors, followed by focus groups with users and non-users. Following this the team held a workshop with library staff and elected officials, enabling the interim results to be discussed.

A fascinating finding of this work was that library staff tended to take on a 'caring' role regardless of their knowledge and familiarity with the local authority's policies in that respect:

> Although the library staff showed little awareness of the County Council's core objectives, there were still many aspects of library policy which were entirely consistent with these objectives, for instance in the widespread commitment to promoting access for people with disabilities. Moreover, individual library staff made decisions based on their own interpretations of what was 'fair' (notably on fines, but also with regard to free photocopying for school children and local policies, which provided free videos for people with certain disabilities).
>
> (Linley and Usherwood, 1998)

This emphasizes that in carrying out a social audit, it is important to investigate the reality of service delivery in the experience of the user, not simply to focus on either staff perceptions or on the policy dimension.

More generally, this work suggested that the value and impact of the public library needs to be examined and demonstrated in terms of:

- the social role of the library
- community ownership
- the educational role of the library
- the economic impact of the library

- reading and literacy
- developing confidence in individuals and communities
- equity in service delivery.

(Usherwood, 2002)

From a performance measurement perspective, the tools of social audit provide a useful way to broaden the scope of investigations into impact. Usherwood (2002) emphasizes that the key tools are qualitative in nature and involve listening to the experiences of those who have, and have not, been engaged by the library. The Museums, Libraries and Archives Council (MLA) provides a number of tools which may be useful, such as the Cultural Diversity Checklist (www.mla.gov.uk/resources/assets//C/cultural_diversity_checklist_pdf_6939.pdf) although these tend to focus on policy and resource inputs rather than outcomes and impact.

■ Economic impact

It is fairly easy to demonstrate that libraries have some kind of economic impact. If a business approaches a library for information on, let us say, standards for packaging products, then that information helps the business in its success and some part of the profits made are attributable to the actions of the library. If a national library, operating at the other end of the spectrum, runs a patent information service which alerts companies to patent applications in their area of interest, that information might save the company enormous expense on wasted research and development, or might help it avoid a case for patent infringement. Again, there is an economic impact. The big question, though, is how to measure it.

In this section we will look briefly at a number of recent studies of the economic impact of libraries to see what lessons they contain for developing performance measures in this area. First, however, we will look briefly at the general methodologies used in this field.

Return on investment

The concept of return on investment (ROI) lies behind many studies of economic impact, especially where either a commercial concern, such as an investment bank, or a government agency is providing significant amounts of funding. As the term suggests, the calculation of ROI is an attempt to quantify the amount generated for each unit (pound, dollar) invested. ROI is one of a number of possible economic measures of economic value, but is perhaps the one most frequently encountered in studies of public sector service-oriented organizations. It is important to recognize that some of the other economic indicators which could be used (such as return on assets or return on equity) may give a very different picture. However, that discussion would take us well beyond the scope of the current book.

Customer preference

There are two broad kinds of studies of the economic value of a service or development to customers. *Stated preference* methods involve asking people to declare their valuations. In other words it is based on what people say that they would do. *Revealed preference* methods, on the other hand, rely on observation of what people have done, and then infer their values from those observations. Related to these are the concepts of *use* and *non-use* values, the former involving assessments from actual use (even if indirect) and the latter from value which is not related to use. An example of the latter would be the value that people put on a pristine landscape, even though they may not themselves ever see it – they feel that it is worth preserving, perhaps for future generations or perhaps as part of their commitment to the environment. But as they never actually 'use' the landscape the economic value they put upon it can only be estimated by using stated preference methods.

Contingent valuation

Among the most common stated preference methods used for assessing economic value is what is known as the *contingent valuation method* (CVM). It involves asking people, through a survey (questionnaire or interview) how much they would be willing to pay for something. The weakness of these methods, of course, lies in the term 'would be willing', because a number of different distortions influence how people reply. For example, interviewees know very well that they will never actually be asked to pay real money, say to preserve the Arctic wilderness (except through general taxation), so they may well overestimate what their price would be. When the topic is controversial – in this case it might be seen as part of a broader campaign to prevent oil exploration – people will naturally overestimate what their real willingness to pay would be. Indeed it has been found in some of these studies that people state that they are willing to pay much more than their actual income!

In response to these criticisms the US National Oceanic and Atmospheric Administration (NOAA) undertook a detailed study in 1993, involving two Nobel Prize winners, which set out a series of recommendations which have won general acceptance (Arrow, 1993):

- Surveys should use personal interviews rather than less direct methods such as telephone interviews.
- Questions should be phrased as 'yes' or 'no' options, so that in effect the interviewees are being asked to vote on a specified amount, perhaps thought of as a tax, to protect a specific resource.
- Interviewees should be given detailed information on the resource in question and on the protection measure they were voting on. For example, they might be told best and worse case scenarios together with scientific evaluation of its ecological importance. They might also be told what the likely outcome of different protection measures might be.
- It should be explained to interviewees that they were being asked to express their willingness to pay to protect a particular resource, not to express their views on more general environmental issues.
- Subsidiary questions should be asked to ensure interviewees understood the main question they had been asked.

The contingent valuation method has been used in a number of studies of the economic value of library services, mostly in the USA. For example, the St Louis Public Library reported in 1997 that 'the library's users are receiving back more than $4 in direct benefits for every $1 of tax revenues that the public is contributing annually to the institution' (Holt et al. 1998?). A number of other studies which have used this approach are described below, while a recent review article can be consulted for a more in-depth analysis of the topic (Missingham, 2005).

The British Library study

In 2004 consultants were commissioned to carry out a study of the economic impact of the British Library, using the contingent valuation approach (British Library, 2004). This revealed that 'each year the British Library generates value around 4.4 times the level of its public funding', or to put it another way 'for every £1 of public funding the British Library receives annually, £4.40 is generated for the UK economy'.

The questionnaires used by the consultants are available on the British Library's website at www.bl.uk/about/valueconf/pdf/quest.pdf. A critical view of the questions asked might query some of the approaches taken. For example, 'The British Library is funded primarily through general taxation. In the unlikely event that this funding ceased to be provided, would you be willing to pay an amount, for example through donation or subscription, to help support the continuation of the British Library and its services?' is likely to have encouraged a response coloured by respondents' views on the desirability of using taxation to support the Library. A follow-up question, 'Imagine that the British Library ceased issuing readers passes but allowed existing readers to sell their pass what is the *minimum* amount you would be willing to accept as a monthly payment in return for your pass?' could be argued to be so unrealistic a scenario that respondents would only make a judgement based on their inference on why the information was being requested – to bolster the argument for continued funding for the Library. The questions posed to representatives of organizations have the additional problem that the individuals contacted may have taken the view that this was a fishing expedition to see if increased charges would be acceptable (in which case the respondent offers a low value) or an exercise to gain stakeholder support for continued grant in aid (in which case the respondent offers a high value) – there is no way of judging. In a number of other respects the study appears to have departed from the detailed recommendations of the NOAA report. These criticisms are not fatal to the study, but they illustrate that survey design for, and responses to, contingent valuation studies need the most careful design and interpretation.

Public libraries in Florida

During 2004 an extensive study was carried out by staff of the School of Information and Library Science, University of North Carolina at Chapel Hill, led by Professor José-Marie Griffiths, the Dean of the School. The study involved a literature review, a workshop for key stakeholder groups, a series of data collection and analysis activities and the use of an economic input/output model known as REMI (after its developers, Regional

Economic Models Inc.). REMI is very widely used by federal, state and local government agencies in the USA for assessments of the economic value of proposed or actual projects and thus has considerable credibility with elected representatives. The model was supported by over 700 telephone interviews and extensive in-library surveys (Griffiths, 2005).

This study provided a wealth of detailed information on who was using the state's public libraries, the amount of use and the many different reasons that people use the libraries. The study also showed that public libraries are regarded as important for all the different kinds of usage identified. However, the headline results related to economic impact. The study showed that 'Florida's public libraries return $6.54 for every $1.00 invested from all sources' (Griffiths et al., 2004; Griffiths, 2005). However, the REMI model enabled the study team to go further and estimate some more specific economic benefits from the investment made in Florida's public libraries. For example:

- for every $6,448 spent on public libraries from public funding sources (federal, state and local) in Florida, one job is created
- for every dollar of public support spent on public libraries in Florida, gross regional product (GRP) increases by $9.08
- for every dollar of public support spent on public libraries in Florida, income (wages) increases by $12.66.

It will be appreciated that these are very powerful arguments for continued investment. Furthermore, the authors were at pains to point out that the benefits of the public libraries accrue to all citizens:

> Public libraries allow users to share knowledge and services at a cost to them as taxpayers and in the time they spend using the libraries; however, all taxpayers in Florida benefit from the public libraries through their considerable contribution to education, the economy, tourism, retirement, quality of life, and so on. While users devote extensive time using public libraries for the reasons stated above (an indication of the value individuals and organizations place on the libraries), it would cost them substantially more in their time, effort and money to use alternative sources of information which, in turn, would affect the State's economy detrimentally.
>
> (Griffiths et al., 2004)

The value of preservation

An interesting question arises when considering the very long term value of library services, especially such activities as conservation and preservation which are intended to benefit future generations. This is clearly an area where there is little apparent immediate economic benefit – the whole point of preservation activity is to create future value. In a paper on this subject Currall and McKinney (2006) point out that decisions on what to preserve are more complex than is often supposed:

> Work has been and is being done on costing digital preservation. However, the methods employed do not take into account the actual assets that need to be preserved (managed), and it is generally assumed that the objects (with little communication of why they are 'assets') must be preserved. Business models must answer not only the question 'how much does it cost?', but also, 'why do we need this?' and 'why should we spend money on this, rather than on the primary business of the organisation?' These questions require very different answers than those that cost models can deliver.

This issue is worth highlighting because one of many libraries' possible roles is to secure the long-term availability of resources, whether these are incunabula, photographs, ephemera or electronic datasets. A limitation of most studies of economic impact is that they have a short timeframe – it is relatively easy to find an answer to the immediate economic impact of a service but enormously difficult to extend that to the economic impact over decades and centuries to come. Yet that is a challenge which needs to be borne in mind when the library's impact is discussed.

■ Conclusion

The social impact of libraries and information services is of critical importance, but is by no means easy to assess. Studies of this issue have relied on a mix of quantitative and qualitative methods, with the latter very much to the fore. Although the causal relationship between a particular social development, such as increased literacy, and the library's services is difficult to establish, listening to the accounts of people who have been directly affected by the service provides important indicators of what is happening.

Recent years have also seen some very interesting studies and approaches to the question of the economic impact of libraries. The application of contingent valuation theories has proved valuable, despite some reservations over their robustness. The results of these studies have shown that in many different situations, libraries are providing a positive return on investment, often of a very high order.

■ Resources

- The Centre for the Public Library and Information in Society at the University of Sheffield has a variety of reports on its research on social impact on its website at http://cplis.shef.ac.uk/.
- A toolkit for evaluating social exclusion has been developed by Suffolk County Council (www.suffolk.gov.uk/NR/rdonlyres/B66D14DB-2420-475A-9EB6-5015CDDEFC2D/0/aspiringtoinclusion.pdf). It is also worth referring to the UK government Social Exclusion Unit's website at www.socialexclusionunit.gov.uk/.
- The American Library Association maintains a bibliography of resources on ROI studies of libraries at www.ala.org/ala/ors/reports/roi.htm.
- The National Library of Australia has recently (2005) published an excellent overview of library economic impact studies. See www.nla.gov.au/nla/staffpaper/2005/missingham8.html.

■ References

Arrow, K. (1993) *Report of the NOAA Panel on Contingent Valuation*, United States. Department of Commerce, National Oceanic and Atmospheric Administration, www.darrp.noaa.gov/library/pdf/cvblue.pdf.

British Library (2004) *Measuring our Value*, www.bl.uk/pdf/measuring.pdf.

Currall, J. and McKinney, P. (2006) Investing in Value: a perspective on digital preservation, *D-Lib Magazine*, **12** (4), www.dlib.org/dlib/april06/mckinney/04mckinney.html.

Griffiths, J.-M. (2005) *Outcomes and Impacts, Dollars and Sense: are libraries measuring up?* In Brophy, P., Craven, J. and Markland, M. (eds) *Libraries without Walls 6: evaluating the distributed delivery of library services*, London, Facet Publishing.

Griffiths, J.-M. et al. (2004) *Taxpayer Return on Investment in Florida Public Libraries*, Tallahassee FL, State Library and Archives of Florida, http://dlis.dos.state.fl.us/bld/roi/pdfs/ROISummaryReport.pdf.

Holt, G. E., Elliott, D. and Moore, A. (1998?) *Placing a Value on Public Library Services*, St Louis MO, St Louis Public Library, www.slpl.lib.mo.us/libsrc/restoc.htm.

Linley, R. and Usherwood, B. (1998) *New Measures for the New Library: a social audit of public libraries*, British Library Research and Innovation Centre Report 89, London, British Library.

Missingham, R. (2005) Libraries and Economic Value: a review of recent studies, *Performance Measurement and Metrics*, **6** (3), 142–58.

Muddiman, D. et al. (2000) *Open to All? The public library and social exclusion*, London, Library and Information Commission.

Pearce, J. (2005) The Future of Social Enterprise, speech made at event to launch Wiselink, Dublin, www.cbs-network.org.uk/Occasional%20Reports.htm.

Pearce, J. and Kay, A. (2005) *Social Accounting and Audit Manual*, Edinburgh, Social Audit Network, www.cbs-network.org.uk/socialacc.htm.

PLB Consulting Ltd (2003) *Users and Non-Users of Museums, Archives and Libraries*, London, Resource: the Council for Museums, Archives and Libraries.

Proctor, R. et al. (1996) *What Do People Do When Their Public Library Service Closes Down?: an investigation into the impact of the Sheffield Libraries strike*, BLRD Report 6224, London, British Library, Research and Development Department.

Roach, P. and Morrison, M. (1998) *Public Libraries, Ethnic Diversity and Citizenship*, British Library Research and Innovation Report 76, London, British Library.

Usherwood, B. (2002) Demonstrating Impact Through Qualitative Research, *Performance Measurement and Metrics*, **3** (3), 117–22.

Usherwood, B. and Linley, R. (1999) New Library: New Measures: a social audit of public libraries, *IFLA Journal*, **25** (2), 90–6.

6
Inputs

■ Introduction

This book has deliberately chosen to put the spotlight on effectiveness, outcome and impact measures in its early chapters, reflecting a concern shared by most professionals to show how much good a library does. However, there are many occasions when it is important to measure inputs – resources which contribute towards the delivery of the service itself; processes – the work done to transform the raw inputs into useful products and services; and outputs – those things, including the intangibles, which are produced. The next three chapters focus on these topics.

■ The library profile

One vehicle for presenting input measures is the 'library profile' and many reports and studies use this approach. In essence the idea is to draw a picture of the library in terms of what resources it has to draw on. These include stock held, contracts for access to information sources, buildings, staff, IT equipment, financial resources and various types of infrastructure. There is always a temptation in presenting such data to imply that 'the bigger the better'. So a larger building, it is implied, is better than a smaller one. A larger bookstock is better than a limited one. All other things being equal, these statements are probably true but it is rare for all things to be equal. Apart from anything else, the purposes of the library and the purposes for which the resources are held will differ over time and between organizations.

■ Library statistics

When measuring inputs, processes and outputs it is common to make use of quantitative (i.e. statistical) data. Indeed, this is so much the norm that it may be taken almost for granted. Such data may be presented in terms of the individual branch, the individual library, a sector or by some other grouping.

Most libraries issue an annual report of some kind, which contains much data of this type. For example the British Library's Annual Report contains a section headed 'Statistics' (the 2004–5 version is at www.bl.uk/about/annual/2004to2005/pdf/statistics.pdf). This includes the data shown in Figure 6.1:

- Service in the reading rooms
  — seats available for users
  — other reader services, including:
      — number of training session attendees
      — number of contacts made by the disability support officer
- Bibliographic services
  — number of records in the British Library catalogues and databases
- Collection development
  — holdings, subdivided by format (e.g. books, philatelic items, music scores)
  — items received on legal deposit
  — serial titles received
- Website usage
- Storage
  — kilometres of storage
  — percentage occupied
- Preservation
  — preservation funding
  — items preserved
  — preservation microfilming (mainly for newspapers)

Figure 6.1 Statistical data about the British Library

The report also contains a financial overview, detailing income from the various different funding sources and expenditures.

A number of different agencies are involved in the collection of quantitative data on the different library sectors. In the UK, LISU (www.lboro.ac.uk/ departments/ls/lisu/index.html) is perhaps the most important of these. LISU undertakes various activities, including work for the public library sector on behalf of the Museums, Libraries and Archives

Council (MLA) and for the academic library sector on behalf of the Society of College, University and National Libraries (SCONUL). Its *Annual Library Statistics* publication includes trend data, showing the changes that have taken place over a ten-year period (see www.lboro.ac.uk/departments/ls/lisu/pages/publications/als05.html for the 2005 edition). Thus, for example, LISU has calculated that in 2003–4:

- public libraries spent an average of £17.80 per person in the UK; of this, 54% was spent on staff and just 9% on books
- higher education libraries spend an average of £293 per full-time equivalent (FTE) student, with 36% being spent on information provision.

In addition LISU publishes data on the average prices of books in a number of categories.

LISU uses a variety of sources for its data. The most important are the SCONUL annual statistical returns for the academic sector and CIPFA data for public libraries. Although extracts and commentaries on the data are published, the databases themselves (see Resources below) are not generally open to the public as access is restricted to contributing libraries. However, for those libraries the databases are accompanied by a number of analysis tools. For example, the SCONUL data can be manipulated to provide ranked lists of data for all SCONUL member libraries according to any particular statistic and can be displayed as a time series giving comparative data for up to nine institutions or for up to nine sets of data at once.

In the USA, the National Center for Education Statistics (NCES) collects data across the major library sectors (see http://nces.ed.gov/surveys/libraries/ – comparative data can be obtained at http://nces.ed.gov/surveys/libraries/compare/Index.asp?LibraryType=Academic and http://nces.ed.gov/surveys/libraries/compare/index.asp?LibraryType=Public). The ALA also maintains a summary of library statistics with pointers to relevant websites (www.ala.org/ala/ors/statsaboutlib/statisticsabout.htm) and issues a series of factsheets (www.ala.org/ala/alalibrary/libraryfactsheet/Default1446.htm) providing detailed information on topics ranging from the number of libraries in the USA to internet use in libraries. The Association of Research Libraries (ARL) publishes statistics for its member libraries and a range of other data about them (see www.arl.org/newsltr/meas.html) and makes this data available through an interactive website hosted by the University of Virginia (http://fisher.lib.virginia.edu/arl/index.html).

Australian and New Zealand library statistics are collected and published by CAVAL (www.caval.edu.au/infosys/prs/libstats/), which works closely with ARL.

In the European Union and adjacent states, the European Commission funded the LibEcon project (www.libecon.org/), which collected data on library provision across all European countries and provided comparative data as well as tools to enable detailed analyses on demand. Among the fascinating statistics made available was the fact that there were 404 million visits to academic libraries in the EU during 2001, of which 119 million occurred in the UK. Spending on libraries of all types across the EU was in excess of €14 billion that year. Unfortunately funding for this initiative was discontinued in 2004, and it seems unlikely that it will be resuscitated.

The International Standard ISO 2789:2003 (library statistics) exists to try and help library managers standardize the way in which they collect and present statistical information so as to facilitate international comparisons. There are six categories in which data are to be collected:

- libraries
- collections
- use and users
- access and facilities
- finance
- staff.

The standard, and the work behind its latest revision, has been described in some detail by Sumsion (2003). Further details will be found in Chapter 14, 'Standards'.

■ Content: acquisition, use and review

Library services are built on information content, so a major issue for library performance measurement concerns the evaluation of the published and perhaps unpublished resources to which access is provided. This section discusses traditional methods, used for example with printed books, and newer methods, for example with selecting and presenting online database services or websites. Robust processes for selecting quality resources are important, because one of the key advantages libraries claim over general purpose search engines is the quality of the resources they point to or provide.

The acquisition process should be guided by a collection management (sometimes called 'collection development') policy, so that a basic question is whether this policy is being followed. Assuming that it is, there remains the issue of whether the policy itself is helping to produce the right acquisition decisions. Further to this, the efficacy of the actual procedures being employed should be monitored.

The procedures used in different library and information sectors will be very different, and evaluation needs to be sensitive to sectoral priorities and nuances.

Book and journal selection

Because the library service relies almost entirely on published resources which the library itself has not created, the question of the quality of the books, journals, reports, CDs, multimedia and other resources acquired is critical. If these inputs to service delivery are of poor quality then the impact created down the line will be the poorer. A variety of methods is used to inform the selection of books and journals in libraries. It is beyond the scope of this book to discuss the selection procedure itself, but the question needs to be asked as to whether the stock acquired is actually meeting the library's purposes. To do this a number of approaches may be taken.

At the simplest level, usage data may be used to check on whether there are significant trends over time. For example, the average number of issues generated by books in their first year in stock would provide a very rough indication as to overall trends – though adequacy of book selection would be only one variable capable of influencing such a trend. A more detailed investigation might involve checking those new acquisitions which have generated little apparent demand and attempting to identify why this might be so.

At a general level, a critical issue will be compliance with input quality criteria in the library's stated collection management policy. This should set out in some detail how the suitability of resources is to be assessed. The kinds of criteria which should be applied include:

- the reputation of the publisher
- the reputation of the author
- recommendations from subject experts
- published reviews (i.e. post-publication).

With journals, a simple approach might be to record and analyse the number of page views of online titles (see below for a longer discussion of the issues surrounding this method). For paper versions the method is not so simple. One popular method is to attach a slip to the cover of each journal issue with a request to users to initial the slip each time they use that issue. Unfortunately, word often gets round and it is not unknown for academics to organize an initialling spree to ensure 'their' journals are not cancelled!

■ Electronic resource usage

By the mid-1990s it had become apparent that the measurement of the use of electronic content was becoming problematic. In the days when such services were mediated by librarians it was relatively easy to keep track of usage. However, with end-user access now the norm, new and more robust methods were needed.

Pioneering work in this field was undertaken by Charles McClure and his colleagues, initially at Syracuse University in the USA. *Assessing the Academic Networked Environment* was a wide-ranging investigation into how academic institutions could measure what was happening as the use of information technologies mushroomed across campus (McClure et al., 1996). It addressed the collection of qualitative and quantitative data to enable institutions to understand both the extent and the nature of networked information and infrastructure usage. Although the long-term goal was to develop ways to assess the *impact* of these services, the authors noted that there was a 'lack of even basic measures that describe and assess the academic networked environment'. A follow-up study used a series of seven case studies to explore the issues in the working environment: six of these were in the USA and one in the UK, namely King's College London.

In the UK, work associated with the Electronic Libraries Programme (eLib) built on the framework of the report *The Effective Academic Library* (Higher Education Funding Council for England, 1995) (see Chapter 1,

'Background'). In 1997, the report *Management Information Systems and Performance Measurement for the Electronic Library* was published, which explored the electronic library's performance from a functional and managerial perspective (Brophy and Wynne, 1997). Table 6.1, taken from that project's final report, illustrates the main areas of concern. Across the top are the functional areas. Down the side are the managerial concerns, ranging from immediate operational requirements to strategic considerations.

Table 6.1 Electronic library services: performance measurement

	Resource discovery	Resource delivery	Resource use	Infrastructure provision	Resource management
Operational management	Ease of use of OPACs	Speed of document supply	Appropriateness of conversion software	Availability of PCs	Peaks in demand for services
Forward planning	Which bibliographic indexes to provide?	Agreements for document supply	Emerging document formats	Number of networked PCs to be provided	Predicted costs of alternative services
Strategic management	Large scale resource discovery ('clumps')	Co-operative (e.g. regional) agreements	New classes of software	Development of off-campus infrastructure	Intellectual property rights (IPR) legislation for electronic sources

In this work it was suggested that the fundamental unit for electronic use should be the user session, rather than database hits. The reasoning was that the session unit 'is time- and process-independent, in that it measures each occasion a user tries to do something (find information or whatever) rather than how (in)efficient they are at it or how they go about it, or whether the network infrastructure is efficient'. This remains the most common method of reporting levels of usage.

In the European context, a number of research and development projects were funded to explore these issues in detail and try to develop sets of performance indicators for the electronic information environment. A collaborative project called CAMILE (Concerted Action on Management Information for Libraries in Europe) ran for two years between 1996 and 1998. A cluster of associated projects – EQLIPSE (Evaluation and Quality in Library Performance: System for Europe), MINSTREL (Management Information Software Tool: Research in Libraries), DECIDE (Decision Support Models: a Decision Support System for European Academic and Public Libraries) and DECIMAL (Decision-making in Libraries: Decision

Research for the Development of Integrated Library Systems) had laid the groundwork for European action. Subsequently work in the EQUINOX project (Brinkley, 1999; Brophy and Clarke, 2001) developed a set of candidate electronic library performance indicators, as follows:

1 Percentage of the target population reached by electronic library services
2 Number of log-ins to electronic library services per capita per month
3 Number of remote log-ins to electronic library services per capita per month
4 Number of electronic documents delivered per capita per month
5 Cost per log-in per electronic library service
6 Cost per electronic document delivered per electronic library service
7 Reference enquiries submitted electronically per capita per month
8 Library computer workstation use rate
9 Number of library computer workstations per capita
10 Library computer workstation hours used per capita per month
11 Rejected log-ins as a percentage of total log-ins
12 Systems availability
13 Mean waiting time for access to library computer workstations
14 IT expenditure as a percentage of total library expenditure.

This work was subsequently taken up within the International Federation of Library Associations and Institutions (IFLA) and the International Organization for Standardization (ISO). IFLA has an active Section on Statistics and Evaluation (www.ifla.org/VII/s22/index.htm) which, during 2006, is leading activity to try to reach agreement, in co-operation with UNESCO, on international standards and protocols for gathering library statistics and calculating performance measures. The aim is to advise libraries and national and international organizations on:

• the adoption of measures facilitating the demonstration of impact and outcome
• appropriate measures to reflect the use of electronic information sources
• the use of appropriate non-library demographic and socio-economic measures
• the construction of appropriate indicators using the recommended statistics

- additional and supplementary avenues to strengthen the collection of data.
(Heaney, 2005)

The ISO standard 11620:1998 (Information and documentation: library performance indicators) is described in Chapter 14, 'Standards'.

The ARL New Measures programme includes the E-Metrics project, which has been gathering comparative data on the usage of individual datasets by academic library users. Although the data are confidential, a sample spreadsheet is available for download at www.arl.org/stats/newmeas/emetrics/TexasUsage03.xls. The background to this work has been described by Shim (2001), who identified several key issues including:

- the problem that acquisitions, accounting and cataloguing systems are not set up to support data collection for electronic services
- definitions of what to collect, and how to collect it, vary between libraries in significant ways
- the fact that electronic resources are dispersed makes it very difficult to consolidate statistical data
- there are varying levels of staff and other resources available in libraries to enable this kind of data to be collected.

It is usually desirable that data on traditional and electronic resources should be collected together and should be as compatible as possible, so that a rounded and integrated picture is obtained, although that is not always possible. For example, SCONUL has added questions on e-resources to its annual statistical return, following an experimental project in 2004 involving 25 member libraries. Conyers (2005) has reported on the initial results of this work, which appear to show a marked shift from print to electronic-only journals over a short period of time, together with a decline in inter-library lending, although problems of definition and data collection are significant. Once a longer period has elapsed these trends should become clearer.

■ Data consistency

One of the issues identified in many of these studies was that there needed to be much greater consistency in defining data elements and capturing statistical information about usage. The International Coalition of Library Consortia (ICOLC) produced its *Guidelines for Statistical Measures of Usage of Web-Based Information Resources*, revised most recently in 2001. This suggested that the following five data elements should be collected:

- number of sessions (defined by logins to the resource)
- number of searches undertaken
- number of menu selections, intended to show how many selections were needed to find resources
- number of full-text units (such as a book or journal paper) downloaded
- number of failed transactions or other measure of peak capacity.

For many years, librarians had been concerned that methods which were being used by publishers to report electronic journal usage were inconsistent. For example, some systems would count every page of a paper as a downloaded item, while others would count each paper. Such inconsistency made interpretation of data well-nigh impossible. To add to the problem it was often simply impossible to work out how the usage data were being generated.

To address this problem, representatives of publishers and libraries came together in Project COUNTER (Counting Online Usage of Networked Electronic Resources) in early 2002. Then, in December of that year, a code of practice was issued containing a series of standard definitions which must be adhered to should a vendor wish to claim COUNTER compliance. For example, an 'item' was defined as

> A uniquely identifiable piece of published work that may be original or a digest or a review of other published work. PDF, Postscript and HTML formats of the same full text article (for example), will be counted as separate items.
>
> (www.projectcounter.org/code_practice_r1.html)

A second edition (Release 2) of the COUNTER *Code of Practice for Journals and Databases* was published in April 2005, followed by the COUNTER *Code of Practice for Books and Reference Works* in March 2006. By that stage 23 publishers were at least partly COUNTER-compliant, including some of the major players such as Springer Verlag and Cambridge University Press.

■ Selection of free online resources

The selection of free online resources raises different issues from those associated with subscription services. Some libraries appear not to treat such resources as their concern, though this would seem to be very short-sighted for any *information* service. In the UK steps have been taken to provide national support for the academic library sector through the Intute (formerly Resource Discovery Network (RDN)) service (see www.intute.ac.uk). There are four subject areas:

- arts and humanities
- science, engineering, technology
- health and life sciences
- social sciences.

The public library based People's Network has developed a Discover service, which is based on records contributed by a range of libraries and also incorporates news from the BBC as well as some specialized data feeds such as 'quicklinks' from the IT for Me project in South Yorkshire (www.itforme.org.uk/it4me/).

The maintenance of quality standards is perhaps the biggest issue for this kind of service. With this in mind, considerable work has been undertaken by Intute and its precursors on the evaluation of resources felt suitable for inclusion in their collections of internet resources (see, for example, Hofman and Worsfold, 1999). The following description is based on this work.

Four major headings – *context, content, use features* and *system features* – provide the basic framework for evaluation. Under these there are specific criteria, described below:

- Context
    - *Provenance*: the authenticity of the resource, whether its source is known and whether this information can be validated
    - *Authority*: the reputation of the author and/or website and whether the material has been quality assured, perhaps by peer review
    - *Uniqueness*: seeking to avoid simply linking to resources which are repetitive of material already available; usually, it is better to link to original sources, although there may be a case for providing clear, explanatory sources as well

—*Relationship to other resources*: concerned with the 'fit' of particular resources within the collection as a whole as well as the completeness of the particular resource

—*Audience*: seeking to match the intended audience of a resource to that of the service; for example, it would be undesirable to include a website explaining chemical reactions to primary school children in a resource intended for university researchers.

- Content
  —*Scope/coverage*: ensuring that the resource is a good fit with the collection's subject or other declared scope
  —*Accuracy*: whether it is possible to verify the accuracy of the content of the resource
  —*Currency*: whether the information is up to date
  —*Substantiveness*: avoiding material that is simply a pointer to something else, including advertising, or which contains trivial amounts of information
  —*Comprehensiveness*: whether the material is complete and contains everything needed to inform the user about the topic
  —*Composition and organization*: the structure of the resource, including issues such as grammar and spelling, as well as the way in which the information is presented.
- Use features
  —*Accessibility*: whether the resource complies with standards for accessibility by differently-abled users, such as the World Wide Web Consortium's Web Accessibility Initiative (see Chapter 11, 'Services for all')
  —*Usability*: the ease with which the resource can be navigated and the clarity of its layout; examples would be clearly labelled links and the judicious use of images to aid navigation, as well as an easy to use search facility
  —*Terms of use*: the resource being available for use on reasonable terms; these may be declared in a Creative Commons licence (see www. creativecommons.org.uk)
  —*Legitimacy*: the resource not breaching anyone else's rights; for example, it should not plagiarize other work or use other resources without permission
  —*Aesthetics*: although to some extent a matter of personal taste,

resources should have a good 'look and feel' and abide by basic design principles
— *User support*: instructions and help facilities where these might be needed, and sites should make some provision for feedback; some sites might provide training materials if the subject matter is complex.
• System features
— *Site integrity*: a minimum of broken links and evidence that the resource is likely to be stable in the medium to long term
— *System reliability*: concerned with the availability and response times of the site
— *Use of technical standards*: the resource conforming to generally accepted technical standards; for example, does the site provide appropriate metadata for records or other objects it contains?

It is unlikely that any resource will completely conform to all of these tests. Instead they form a basic checklist against which candidate resources can be judged. They should also be used to check that resources currently in the collection are still valid, since the nature of internet resources means that they often quickly date.

Criteria of this type have been adapted by many of the different libraries and broader services which provide internet resource collections. (For an example, see www.sosig.ac.uk/about_us/ecrit.html.) An interesting example of the possible application of such criteria would be the collaborative resource, Wikipedia – see www.nature.com/news/2005/051212/full/438900a.html for a report on *Nature*'s comparison of Wikipedia and the online Encyclopaedia Britannica.

■ Collection strength

Assessing the quality of the resources offered is not just a matter of assessing individual items being selected for acquisition. For as long as the physical library remains important, it will be vital to be able to measure the strengths of its *collections* of books, journals, etc., since the collection rather than the possession of a single title is usually what makes a visit to the library worthwhile. At the same time, it is of course important to be able to assess the appropriateness and strength of the collections made available by electronic means. Different approaches will be needed to these two issues.

With regard to physical collections, one systematic method is to compare the collections of a particular library with the best known examples. The Conspectus methodology was originally developed by the Research Libraries Group (RLG) in the USA to formalize this approach, although it is no longer widely used in the original form (see www.rlg.org/en/page.php?Page_ID=206). However, the approach was further developed by the Western Library Network (WLN) and the methodology is worth noting as it can still be useful as a means for libraries to describe their collection strengths. WLN's work forms the basis for current Conspectus-related methodologies such as that supported by OCLC (see below).

Under Conspectus 24 subject divisions were defined and two codes were assigned to each collection (or subject area), one describing its existing collection strength (ECS) and the other the current collecting intensity (CCI). Levels were defined in the following way:

- Level 0: out of scope: the library does not collect in this area.
- Level 1: minimal: a collection for which only few selections are made beyond introductory/very basic material.
- Level 2: basic information: a collection of up-to-date materials which serves to introduce and define a subject; a basic information collection which can support general enquiries, school and some undergraduate instruction, but is not sufficient to support advanced undergraduate courses.
- Level 3: intermediate: a collection containing a broad range of resources adequate to support undergraduate instruction and work at less than research intensity.
- Level 4: research: a collection containing current and retrospective resources which can support postgraduate and independent academic research; the collection will provide materials in all appropriate formats and languages.
- Level 5: comprehensive: a collection which includes, as far as is reasonably possible, all significant works of recorded knowledge in all applicable languages for a defined and limited field; the aim, if not the achievement, is comprehensiveness.

(www.ukoln.ac.uk/metadata/cld/study/collection/conspectus/)

This approach proved useful in the 1980s and 1990s when attempts were being made to identify and characterize research collections and is still used by some libraries (for a recent example see Skaggs, 2006). OCLC developed a number of tools to assist libraries in using Conspectus and maintains a WLN/Conspectus subject hierarchy based on the original 24 subject divisions. OCLC has further developed its Conspectus-related services and launched a new facility in 2005 (the *WorldCat Collection Analysis Service* – www.oclc.org/collectionanalysis/default.htm), which enables subscribing libraries to analyse and compare their collections with others represented in WorldCat, OCLC's shared catalogue service. This includes reference to the Conspectus subject hierarchy, which is linked to the Dewey Decimal, Library of Congress and National Library of Medicine Classifications. Quite sophisticated analyses can be performed, including sub-divisions by date of publication, audience (adult or juvenile), language and format.

■ Conclusion

It is important for managers to have a clear grasp of the inputs which are available to them in terms of resources such as finance, buildings and stock and to be able to identify significant changes. Although such data do not indicate use, still less impact, without them managers cannot organize resources or put in place appropriate processes for service delivery. Of particular importance is the comparability of data over time and where possible between services, so that trends can be discovered and tracked.

■ Resources

- Library and Information Statistics Unit (LISU): www.lboro.ac.uk/departments/ls/lisu/index.html.
- SCONUL statistical data (requires password for access): www.sconul.ac.uk/pubs_stats/stats.html.
- CIPFA public libraries statistical data (requires password for access): www.cipfastats.net/. A summary and commentary on each year's results is published: see www.cipfastats.net/download.asp?filename=www.cipfastats.net/uploads/commentary412006271558.pdf for the most recent.
- COUNTER codes of practice can be consulted at www.projectcounter.org/code_practice.html.

- At the time of writing the *Intute Collection Development Framework and Policy* was being revised. It will be available at www.intute.ac.uk/policy.html when published.

■ References

Brinkley, M. (1999) The EQUINOX Project: library performance measurement and quality management system, *Exploit Interactive*, (03), www.exploit-lib.org/issue3/equinox/.

Brophy, P. and Wynne, P. (1997) *Management Information Systems and Performance Measurement for the Electronic Library*, London, Library Information Technology Centre, www.ukoln.ac.uk/dlis/models/studies/mis/mis.doc.

Brophy, P. and Clarke, Z. (2001) *EQUINOX: library performance measurement and quality management system: deliverable D2.5: edited final report*, Dublin, Dublin City University, http://equinox.dcu.ie/reports/d2_5.html.

Conyers, A. (2005) E-resources in SCONUL Member Libraries: what the statistics tell us, *SCONUL Focus*, (36) 65–7.

Heaney, M. (2005) Global Statistics, *IFLA Statistics and Evaluation Section Newsletter*, December, 3.

Higher Education Funding Council for England (1995) *The Effective Academic Library: a framework for evaluating the performance of UK academic libraries: a consultative report to HEFC(E), SHEFC, HEFC(W) and DENI by the Joint Funding Council's Ad Hoc Group on performance indicators for libraries*, HEFCE(E), Bristol, HEFCE.

Hofman, P. and Worsfold, E. (1999) *Specification for Resource Description Methods Part 2: selection criteria for quality controlled information gateways*, ILRT, University of Bristol, www.ukoln.ac.uk/metadata/desire/quality/.

McClure, C. R. et al. (1996) *Assessing the Academic Networked Environment: strategies and options*, Washington DC, Coalition for Networked Information, www.ii.fsu.edu/~cmcclure/network/toc.html.

Shim, W. (2001) Measuring Services, Resources, Users and Use in the Networked Environment, *Journal of Library Administration*, **35** (4), 71–84.

Skaggs, B. L. (2006) Assessing an Integrated Government Documents Collection, *Collection Building*, **25** (1), 14–18.

Sumsion, J. (2003) ISO2789: what's new in and around the revision? *Performance Measurement and Metrics*, **4** (3), 103–12.

7
Processes

■ Introduction

Efficiency of operation – essentially the transformation of available inputs into the maximum number of high quality outputs, or the production of the required number of high quality outputs from as few inputs as possible – is an important part of performance measurement. Apart from any other consideration, accountability for the use of, often public, funding requires that processes are as efficient as possible. Libraries have addressed this requirement for many years. In this chapter we will look at some of the ways in which efficiency can be measured.

A useful perspective on assessing process performance is to think of the organization as a series of units which are dependent on each other, acting as each other's suppliers and customers. The following example illustrates the point:

> The professional librarian may decide to order the book in the first instance on the basis of either an earlier request or an assessment of likely demand. He or she then becomes the customer of the acquisitions department which is to arrange for the item in question to be purchased. In turn the acquisitions department becomes the customer of an external supplier. When the book is delivered, the acquisitions department supplies it to the cataloguer – another customer/supplier relationship. Each department of the library will in turn be the customer and the supplier as the book travels down the chain until eventually the circulation department supplies it to the end user, the external customer.
>
> (Brophy and Coulling, 1996)

This idea has been encapsulated in the concept of *quality chains*, encouraging a stress on the importance of internal customer satisfaction. Using classic definitions of quality, we can ask whether the product which is handed over to the next person in the chain is fit for that person's purpose and meets that person's requirements. Asking these questions provides a powerful tool for identifying where things may be going wrong, or where inefficiencies may be occurring. As with all chains, the strength of the whole is defined by the strength of the weakest link. Identifying this weakness provides staff with opportunities to improve overall performance. A useful discipline is therefore for all staff to be challenged to answer a series of questions at regular intervals:

- Who are my customers?
- What are their requirements?
- How do I find out about their requirements – and how do I know when their requirements change?
- How do I know whether or not I'm meeting their requirements?
- What prevents me from meeting their requirements – and what can I do about it?

■ Throughputs

An obvious way to perform external checks on efficiency is to calculate how many units, of whatever kind, are processed in a given time period. For example, the number of books catalogued per month could be used as a measure of the efficiency of a cataloguing department, or perhaps of individual cataloguers. Such data are readily available, either from the cataloguing system or perhaps by manual record keeping. The data can be tabulated and graphs drawn, perhaps comparing results month by month. However, the interpretation of such data needs considerable care. Factors such as the following may be relevant:

- the type of books being catalogued; for example, it would be expected that foreign language material would take longer to catalogue than books in the native language
- the number of working days, so, for instance, a monthly calculation of efficiency would need to take account of public and personal holidays,

even the movable date of Easter can have a significant effect, as it may occur in March one year and in April the next
- the availability of material to catalogue; if staff have been so efficient as to complete all the cataloguing, and so moved on to other tasks, this needs to be taken into account.

One way to examine the data produced from this kind of exercise is to benchmark the results against those from other libraries. This is discussed in Chapter 12, 'Benchmarking'.

■ The ISO 9000 standard

A rather different approach to measuring performance in the context of processes is represented by the ISO9000 quality management standard. The idea behind this standard is that by monitoring conformance to agreed processes and reducing the number of errors made, performance can be maximized. The antecedents of this standard, notably its British Standards equivalent BS5750, set out the principle that performance can be improved by having detailed procedures in place, monitoring that they are being followed, and then tracking exceptions back to a faulty procedure or faulty application of the procedure. The former problem implies that the procedure needs to be changed, the latter that better staff training or better management control is needed.

At the heart of this approach is the idea that services should be delivered consistently and that only through consistency can quality of service be guaranteed. It is important to emphasize, therefore, that the ISO 9000 approach differs fundamentally from the kind of process control which relies on inspection at the end, or after the end, of service or product delivery.

The standard has been used in a number of libraries and a useful guide to library applications has been published (Ellis and Norton, 1993). This demonstrates, among other considerations, how a quality system like ISO 9000 can be applied to typical library procedures such as acquisitions. As Ellis and Norton remark:

It is not sufficient to *say* that suppliers are checked for delivery times every month; this has to be checked, documented and demonstrated. A quality record will show what action is taken and what is done if supply times are consistently unsatisfactory.

ISO9000 compliance is accredited by an external auditor, who examines both the basic documentation and the organization's records of exceptions and corrective actions. In this way the organization is encouraged not just to identify problems but to take systematic steps, often by changing procedures or improving training, to ensure long-term corrective action is taken.

▪ Business process reengineering

The importance of monitoring and improving the library's processes can be seen in the parallels with the emphasis which the commercial sector has placed on business process reengineering (BPR). Hammer and Champy (2001), who wrote one of the seminal books on the topic, defined BPR as 'the fundamental rethinking and radical redesign of business processes to achieve dramatic improvements in critical contemporary measures of performance, such as cost, quality, service, and speed'. One of their insights is that technological change has made it imperative for organizations to rethink their processes from the viewpoint of essential outcomes. A particularly good example of BPR in the library sector is provided by Stanford University Libraries Technical Services team, who have made their investigation and action plan available at http://library.stanford.edu/depts/ts/about/redesign/report/index.html. Their use of this approach resulted in eight specific changes to processes, designed within a new concept of technical processing.

From a library performance measurement perspective the actual use of BPR would follow on from the identification of process questions, with relevant data being fed into the process. Usually there would be some emphasis on costs as well as use of resources. These considerations imply that suitable performance indicators will need to be in place *before* a BPR exercise is carried out and they will be needed during and after the exercise. Representative process indicators, such as throughputs, would typically be needed. An essential consideration is that the chosen indicators will need to be valid before, during and after the exercise – there is no point implementing revised processes and then finding that the available data cannot tell you whether there have been any consequent improvements!

■ Electronic delivery

Process issues are particularly important with electronic service delivery because the lack of a human intermediary when a transaction occurs reduces the opportunity for immediate corrective action. The irritation of users who find that the system is behaving illogically yet offering no escape route is obvious. The result of such experiences can all too easily be that the user goes elsewhere – which is very easy in a world of information glut – and never returns.

Most IT-based services are delivered using a web browser, although there are some proprietary interfaces in use. As far as their processes are concerned, the performance of these systems can be monitored in relation to consistent delivery of the service when required. For example, dead links on the library website are a process failure, as is unscheduled system downtime. Procedures need to be in place to monitor both problems. Issues related to website usage are a somewhat different matter and are discussed in Chapter 8, 'Outputs'.

A more complex process issue arises from considerations related to the interoperability of IT-based systems. A great deal of effort is being expended in trying to ensure that a wide range of heterogeneous information systems can present data to the user seamlessly. From a technical performance measurement perspective, this issue is best expressed in terms of conformance to relevant standards. For example, if a system is to cross-search a series of remote target databases, then compliance to the Z39.50 standard may the critical issue. If the library is to harvest records from a range of external repositories in order to perform its own processing, then OAI-PMH (Open Archives Initiative – Protocol for Metadata Harvesting) is the appropriate standard. To complicate matters, conformance is not a simple yes/no dichotomy, since there are levels of conformance that need to be related to the service which the library wishes to offer.

Process conformance in relation to ICT-based systems is further complicated by the rapid development of new standards and protocols and it can be difficult to strike the right balance between being up to date and achieving stable systems. It is helpful that, in the UK, the Joint Information Systems Committee (JISC) has spent considerable effort in developing a model 'information architecture', described at www.ukoln. ac.uk/distributed-systems/jisc-ie/arch/. The aim of this work is to demonstrate how libraries and other services within academic institutions can develop coherent services by adopting common standards and sharing infrastructure and 'middleware' services. From a performance measurement point of view, this suggests that there is a need for conformance to standards in the following areas:

- web standards and file formats
- distributed searching
- metadata harvesting
- news and alerting
- context-sensitive linking
- transactional services
- authentication and authorization
- metadata usage (essentially following guidelines on the application of Dublin Core)
- service registries.

The situation with technical infrastructure is further complicated by the presence of disparate systems within a marketplace peopled with competing commercial suppliers as well as sector-specific services.

An even more complex issue arises when the performance of electronic processes is considered in relation to users' tasks, activities and workflows. Where the library is effectively a data provider to other services, such as VLEs, MLEs or search engines, there are considerations of visibility and integration which may be driven by other providers' decisions and solutions. BPR offers a possible methodology for exploring these implications and designing appropriate solutions.

■ Conclusion

Consistency of processes has a great deal to do with the achievement of excellent services, provided those processes are being monitored continuously to ensure that they are producing the required outputs, which then lead on to outcomes and impacts. The ISO 9000 standard provides a formal mechanism, with external audit, to ensure that processes are appropriate and being applied properly, while encouraging the use of exceptions to flag where management action is needed. BPR is a less formal methodology which has proved effective in the commercial sector with a few examples emerging in library management. Processes associated with the delivery of electronic services are complex, especially where they imply integration into non-library workflows, but require attention if the delivery of excellence is to be achieved.

■ Resources

- The eVALUEd Toolkit contains a section on technical performance, which addresses a range of process issues, at www.evalued.uce.ac.uk evaluating/management/technicalperformance.htm. Some other sections of the Toolkit are also relevant to these issues.
- ISO 9000 is explained in detail on the British Standards Institute website at http://emea.bsi-global.com/Quality/Overview/WhatisISO9000.xalter.
- In addition to the UKOLN web pages describing the JISC Information Architecture, there are pages on the key technical standards (www.ukoln.ac.uk/distributed-systems/jisc-ie/arch/standards/) and on the relationship of this with other architectures (www.ukoln.ac.uk/distributed-systems/jisc-ie/arch/vle/). Organizations like CETIS (www.cetis.ac.uk/) are also important, especially for libraries implementing learning systems.

■ References

Brophy, P. and Coulling, K. (1996) *Quality Management for Information and Library Managers*, Aldershot, Gower.

Ellis, D. and Norton, B. (1993) *Implementing BS5750 / ISO 9000 in Libraries*, London, Aslib.

Hammer, M. and Champy, J. (2001) *Reengineering the Corporation: a manifesto for business revolution*, London, Nicholas Brearley.

8
Outputs

■ Introduction

While the importance of outcomes and impacts has been stressed in earlier chapters, it remains the case that assessing outputs is an important way of measuring performance. While bigger does not necessarily mean better, it is certainly true that the average reader is likely to find more of interest in a large library than in a small one – all other things being equal. Because a larger stock almost always means a more varied stock, the large library has an inbuilt advantage. Of course other factors are at play. We would want to ask how old the stock is. How well is it described in the catalogue? How readily can items be found on the shelves? How liberal are the lending policies? How helpful are the staff? Each of these issues will be reflected in the volume of business that the library transacts, so that measuring those outputs will be helpful as we seek to measure overall performance.

Outputs often feature prominently in libraries' reports. The statistical summaries which were discussed in Chapter 6, 'Inputs', contained a considerable amount of data on outputs as well as inputs, not surprisingly since quantitative data are often reported as a whole. Although there is a huge range of potential outputs that could be counted, the most common ones that libraries report are volume of issues, which measures items that users have borrowed, and number of visits, which measures physical visits to library services; LISU calls these 'the most prominent output measures' (Creaser et al., 2005).

■ Usage of library materials
Usage counts

The amount of usage of library materials is one of the most frequently measured outputs and this is often presented under the heading of 'document delivery'. The performance of the library is assessed in relation to the number of items delivered during a specified time period, sometimes associated with factors such as delivery times. For example, the inter-library loan (ILL) service may best be judged by a combination of its success rate in obtaining items requested by users and the speed with which it is able to arrange delivery of those items to them. Monitoring this activity regularly will be fundamental to assessment of the library's ongoing performance.

Electronic materials usage may be handled similarly. There have been a number of attempts to standardize the way in which the usage of electronic resources is counted. The discussion of these, including the COUNTER project and the ICOLC guidelines, will be found in Chapter 6, 'Inputs'.

The British Library's Zetoc Table of Contents service provides a good example of the kinds of statistical data that are produced by electronic services (see http://zetoc.mimas.ac.uk/stats/). For example, it showed that for the first five months of 2006, users registered at Manchester Metropolitan University used the service as shown in Table 8.1:

Table 8.1 Usage of Zetoc at Manchester Metropolitan University

	Sessions	Searches
January	173	365
February	193	414
March	176	418
April	105	224
May	101	222
Total	748	1643

Although this covers a short time period it illustrates that use of the service is quite variable. By monitoring these kinds of statistics over a longer period, and comparing trends across different products, apposite questions can be asked about the ongoing suitability of different services.

For many library services, output data of this kind will be the main, readily available information which can be obtained regularly. It is often produced as a by-product of service delivery, with statistics being collected by the library's IT systems and output via a report generator – indeed most library systems include this feature. For example, Talis provides two products, Talis Reports and Talis Decisions, which provide a variety of features for outputting management information, including data tailored for specified performance indicators (see www.talis.com/products/talis_reports/index.shtml and www.talis.com/downloads/white_papers/BusinessIntelligencePaper.pdf). Typical reports might include the performance of the reservations system (average time taken to fulfil a request over a specified time series) or a list of titles receiving the highest number of requests. Aggregated data, presented as a time series, will be useful for senior management while the detailed information is vital for efficient operational management.

As an example, the LISU *Annual Library Statistics 2005* report (Creaser et al., 2005) highlights the following output statistics collected by academic libraries:

* loans: 'loans have kept pace with student numbers over the period . . . Loans per FTE student . . . has increased by 8.7% since 1993-4'
* visits: 'although the number of visits to library premises has increased by 20% over ten years, visits per student have fallen by 22%'.

This also illustrates that very often output data are most meaningful when presented as a ratio (*x* per unit *y*) and examined as a trend over time.

Bibliometrics

The characteristic of bibliometrics lies in the statistical analysis of data, generated by large volumes of information usage, to identify trends and patterns from which generalizations can be drawn. The approach has been most heavily used in relation to the scholarly journal literature and electronic equivalents, where it is possible to analyse both direct usage and citation patterns. The latter have proved a powerful tool in identifying significant publications in different disciplines. Furthermore, the ranking of citations to journals in a particular discipline forms an authoritative source of information on which journals are the most influential and most prestigious. In some countries, including the UK, such data have also been used as a metric for determining research funding. Thus in the research assessment exercise (RAE) some subject-based assessment panels have stated formally that publications in ranked journals will be more highly rated than others. However, other panels, notably in the arts and humanities, have argued that a metrics-based approach is less effective than peer review, mainly because there is much higher reliance on monographs for the publication of excellent research in these disciplines. Thus the Arts and Humanities Research Council (AHRC) is on record as stating that 'expert judgements are the only appropriate way to arrive at assessments of quality in the arts and humanities, with judgements driven by qualitative rather than purely quantitative indicators' (www.ahrc.ac.uk/about/policy/response/funding_councils_review_of_research_assessment.asp).

Libraries wishing to use bibliometrics to aid selection of content can refer to the *ISI Journal Citation Reports* (JCR) (http://scientific.thomson.com/products/jcr/), which provide an authoritative source of data on the ranking of journals across the sciences and social sciences. As such they stand in a long tradition of the use of citations as a method of establishing relative value, stretching back to the 1920s (Gross and Gross, 1927). For many years the *Science Citation Index* (SCI) and its associated titles formed a key resource for academic libraries and it is on this accumulation of data that the JCR are based. It is also worth noting that Google's PageRank algorithm is in effect based on citation analysis (Page et al., 1999).

A number of studies have been made of bibliometric and associated data to illuminate the use of published information in electronic environments. The Centre for Information Behaviour and the Evaluation of Research (CIBER) at University College London has used deep log analysis (DLA) to analyse what users do when searching online. For example, they use the concept of site penetration as 'a deep log technique which takes log data much further than is the norm and offers an extremely good platform for characterizing the information-seeking behaviour of sub-groups of users' (Nicholas et al., 2005). This produces intelligence on what users actually do, as opposed to what they say they do. However, it needs to be supplemented with qualitative studies of *why* users act as they do.

■ Usage of websites

One of the common output measures which libraries now calculate is activity related to the use of their websites – we saw in Chapter 6, 'Inputs', that this is one of the statistical measures which the British Library publishes in its annual reports. It is interesting to note that in fact the Library uses two measures: page hits, also defined as 'successful requests for pages', and 'unique hosts served'. The latter measure is used as the best available approximation to the number of individual users of the website. This points up some of the problems with trying to assess website usage:

1 A lot of traffic on websites is generated automatically, for example by spiders and robots which are indexing pages for search engines and other services.
2 The number of page hits depends on the design of the site. For example, some sites may contain a lot of information on one page, while others use multiple pages to present similar information.
3 The fact that someone has visited a page does not necessarily mean that they have even read its content. They may have been directed from a search engine and immediately realized that the page is irrelevant.
4 The number of hits recorded will depend on the extent to which the page is cached by other service providers or in the user's PC (i.e. a copy kept in case of repeat requests) and how the server handles cached pages.

Despite these difficulties it is important to monitor the available web usage statistics regularly. Apart from anything else, a severe drop in hits on a page, or a page which repeatedly reports zero hits, clearly deserves investigation.

■ Presentation via the web

A more general framework for the assessment of academic, and by extension other sectoral, library websites has been suggested by Chao. This makes use of eight criteria:

1. Presentation
2. Content
3. Graphic design
4. Compatibility
5. Services
6. Search capability

7. Institutional information
8. Information about links. (Chao, 2002)

This is a useful framework, which has been tested empirically, but it needs to be complemented by user-focused design and evaluation. There are a variety of tools available to achieve this, ranging from the Internet Detective (www.vts.intute.ac.uk/detective/), which is essentially a tutorial, to formal usability tools, discussed in the next section.

■ Usability

It has been recognized almost since the inception of the web that the usability of websites is a critical issue. Just as customers will walk away from a physical facility which they find difficult or impossible to use, so they will click away from web pages with poor usability – and they always have plenty of alternatives to visit.

Usability testing derives from work in human–computer interaction (HCI) and seeks to answer questions such as:

- How easy is it to learn to use a website? If someone has never come across it before, how quickly would they be able to find their way around it?
- Once the layout and other features of the website have become familiar, how quickly can users complete their tasks? What barriers might they encounter?
- How easy is it to remember the features of the site, so that on returning the user can readily use it effectively?
- How error-prone is use of this website? What happens when users make an error – how quickly and easily can they recover?
- What kind of overall impression does the site leave on the user? Was use a pleasant experience?

In other words 'a usable Web interface is one that is accessible, appealing, consistent, clear, simple, navigable and forgiving of user blunders' (Murray and Costanzo, 1999). An approach to usability testing might encompass:

1 *User-centred design*. In other words the initial design of the website tries to take into account usability as far as possible. One way to do this is to

develop *personas* of fictional users, representative of the intended users of the site. A persona does not simply describe the tasks that might be carried out but includes motivation and expectations. It tries to depict a rounded picture of a typical individual user, sometimes even going so far as to describe feelings and provide a photograph so as to make the individual 'come alive' to the designer. Test versions of the new website should however be tested with real users to check on usability in practice.

2   *User testing* of the established website at intervals. There is a range of protocols available to assist in this process, but commonly the users will be asked to complete predetermined tasks and either to record their comments or 'talk-aloud' as they progress. An end-of-task questionnaire may be used to gather overall impressions. However, this is expensive to conduct and so a number of other techniques may be used.

3   A *cognitive walkthrough* is undertaken by a member of staff acting as a user, undertaking a typical task and noting the results. This method may re-use the personas developed during the design stage. It is very important that this is carried out with a full appreciation of what the users' prior knowledge and understanding will be – it is not an 'expert walkthrough'!

4   *Heuristic evaluation* consists of a test of the website against a checklist of usability 'dos and don'ts', again usually carried out by staff. The Interactive Heuristic Evaluation Toolkit (www.id-book.com/catherb/) is a very useful tool for generating these checklists.

The leading guru of usability is Jakob Nielsen, whose website (www.useit.com/) contains a wealth of resources on the subject (see also his latest book, *Prioritizing Web Usability* (Nielsen and Loranger, 2006)).

Libraries which have reported on website usability testing include the University of Hull (Holland, 2005), which recruited 15 students to test its website using a series of tasks, such as: 'Your lecturer has told you about a database of images called the "Education Image Gallery", and you want to find it on the library web pages.' Each student undertook the tests in controlled conditions, with one member of staff reading out the task and another making notes on what the student did. They were then shown another library's website, selected as an example of the type of design that Hull was thinking of adopting and asked to comment on it. The Hull site was then redesigned using the data collected and a further round of user testing undertaken on the new site. Holland concluded: 'While time-consuming and staff intensive, usability testing provided the key evidence required to successfully redesign the library website and make it more "user-friendly".'

A specific concern, associated with usability, relates to ensuring the *accessibility* of electronic services. This will be discussed in Chapter 11, 'Services for all'.

■ Conclusion

Assessment of the performance of libraries and information services will usually involve the collection of data on outputs. While traditional services may concentrate on data such as loans and visits, the development of electronic services has made the collection and analysis of output-related data more complex, but also more powerful. Analysis of huge quantities of bibliometric data enables authoritative data to be generated on patterns of user activity. Web-based services present particular challenges, with usability a primary consideration.

■ Resources

- Refer to the Resources section of Chapter 6, 'Inputs', for examples of statistical data series.
- *Journal Citation Reports* are produced by Thomson Scientific and require a subscription. UK academic institutions can access them through MIMAS (www.mimas.ac.uk/).
- Although very dated, it is still worth reading Jeffrey Goldberg's *Why Web Usage Statistics Are (Worse Than) Useless* at www.goldmark.org/netrants/webstats/.
- There are a huge number of web traffic analysis packages available. *Webalizer* (www.mrunix.net/webalizer/) is a free package while among the most popular commercial, and very sophisticated, products is *Wusage* (www.boutell.com/wusage/).
- Similarly, there is a vast range of products for usability testing, and an ever greater number of consultancies offering usability testing services. The Nielsen Norman Group is the leading usability consultancy, although it is likely that most libraries would wish to employ a more local (and less expensive!) consultant.

• An example of library website usability testing can be found at http://macfadden.mit.edu:9500/webgroup/usability.html where the results of tests on MIT Libraries websites are presented.

■ References

Chao (2002) Assessing the Quality of Academic Libraries on the Web: the development and testing of criteria, *Library and Information Research*, **24** (2), 169–94.

Creaser, C. et al. (2005) *LISU Annual Library Statistics 2005: featuring trend analysis of UK public and academic libraries 1994–2004*, Loughborough, Library and Information Statistics Unit, Loughborough University.

Gross, P. L. K. and Gross, E. M. (1927) College Libraries and Chemical Education, *Science*, **66**, 385–9.

Holland, D. (2005) Practical Experiences of Using Formal Usability Testing as a Tool to Support Website Redesign, *SCONUL Focus*, (36), 31–5.

Murray, G. and Costanzo, T. (1999) *Usability and the Web: an overview*, Library and Archives Canada, www.collectionscanada.ca/9/1/p1-260-e.html.

Nicholas, D. et al. (2005) Scholarly Journal Usage: the results of deep log analysis, *Journal of Documentation*, **61** (2), 248–80.

Nielsen, J. and Loranger, H. (2006) *Prioritizing Web Usability*, Berkeley CA, New Riders Press.

Page, L. et al. (1999) *The PageRank Citation Ranking: bringing order to the web*, Stanford Digital Library Technologies Project, http://dbpubs.stanford.edu/pub/showDoc.Fulltext?lang=en&doc=1999-66&format=pdf&compression=&name=1999-66.pdf.

9
Staff

■ Introduction

Libraries, as do many other organizations, often state that their staff are their most valuable asset. If this is to be more than a platitude then it is important that they too form part of the performance measurement processes of the library. Such assessment must be undertaken with the utmost sensitivity and it is important that staff do not feel that they are on trial. Indeed, it is almost always the case that if staff are not performing to expectations then lack of training and/or lack of leadership are to blame rather than incompetence. Any action to evaluate staff performance should be undertaken with this in mind.

Measuring the effects of investment in staff, including training, is never easy because there are so many variables in play. As Oldroyd (1995) noted:

> it is usually simple to measure the time taken up by training, but extremely difficult to measure its benefit. It becomes progressively more difficult the further one moves from tasks towards responsibilities. Some benefit is self-evident and shows itself in improved competence (particularly in a crisis), positive feedback from customers and good working relations. Other visible benefits are seen in high motivation, openness to change, trust and flexibility. A library with high morale, a good reputation among its users, and a good 'feel' can be an important factor in successful outcomes.

■ Staff surveys

One starting point for the assessment of staff performance is to begin with the staff themselves and undertake a staff satisfaction survey. It is surprising how infrequently this is done given the prevalence of user satisfaction surveys. Many of the principles discussed in Chapter 3, 'User satisfaction', are relevant to this kind of survey. In addition, there are sensitivities to observe and it is wise to gain institutional approval (you may be setting a precedent for other departments!) and to ensure that staff members, where appropriate including union representatives, are fully engaged with the process. This means, among other things, that data produced from such surveys should always be confidential and almost always anonymous.

The results of a staff satisfaction survey can be used to highlight issues of which senior managers may either be unaware or whose significance to their staff they may not realize. Very often these can be apparently mundane issues but ones which greatly affect people's ability to work effectively. An outcome of this better understanding might be to find ways to empower staff to take control of such matters themselves. This in itself may suggest that the staff survey could profitably be organized by more junior staff, who might analyse the results and present them to management. What is then vital, of course, is that action is seen to be taken on the key issues which have been raised.

■ Appraisal

Appraisal is a well established practice in most large organizations. It usually takes place on an annual cycle, although that does not necessarily mean that there is only one appraisal event each year since activity may be spread out. In any case the appraiser and appraisee should be reviewing activity regularly. It is important that the appraiser has detailed knowledge both of the appraisee's work and of the broader needs of the organization. The process should be confidential, although reports should be available if there is a change of appraiser. In essence, appraisal consists of a dialogue, a two-way process of reflection on an employee's activities during the past year, on the organization's requirements of them for the future and of their personal development needs. It is worth looking at these aspects in more detail.

Reflection on past performance

It is as well to start with the clear statement that appraisal is *not* an opportunity for disciplinary action. If there are serious concerns with an individual's performance then these should be tackled separately, using procedures devised for the purpose. Appraisal is an opportunity for the appraiser (usually the manager) and the appraisee to reflect on the previous year's performance. It is an opportunity for the appraiser to give positive feedback on what has gone well and for discussion about problems and difficulties that have been encountered. A useful mantra for appraisal interviews is 'there shall be no surprises'.

The starting point for this discussion will usually be a formal record of the previous year's appraisal, which will have included agreement on targets and priorities, coupled with the employee's job description.

The organization's requirements

All organizations are undergoing continuous change. It is therefore inevitable that the demands they place on their staff will change and the appraisal interview is an opportunity to discuss these and to update such documents as job descriptions. Far too often these lie untouched until a post falls vacant and there is a scramble to update them.

At the end of the appraisal interview a record should be created of the targets and priorities agreed for the coming year – the performance indicators of staff achievement. It is important that each of these should be *measurable*, *recognisable* and *achievable*. They will form the base for the next year's interview, and this will be a wasted opportunity if there is no clear record of what the member of staff should have achieved.

Personal development needs

In order to be an effective employee, every member of staff needs access to personal and professional development opportunities. These may relate to learning new skills or could be more a matter of updating what is already known. If there is a major change in role, the development requirements will probably be equally significant.

It is important that the appraiser is able to authorize or negotiate for the required personal and professional development support. This is one of the reasons that appraisers are usually line managers, although of course not all managers have the necessary resources at their disposal.

Following up appraisal

At the conclusion of a round of appraisal interviews it is important that the outcomes are summarized and considered by management although confidentiality of individuals must of course be maintained. In particular, the resource requirements of appraisal outcomes need to be considered and authorized; for example, to ensure that promised professional development activities can be undertaken. The overall performance of staff, as revealed by the process, should also be considered.

Other forms of appraisal

There has been growing interest in recent years in what is termed 180 degree or upward appraisal, where the member of staff has the opportunity to appraise the manager's performance. A further variant is 360 degree appraisal, which involves a group of employees – nearly always managers – in appraising each other. Each of these can provide useful performance data for management.

■ Investors in People

In the UK, a group of major business and other national organizations came together in 1990 to develop a standard for the management and development of their people. Over time, this Investors in People (IIP) standard has become the accepted benchmark for human resources management. As of mid-2006 over 25% of the UK workforce was employed in organizations which had IIP recognition. While it is concerned with far more than the measurement of staff performance, it forms a framework within which the contribution of people to performance can be managed and monitored. The basic framework is deliberately mapped onto the classic business planning cycle of Plan, Do, Review. There are ten indicators for which evidence must be provided if an organization is to qualify for IIP status:

1. A strategy for improving the performance of the organization is clearly defined and understood.
2. Learning and development is planned to achieve the organization's objectives.
3. Strategies for managing people are designed to promote equality of opportunity in the development of the organization's people.
4. The capabilities managers need to lead, manage and develop people effectively are clearly defined and understood.
5. Managers are effective in leading, managing and developing people.
6. People's contribution to the organization is recognized and valued.
7. People are encouraged to take ownership and responsibility by being involved in decision-making.
8. People learn and develop effectively.
9. Investment in people improves the performance of the organization.
10. Improvements are continually made to the way people are managed and developed.

(www.investorsinpeople.co.uk/)

IIP has also developed three models to assist in the management of the people aspects of organizational management: a *leadership and management* model, a *recruitment and selection* model and, most recently, a *work–life balance* model.

■ Reflective practitioners

A staff survey can be a one-off or at least irregular way to explore overall staff experiences and attitudes, while appraisal enables individuals to express their experience and to discuss targets and attainment. However, to achieve the best performance from staff it is necessary to inculcate the habit of continuous *reflective practice*:

> Without understanding the underlying theoretical principles of practice, we are merely skilled mechanics trying out one tool after another without understanding what tool would be appropriate to the task. We apply techniques and interventions without full consideration of the reasons behind such approaches, without understanding their likely consequences, without the ability to evaluate the success or failure of those interventions, and without the tools and resources to learn from each experience. (Lang, 1998)

The idea that those who practise a profession should reflect continuously on what they are doing emerged in education through the work of Donald Schön, one of the most influential theoreticians in that and related fields. His work on this topic was published in his book, *The Reflective Practitioner* (Schön, 1983). The central idea behind this work is that professional practice must be a process of lifelong learning. It is not enough to simply do a job, task after task. Each task and especially each interaction with a client, whether a school student or a library user, has to be reflected on and used as an opportunity to become more effective. This reflection should take place both during the interaction with the client and after the interaction – reflection *in* action and reflection *on* action.

It is worth noting that the idea of reflective practice fits well with Kolb's experiential learning cycle (Kolb, 1984), an influential theory of how human beings learn. This suggests that *concrete experience* leads to *reflective observation* on that experience, which in turn leads to the application or derivation of theories or rules about that experience (*abstract conceptualization*), which in turn is followed by *active experimentation*, by which we test and modify our thinking. The cycle is completed when the next concrete experience is undertaken using the learning from earlier iterations. The relationship with constructivist approaches to learning, described in Chapter 2, 'Theoretical considerations', is clear.

It follows from these theories, which have gained widespread acceptance, that one of the keys to measuring the performance of staff actually lies with the staff themselves. Ways have to be found to encourage reflective practice, so that staff are assessing their own performance and learning from it all the time. Reflective practice can also be a group activity when staff come together, sometimes with colleagues from other organizations, to think about their experiences in delivering services and to learn from each other's insights. As part of this reflection they need to explore the evidence available to them and the indicators which signify achievements. Providing time for such activity is thus a vital part of performance measurement.

■ Conclusion

Because staff are the most important asset of any service organization, it is important that the measurement of the organization's performance is fully informed by knowledge of their performance, and that evidence is used to identify weaknesses and training requirements. Various systematic methods are available to assist in this, from the formality of Investors in People to the encouragement of reflective practice among all employees.

■ Resources

- CILIP has published *Top Tips on Conducting a Performance Appraisal* (see www.cilip.org.uk/professionalguidance/needadvice/toptips/appraisal. htm).
- Oldroyd, M. (ed.) *Developing Academic Library Staff for Future Success*, Facet Publishing, 2004, is a useful guide to library staff management issues including performance assessment.
- Information on Investors in People is available at www.iipuk.co.uk/IIP/ Web/default.htm. The site includes a number of short case studies, one of which concerns a university library: www.iipuk.co.uk/IIP/Web/ Case+Studies/University+of+Wollongong+Library.htm.

■ References

Kolb, D. A. (1984) *Experiential Learning: experience as the source of learning and development*, London, Prentice-Hall.

Lang, M. (1998) Becoming Reflective Practitioners, *Consensus*, www. mediate.com/articles/reflect.cfm.

Oldroyd, R. (1995) Staff Development and Appraisal in an 'Old' University Library, *Librarian Career Development*, **3** (2), 13–16.

Schön, D. A. (1983) *The Reflective Practitioner: how professionals think in action*, London, Temple Smith.

10
Infrastructure

■ Introduction

Libraries rely heavily on their infrastructure for the delivery of services. The library building is the most prominent and probably most expensive part of that infrastructure but information and communications technology facilities will be of almost the same importance. Clearly it is imperative that the performance of these investments be monitored to ensure that they are helping the library deliver value, and that they are not in themselves an untoward constraint.

■ The library building

The building from which services are delivered is a very significant input to library service as a whole, especially in relation to those services that require the user to come to the building, such as physical book lending or access to workstations. At one time it was usual for detailed norms to be published for the building itself, often by government agencies, and although this is now less common it is an approach which can still be found. Compliance with such standards is then the basic measure of performance. An example of this approach can be found in the 'Library building standards' published by the State of Queensland in Australia (www.slq.qld.gov.au/serv/publib/policy/guidelines/four). These suggest, for example, that for a main branch library the total floor area should be related to population size:

- Population: 10,000–15,000 there should be between 49 and 45 m^2 per 1000 population

- Population: 15,000–50,000 there should be between 45 and 41 m² per 1000 population
- Population: 50,000–100,000+ there should be between 41 and 37 m² per 1000 population.

The standards also state that for a new library there should be space for each of the functions listed in Figure 10.1. This then becomes a checklist against which performance can be measured.

Note that all of these are inputs to the service. The fact that there is, for example, a 'toys and games area' tells us nothing about what has been provided there, who has used that area or what effect that use had on them. This is not to say that such information is useless: unless a library has this kind of designated area it might be very difficult to attract very young children. As was stressed in Chapter 6, 'Inputs', these performance indicators thus take us to the first stage and tell us something about that library's capabilities.

In the academic sector, CILIP has published *Guidelines for Colleges* (Eynon, 2005), which contain detailed space norms. For example:

- the space for learning resource centres should be at least 10% of total college area or a minimum of 20% of the total teaching space
- there should be 1 seat per 10 FTE students in further education and 1 per 6 FTE students in higher education
- there should be 1m² of floor space per 10 students.

CILIP has similarly published *Guidelines for Secondary School Libraries*, again containing advice on norms (Barrett and Douglas, 2004).

A broader assessment process in relation to library buildings is exemplified by the work undertaken by SCONUL in relation to its Library Design Award. The Society established an assessment panel under its Advisory Committee on Buildings (now Working Group on Space Planning), which is responsible for examining new academic libraries in Britain and Ireland, using the following criteria (McDonald, 2002):

- functional: space which works well, looks good and is lasting well
- adaptable: flexible space, the use of which can easily be changed
- accessible: social space which is inviting, easy-to-use and promotes independence

- AV equipment storage and usage areas
- children's area, including space and facilities for activities and programmes
- circulation desk and self check-out space
- cleaners' storeroom
- coffee and tea making facilities for the public
- collections areas with an emphasis on face-out display
- community information area
- entrance and foyer (single public entrance for ease of supervision)
- exhibition and display area
- informal reading and browsing areas (both adult and junior) with a range of seating and desk types
- kitchen facilities, with provision for catering for staff and public events
- librarian's office
- listening posts for using audio resources
- loading and delivery area
- local/family history space
- meeting room/s
- newspaper and periodicals area
- photocopying
- public toilets, unisex parenting room
- public use PC areas for OPACs, internet and a range of other applications and peripheral equipment, with provision for public access computers to also be available in all areas of the library
- reference area
- returns room, fireproof
- self-opening doors to ensure equal access for all clients
- stack/storage areas
- staff room
- staff toilets, sick bay and shower
- staff work areas
- study areas, including areas suitable for group study
- telephone system facilitating staff connectivity while moving throughout the library
- toys and games area
- training rooms for use by staff and public
- volunteer work areas (for example, friends of libraries)
- youth space.

Figure 10.1 Library building standards checklist for Queensland Public Libraries

- varied: with a choice of learning spaces and for different media
- interactive: well-organized space which promotes contact between users and services
- conducive: high-quality humane space which inspires people
- environmentally suitable: for readers, books and computers

- safe and secure: for people, collections, equipment and data
- efficient: in space, staffing and running costs
- suitable for information technology: with flexible provision for users and staff
- 'oomph': combining these qualities to capture the minds of users and the spirit of the institution.

Examples of buildings winning the SCONUL award, and the reasons for their selection, can be found at www.sconul.ac.uk/activities/space_planning/events/buildings/sconullibrarydesignaward02.html.

In the USA a biennial competition to recognize the best in library buildings is organized jointly by the ALA and the American Institute of Architects (AIA). The description of the eight winning buildings in 2005 (www.aia.org/aiarchitect/thisweek05/tw0401/0401libraryawards.htm) includes the criteria for their selection.

A rather more formal approach to the evaluation of new buildings was undertaken in the mid-1990s in the UK by the Chartered Institute of Building Services Engineers (CIBSE) with the government department responsible for the environment (then the Department of the Environment, Transport and the Regions). Known as Post-occupancy Review Of Buildings and their Engineering (PROBE), these studies are intended as a way of checking how successful new building projects had been by evaluating them under 14 headings:

- procurement route
- design and construction
- initial occupancy
- occupant satisfaction
- management perceptions
- energy and water consumption
- operation and management
- maintenance and reliability
- controls and controllability
- design intentions
- alterations made
- benchmark comparisons
- strengths and weaknesses
- key messages.

While this type of evaluation is structured towards an engineering view of buildings, it is important for librarians to appreciate how those responsible for building projects may view outcomes. PROBE includes occupant surveys so that the user perspective on buildings is assessed. Although much more wide-ranging than libraries, a number of learning resource centres and library buildings have been included in PROBE studies, including Anglia Polytechnic University's Learning Resource Centre in the first round of studies.

Post-occupancy studies of public libraries have been carried out in the UK by the professional bodies, notably through the Public Library Building Awards scheme of the Public Libraries Group (PLG) of CILIP. There is considerable emphasis on aesthetics in these awards, the criteria including the appearance and design of the library but also encompassing its impact on the community, the quality of its services and its capacity for development.

More recently, a general methodology for post-occupancy studies of public libraries has been suggested by Lackney and Zajfen, who found that in three studies they undertook in the USA similar problems emerged, including lack of staff space, lack of quiet spaces and so on. This suggests that such studies could provide generalizable checklists of issues for use in evaluating the adequacy of new library buildings (Lackney and Zajfen, 2005).

Enright (2002) suggests that the importance of post-occupancy evaluations of buildings lies in their ability to:

- introduce a culture of feedback, service to community and continuous improvement based on good practice, dissemination of expertise and a degree of self-assessment, so avoiding confrontation and blame cultures
- identify and quantify value-for-money projects and cost-effectiveness, demonstrating money has been well spent
- introduce appropriate record management, technical information, support and training of technical staff
- identify and quantify the need to improve building services and controls and evaluate performance issues such as space efficiency, functional performance and environmental and energy performance to allow fine-tuning and learning lessons for the future
- help address occupant dissatisfaction or complaints about basic comfort, health or safety issues such as noise (staff and users) resulting in

occupants understanding more about the operation and management of the building
- assess the current occupancy situation rapidly and in advance of alteration, refurbishment or new construction.

■ ICT systems infrastructure

The ICT systems infrastructure used by the library is now absolutely critical to the successful achievement of its mission. In terms of performance measurement, it is useful to think in terms of the physical network, hardware, internal library systems and remote systems which are accessed to provide services. However, it is very hard to draw boundaries around each of these topics, and it is best to start the discussion by considering the IT infrastructure as a whole.

A useful way to do this is by reference to an 'information systems architecture', of which the best known is that developed for the JISC Information Environment (see www.ukoln.ac.uk/distributed-systems/jisc-ie/arch/). This suggests that there are three 'layers' to the information architecture needed to provide services to the library's users, together with a collection of shared infrastructure components. In brief there is:

1 A user-facing *presentation layer*, which is perhaps best thought of as consisting of those components which users might see on their workstations as they explore the various resources which the library makes available. This would include the library's OPAC interface, various subject-related or media-specific portals, search engines, the virtual learning or virtual research environment (VLE or VRE) and some additional facilities such as resolvers which enable the user to negotiate delivery of the appropriate copy of a resource available from different locations.
2 A bottom level *provision layer*, which contains the raw data and information services that are drawn on to provide the information services to which the library provides access. These would include the major private sector document supply companies, collections and services that are set up for the sector as a whole, possibly through public funding – national data repositories might be an example – and local services such as institutional repositories.
3 A central *fusion layer*, which contains a series of services that enable the

most appropriate raw information source to be located and used to provide the end-user service. These include various kinds of catalogue and index, as well as commercial services that aggregate content from different suppliers to provide value-added services.

4 A set of *shared services*, which enable the library to deliver each of its services efficiently and effectively. These would include:

—authentication and authorization services, which check that users are who they say they are and that they have the right permissions, such as through membership of a particular library, to use the resources requested

—terminology services, which are able to 'translate' a query provided by the user, through a presentation layer service, into the correct terminology to extract results from a fusion or provision layer service

—service registries, which hold details of as many of the available fusion and provision layer services as possible. They may be queried to find the best resources to search for a given request, for example through subject metadata held about the whole range of possible services. They thus help the local library avoid having to maintain up-to-date technical information about how to access every individual service.

In addition to this functional view of the infrastructure, it is important not to neglect the physical infrastructure of networks and workstations. Taken together these offer a very considerable challenge from a performance measurement perspective.

A useful way to think of this problem is:

1 To assess the contribution, positive or negative, that the infrastructure is making to the achievement of excellence in responses to library surveys, using the approaches and tools described elsewhere in this book. For example, when examining the impact of library services it is important to make judgements about the ways in which the IT infrastructure is facilitating or obstructing achievement.

2 Acknowledging that the critical issue with a complex information infrastructure is that of interoperability between components, to focus attention on:

—any evidence of interoperability failures, as when one system does not have the ability to query another, possibly forcing the user into extra steps to retrieve information

—the compliance of components to appropriate international standards (see Chapter 7, 'Processes').

3 To make as much use as possible of performance data that are provided by service components. For example, the COUNTER project (see Chapter 6, 'Inputs') focuses attention on the provision of helpful usage data from electronic journal and electronic database providers. The JISC publishes performance data about the Joint Academic Network (JANET), which can help identify the location and responsibility for problems or failures (see below).

4 To make use of infrastructure performance data provided locally by, for example, IT systems departments.

As an example, the UK JISC Monitoring Unit (www.mu.jisc.ac.uk/) produces an annual report on the basis of its survey of network usage across the higher and further education sectors. Its 2005–6 report (www.mu.jisc.ac.uk/reports/getreport.php?id=p12) contains quantitative and qualitative data on network services:

* the network was very highly regarded with 62% of respondents considering it *excellent* and 35% *good*
* comments from users and technical personnel: '[RSC North West] are very good at handling connectivity problems. I am impressed that their staff always notice when we switch our end of the connection off for systems work, they always call us to make sure we are aware. We are very happy with the quality of service we have experienced. Our internet connection is very reliable'.

Not only can such reports be useful for internal purposes, but they provide a cross-sectoral benchmark against which local performance can be assessed.

■ Other considerations

It is important to apply considerations of usability (Chapter 8, 'Outputs') and accessibility (Chapter 11, 'Services for all') to the library's infrastructure. From both perspectives there is a strong case for adopting 'Design for All' principles, so that as little as possible of the building and the IT infrastructure is designed for special purposes. For example, all workstations should, as far as possible, be multifunctional and capable of supporting users with differing abilities. A useful performance measure would be the extent to which this has been achieved.

■ Conclusion

The library's infrastructure is critical to the delivery of excellent services, even though much of it is either hidden or taken for granted a lot of the time. Performance indicators need to be established to enable the contribution of the infrastructure to be monitored and particularly to track any failures which are impacting on service delivery.

■ Resources

- Designing Libraries: library buildings online (www.designinglibraries. org.uk/) has a considerable amount of useful information. There is a toolkit of resources at www.designinglibraries.org.uk/resources/toolkit/.
- The SCONUL Library buildings project database is available at www.sconul.ac.uk/lib_build/buildings/.
- The American Library Association has issued a fact sheet called 'Building Libraries and Library Additions'. See www.ala.org/Template. cfm?Section=buildings&template=/ContentManagement/Content Display.cfm&ContentID=130003.
- Each year the April issue of *American Libraries* focuses on library buildings.

■ References

Barrett, L. and Douglas, J. (eds) (2004) *The CILIP Guidelines for Secondary School Libraries*, 2nd edn, London, Facet Publishing.

Enright, S. (2002) Post-occupancy Evaluation of UK Library Building Projects: some examples of current activity, *Liber Quarterly: the Journal of European Research Libraries*, **12** (1), 26–45.

Eynon, A. (ed.) (2005) *Guidelines for Colleges: recommendations for learning resources*, London, Facet Publishing.

Lackney, J. A. and Zajfen, P. (2005) Post-occupancy Evaluation of Public Libraries: lessons learned from 3 case studies, *Library Administration and Management*, **19** (1), 16–25.

McDonald, A. (2002) Celebrating Outstanding New Library Buildings, *SCONUL Newsletter*, (27), 82–5.

11
Services for all

■ **Introduction**

In measuring the performance of a library or information service, it is easy to concentrate almost entirely on the broad picture and thus lose sight of the service being received by particular user groups. In this chapter we will be looking at ways in which success in meeting the needs of such groups can be assessed. A particular emphasis will be placed on users with disabilities (or, more properly, different abilities). However, all libraries should carefully consider how they are addressing the needs of all the sub-groups in their populations, bearing in mind comments such as that in Chapter 5, 'Social and economic impact', that 'the public library service has not yet managed to engage freely with ethnically diverse communities' (and there is no evidence that other sectors are any better). By developing the library profile (see Chapter 6, 'Inputs') to include such groups, regular measurement of performance in meeting specific requirements can be encouraged. Williams (2004) suggests that libraries should be considering, and monitoring their performance in serving, people who are 'different' in all of the following ways:

- age
- ancestry
- cognitive style
- cultural background
- economic background
- ethnicity
- gender
- geographic background

- language(s) spoken
- marital/partnered status
- nationality
- disability (mental, learning and physical)
- physical appearance
- political affiliation
- race
- religious beliefs
- sexual orientation.

As a general principle, the more that services can be differentiated to meet the specific needs of individuals and groups, the greater satisfaction with those services is likely to be and the more probable it is that customers will return time and time again. For this reason, there has been considerable interest in the possibilities of personalization, and this is the topic we turn to first in this chapter.

■ Personalization

The idea behind personalization, in terms of electronic services in particular because it is there that the scope is greatest, is that each individual should be able to tailor the 'look and feel' of the information which is displayed on their workstation, so that it matches their personal requirements both in terms of content and presentation. An advantage of this approach is that it enables people to express their individuality and their personal needs for themselves. Personalization increasingly requires that the library service is integrated into the individual's natural workflow, so that, for instance, a student undertaking an assignment within a VLE can tune the information delivery and display to synchronize with their personalization of the VLE workspace. At the same time, the student may adjust display preferences to meet particular requirements, such as for low vision or colour blindness.

It follows that the issue from a library performance measurement perspective is whether service delivery meets the agreed service aim in this respect – the extent to which the library has committed to offer personalization. It is important to be clear about the implications of policy decisions in this area. While individuals should be able to adjust information displays to meet specific ability requirements, meeting individual personal aesthetic preferences may not always be as desirable. A high level of personalizability makes maintenance more difficult and may introduce additional scope for conflicts between systems. The type of issues that need to be checked, therefore, are:

- Does the level of personalization achievable by the individual user match the agreed standard?
- How easy is it to personalize the service? This will bring to the fore questions of usability (see Chapter 8, 'Outputs').
- How easy is it to maintain the service, including providing helpdesk and similar support?
- How easy is it to revert to the default display? This may be important to enable library staff to check whether the source of a problem is the personalized display or the underlying service.

■ Group differentiation

The discussion above relates largely to individual use of services. However, it is equally important that the needs of different, especially minority, groups are recognized. An obvious example would be the provision of signage and IT-based systems help screens in minority languages. From a performance measurement perspective, the critical issue is ensuring that whatever overall assessments are carried out, they are sensitive enough to capture the experience of such groups. Thus, for example, a user satisfaction study needs to enable managers to judge whether each of the groups the library is serving is satisfied, not simply that there is an acceptable overall level of satisfaction with the service. Ågot Berger has provided a useful summary of the issues involved in assessing services for multi-ethnic populations, using the example of Denmark and its recent move towards a multicultural society, noting that 'libraries play an important role in the overall process of societal integration' (Berger, 2002).

■ Accessibility for users with disabilities

Anyone who has a disability faces barriers in many different walks of life and libraries are no exception to this rule. Physical accessibility of library buildings, including bookstock and services, has been an issue for many years. This is now coupled with problems of accessibility of electronic services, made challenging by the combination of abilities needed for access, such as the ability to see and interpret images, manipulate a pointing device such as a mouse and handle information streamed in multimedia formats.

Physical accessibility

The ability to access the building and its contents is of course critical to the success of the library in serving disadvantaged groups. There are a considerable number of factors which need to be considered, ranging from the ability to park a car near the entrance to how a user with a physical disability can obtain books from high shelves. Two approaches are useful here:

* regular checking of a comprehensive guideline or checklist (see for example http://bpm.nlb-online.org/chapter12.html)
* regular physical walkthrough audits; if it can be arranged for these to be undertaken by people with disabilities, so much the better.

In the UK it is a legal requirement under the Disability Discrimination Act (DDA), which originally came into force in 1996 with physical access provisions operative from 1 October 2004, to take reasonable steps to make all library services available to disabled people. The Disability Rights Commission (DRC) has published a good practice guide for libraries and learning resource centres (downloadable at www.skill.org.uk/info/drc_ guides/libraries.doc). This points out that 'institutions are expected to make "anticipatory" adjustments, not simply wait until a disabled person requires a particular adaptation'. It follows that the assessment of the library's capability to deliver services to all users is an ongoing, proactive requirement and cannot be left to a responsive approach.

A particular issue is that where assistive technologies are provided, library performance will not be satisfactory unless frontline staff are confident in their use and able to provide immediate and knowledgeable assistance to users.

Web accessibility

The world wide web has now become such a ubiquitous medium that it is impossible to access anything approaching a full range of library services without it. Library catalogues are usually web-based and if not use online delivery that mimics the web. Bibliographic information services are largely delivered through the web and web-based versions of journals, books, visual and audio media, to say nothing of multimedia presentations, are commonplace. This presents problems for people with disabilities. For example, anyone who is Deaf/deaf is potentially disadvantaged if an audio stream forms or accompanies an information resource (note that deaf people may prefer to describe themselves as Deaf with a capital D to emphasize their Deaf cultural and linguistic identity – see www.rnid.org.uk/information_resources/aboutdeafness/meaning_of_deafness/). Anyone with motor impairment, such as difficulty in manipulating hand-controlled devices, encounters problems when faced with a mouse or trackball. Anyone with learning difficulties is excluded when faced with complex language and concepts or impenetrable layout. Perhaps most seriously of all, anyone with visual impairment, including people who are blind, is potentially disadvantaged and excluded when web pages use images to convey content. Given that the web is a very visual medium, these are extremely serious problems and there is a clear duty for libraries to address them. Performance cannot be said to be satisfactory while some users are excluded.

These problems have been recognized since the early days of the web, although that is not to say that solutions have always or even frequently been implemented. The lead has been taken by the World Wide Web Consortium (W3C), through its Web Accessibility Initiative (WAI – pronounced 'way'). Prominent among WAI's work has been the development and promotion of a set of web accessibility guidelines. These include the Authoring Tools (ATAG), User Agents (UAAG) and, probably the most widely known, the Web Content Accessibility Guidelines (WCAG).

WCAG defines a set of checkpoints, which can be tested to ensure theoretical accessibility. However, it should be noted that in reality accessibility depends on the presentation of the source (i.e. the issues covered by WCAG) *and* the individual's circumstances *and* the task being carried out. For this reason, a combination of automated compliance checking, expert testing and user testing is needed to ensure accessibility – these are discussed further below.

A particular issue relates to the overall design strategy behind the website. For some time the dominant approach was to create a 'main' site and a parallel 'text-only' site, the latter being intended for use by people with disabilities. The main disadvantage of this tactic, however, is that in practice it is frequently found that maintenance of the text-only site fails to keep pace with that of the main site. It also has to be said that creating what is in effect two websites is a very inelegant solution to the problem. In recent years, therefore, there has been a much greater emphasis on what is known as the 'design for all' approach, whereby a single site is designed to be accessible to everyone. The WAI development supports this view.

A major study by the UK Disability Rights Commission (DRC) in 2004, using both automated testing and a panel of users, checked 1000 websites and identified 585 potential accessibility problems (Disability Rights Commission, 2004). It is useful to note that the most common failings related to the following checkpoints:

- provision of a text equivalent for every non-text element (the ALT tag) [WCAG Checkpoint 1.1]
- ensuring that foreground and background colours provide adequate colour contrast [WCAG Checkpoint 2.2]
- ensuring that pages remain usable when scripts are turned off, or if this is not possible providing an alternative [WCAG Checkpoint 6.3]
- avoiding moving content in pages, until browsers enable the user to freeze content [WCAG Checkpoint 7.3]
- ensuring that pop-up windows are not spawned without informing the user [WCAG Checkpoint 10.1]
- dividing large blocks of information into manageable groups where this is possible [WCAG Checkpoint 12.3]
- identifying the target of each link clearly [WCAG Checkpoint 13.1]
- using only the clearest and simplest language for a site's content [WCAG Checkpoint 14.1].

It will be seen that most of these failings are easily addressed. Even if library web managers were to address only these eight issues, overall accessibility would be much improved.

In order to check accessibility, as was noted above, three approaches need to be used:

1 *Automated accessibility checkers* – a wide range of online checkers is available to which web pages can be submitted. Both Cynthia Says™ (www.cynthiasays.com) and WAVE (http://wave.webaim.org/wave.index.jsp) are free of charge to users.
2 *Expert checking*, which involves someone with expertise in disability issues and in web page design checking for observable errors. Experts will usually check the source HTML in order to pinpoint the cause of errors which they find.
3 *User checking*, which involves a panel of users with disabilities, together with a control group, undertaking structured tasks to identify any inaccessible content or other features.

As with physical devices, frontline staff should have some familiarity with the technology, such as basic knowledge of HTML and CSS, so as to be able to assist users.

A more detailed overview of accessibility challenges posed by library services delivered via the web will be found in Brophy and Craven (2007).

■ Guidelines and standards

A more general discussion of the use of guidelines and standards will be found in Chapter 14, 'Standards', but it is worth noting here that this approach has been used quite widely in relation to services to disadvantaged groups and individuals. Examples include the WAI publications already described as well as:

- *Library Services for Visually-Impaired People: a manual of best practice* (Hopkins, 2002) prepared for Resource (now the Museums, Libraries and Archives Council). Although only one of the chapters in this manual is actually headed 'Guidelines and standards', all contain useful information and/or checklists for libraries to use in assessing this aspect of service performance. One example will illustrate the kinds of issue which need to be considered. Recommendation 12.7.2 states that 'Wall-mounted furniture such as vending machines for photocopier tokens should not project more than 100mm from the wall, and need a hazard warning in the form of a kerb or barrier which can be detected by someone using a mobility cane if they are located adjacent to a circulation route or on a corridor' (http://bpm.nlb-online.org/).

- The IFLA Section of Libraries Serving Disadvantaged Persons *Guidelines for Library Services to Persons with Dyslexia* (www.ifla.org.sg/VII/s9/nd1/iflapr-70e.pdf).
- The *Calimera Guidelines on Social Inclusion*, part of a more comprehensive set of guidelines prepared for local library, museum and archive organizations across Europe (www.calimera.org/Lists/Guidelines/Social_inclusion.htm).

See also the Resources section below.

■ Conclusion

The temptation to adopt a 'one size fits all' approach to library service delivery can be countered by designing performance measures that differentiate between groups and enable the appropriateness and success of services to each group to be assessed. Personalization, where individuals are empowered to adjust the display of results and other service delivery for themselves, provides one option, although maintainability can become an issue. Where possible, software or hardware devices can be used to enable a 'design for all' approach to deliver differentiated outputs so that creation and maintenance of the underlying presentation is efficient.

There is now an enormous literature, including well-established guidelines and standards, on serving people with differing abilities. Libraries have been well to the fore in this area, and careful monitoring of performance in delivering to individuals and groups using these approaches can bring real benefits to users and to the service as a whole.

■ Resources

- IFLA's Library Services to Multicultural Populations Section has published *Multicultural Communities: Guidelines for Library Services* (www.ifla.org/VII/s32/pub/guide-e.htm), which contains criteria for establishing and monitoring such services. It is available in seven languages.
- Library and Archives Canada has an online Multicultural Resources and Services Toolkit at www.collectionscanada.ca/8/25/r25-300-e.html. This is particularly useful because of Canada's long experience of integrating services for diverse language communities.

- A good place to start with understanding and monitoring web accessibility is the W3C's Web Accessibility initiative website (www.w3.org/WAI/) and the Introduction to Accessibility on that site (www.w3.org/WAI/intro/accessibility.php).
- The Royal National Institute for the Blind has a web-based Web Access Centre, which contains advice for web developers and designers (www.rnib.org/xpedio/groups/public/documents/code/public_rnib008789.hcsp).
- The British Standards Institution (BSI) has published *Publicly Available Specification 78: guide to good practice in commissioning accessible websites* (2006), which is available to purchase from BSI, although single electronic copies can be downloaded from the DRC website (see www.drc-gb.org/library/website_accessibility_guidance/pas_78.aspx).

■ References

Berger, Å. (2002) Recent Trends in Library Services for Ethnic Minorities: the Danish experience, *Library Management*, **23** (1/2), 79–87.

Brophy, P. and Craven, J. (2007) Web Accessibility, *Library Trends*, **55** (4), in press.

Disability Rights Commission (2004) *The Web: access and inclusion for disabled people: a formal investigation carried out by the Disability Rights Commission*, London, The Stationery Office.

Hopkins, L. (ed.) (2002) *Library Services for Visually-impaired People: a manual of best practice*, rev. edn, London, Resource: the Council for Museums, Archives and Libraries, http://bpm.nlb-online.org/.

Williams, J. (2004) *How to Know if it's Real: assessing diversity and organizational climate*, National Diversity in Libraries Conference, Atlanta, GA, www.librarydiversity.org/how_know_real.pdf.

12
Benchmarking

■ **Introduction**

No library exists in isolation, for within any sector the services offered will share many common characteristics. The user populations may be similar, though clearly not identical, equivalent types of resource will be stocked or made available and the processes engaged in will be comparable. For this reason it can be very useful to compare the performance of one library with others. It can also be useful to make internal comparisons between branches, departments or sections. The term *benchmarking* is used to describe such processes of formal comparison.

Over ten years ago Charles Handy recounted an anecdote about benchmarking in his book *Beyond Certainty*. He said:

'Help us to be better', a firm's management said to me once. They were not even clear about which areas they wanted to be better in. 'I cannot help you', I replied. 'But you will know some people who can. Think of the different organizations you have met whom you admire for some aspect of their work. Go to them, ask them if you can study their methods . . . then come back and apply them to your business.'

They went, they saw and they learnt – but not what they expected. They learnt no new techniques or pieces of electronic wizardry, but discovered instead that some firms expected failure rates up to 100 times better than theirs or had absenteeism levels ten times lower and, in one comparable case, new product development times five times shorter. Standards were different, that is all.

Handy continued:

> This form of organized learning has recently acquired a label – benchmarking, the discipline of measuring yourself against best practice in any function or field, often in industries very different from your own. The label, however, reduces to a technique what surely ought to be an ingrained habit – to aim to be not just good enough but as good as can be, to look beyond oneself in setting standards for oneself, to shun complacency and the false comforts of talking only to people like oneself. (Handy, 1995)

That story is a useful antidote to any idea that benchmarking is either an arcane art or an optional extra. Handy's argument is that it must become an integral part of everyday organizational life. Libraries are particularly well placed to benefit from benchmarking, partly because so many of their procedures are similar to one another, and partly because most are publicly funded and much less constrained by considerations of commercial confidentiality than many other organizations.

■ Benchmarking defined

There are numerous definitions of benchmarking to choose from. The following summarize the generally accepted understandings (see www.benchmarking.gov.uk/about_bench/whatisit.asp):

> Benchmarking is simply about making comparisons with other organisations and then learning the lessons that those comparisons throw up.
> (The European Benchmarking Code of Conduct)

> Benchmarking is the continuous process of measuring products, services and practices against the toughest competitors or those companies recognised as industry leaders (best in class). (The Xerox Corporation)

> Improving ourselves by learning from others.
> (UK Public Sector Benchmarking Service)

Although benchmarking is concerned with comparing one service with others, it is important to be clear as to what it is not. Benchmarking is not about:

- *Checking your position in league tables.* Benchmarking seeks to understand *why* you're not at the top (or, if you are, why your competitors or colleagues are edging closer!). It is not aimed at self-justification or self-congratulation.
- *Competitor analysis.* The best benchmarking involves collaboration rather than an attempt simply to beat the competition. The motivation is to be the best, not just to squeeze ahead of a competitor, but to provide the best possible service or product.
- *A way to fix a perceived problem.* Benchmarking is long term and involves repeated analysis of performance compared with that of others, followed by continuous improvement. While it is possible to observe or take advice from others in order to resolve a specific issue, that is not what is usually meant by benchmarking.
- *Doing things differently.* Because someone else does it a different way does not mean that you should. You benchmark to *learn*, not just to copy.
- *Professional tourism.* You don't examine other people's services just out of curiosity or so you can talk about your visit to your colleagues as you swap 'war stories' round the water fountain. Failing to follow up what is learned with action is a waste of time.
- *Espionage.* Benchmarking is not designed to enable you to steal someone else's secrets (not that there tend to be many in librarianship!) but works best in a spirit of openness and honesty where the learning is shared.

Benchmarking is concerned with developing systematic and structured approaches to finding and implementing best practice. It links the identification of what is currently the best way of doing things in the sector (or outwith the sector if useful examples can be found) with a determination to improve one's own organization and 'to be the best'.

One further point should be made: the term *benchmark* is sometimes used as a synonym for *target*, especially for pan-sectoral performance management. Thus the requirement for UK public libraries to pursue and demonstrate Best Value, introduced in April 2000, involved the setting of a series of performance indicators some of which were targets set by central government (see Chapter 3, 'User satisfaction'). These are sometimes referred to in the literature as 'benchmarks'. However, while they involve comparisons, they are not what is normally meant by benchmarking.

■ Types of benchmarking

Benchmarking can be *internal* or *external*. That is, it can be done within the organization, maybe across divisions or sections or simply by comparing new and old ways of doing things. Or it can be undertaken externally, by comparing the organization with others. Some sectors have developed their own 'benchmarking clubs', where organizations agree to work together to share benchmarking methods and data. A number of these have been established among libraries, notably in the public library sector.

A useful distinction is often drawn between *process benchmarking* and *data benchmarking*. The former is primarily concerned with comparing processes and activities by looking at similar functions in different organizations. Organizations may then be able to spot ways they could improve their own internal processes. The latter is more concerned with looking at inputs, outputs and outcomes, and often focuses on quantitative data analysis. This enables differences to be identified and the need for further investigation to be highlighted, especially where it appears that the data show that one organization is significantly more efficient than another. In practice the two are often used together.

■ The benchmarking wheel

The process of benchmarking is often guided by what is known as the *benchmarking wheel*, which depicts the different stages of the process but emphasises iteration and continuity. It is illustrated in Figure 12.1.

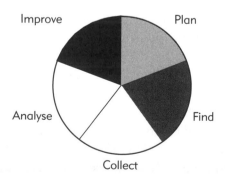

Figure 12.1 The benchmarking wheel

The first part of the process, obviously enough, is *plan*. This covers ensuring clarity of purpose, identifying the critical internal processes that need to be compared and considering how information might best be gathered to support the exercise. It is then necessary to *find* suitable benchmarking partners. Here it is best to develop some explicit criteria. For example, you might be looking to benchmark reference services, in which case the criteria might ignore sectoral differences by seeking to gather information about such services from a wide spectrum of library types. In another case, say where the comparison was between information skills delivery within the secondary school curriculum, then the sector might be an explicit criterion. However, it is always good to range as widely as possible. In addition to criteria about what is to be benchmarked, it is also useful to think about how the process will happen. So, for example, you might have expectations about who needs to be involved at each organization.

Having found benchmarking partners and agreed exactly how the process will operate, a formal agreement should be placed on record. The next step is to *collect* data, for which many different methodologies might be used. Appendix 1, 'Data collection methods', lists the main ones that libraries would tend to employ, but what is critical is that they are operationalized in such a way that data collected are truly comparable. Of course, in some circumstances, particularly where process benchmarking is being employed, it may be that the method is limited to discussions between and perhaps demonstrations by staff. Where quantitative approaches are being used, discussions will be needed to illuminate the data.

This brings us to *analysis*, where the meaning of the data is elucidated in useful ways. So the questions are 'what do these data tell us?' and 'what implications are there for the way we conduct our business?'. Asking these questions, which in essence relate to validity and relevance, enables a plan of action to be drawn up.

The next stage is to take action to *improve* the existing processes and services. Staff will need to be informed as to what is happening and the reasons for it, as would be the case for any change, but care is needed not to imply that the need for change is due to staff failings! Alongside implementation of changes, steps should be taken to ensure that change is being monitored. So, for example, if changes have been designed to address a situation where it appears that the library is not very efficient, efficiency measures need to be in place to monitor what happens as a result of the benchmarking exercise.

The benchmarking wheel then indicates that the process is repeated. A new stage of planning might identify that a different service needs to be benchmarked, or perhaps the criteria for choosing partners need to be modified. And so the process continues, encouraging continuous, purposeful change in the organization.

■ Benchmarking and quality management

There are close links between the use of benchmarking and quality management, with systematic approaches such as total quality management (TQM) incorporating benchmarking as an important tool. The Business Excellence Model of the European Foundation for Quality Management (EFQM) is explicitly recommended by EFQM as a basis for benchmarking between organizations. It divides the criteria for excellence into nine sets, five being 'enablers' and four being 'results'. See the definitions in Table 12.1.

Table 12.1 EFQM Business Excellence Model

Enablers
Leadership: providing direction and inspiration to the organization: 'Excellent leaders develop and facilitate the achievement of the mission and vision.'
Policy and strategy: having meaningful and actionable policies and strategies in place and acting on them: 'Excellent organisations implement their mission and vision by developing a stakeholder focused strategy that takes account of the market and sector in which it operates.'
People: the staff who work in the organization are its greatest asset: 'Excellent organizations manage, develop and release the full potential of their people at an individual, team-based and organizational level. They promote fairness and equality and involve and empower their people.'
Partnerships and resources: EFQM sees the management of partnerships with external suppliers and internal management of resources as a single issue: 'Excellent organisations plan to manage external partnerships, suppliers and internal resources in order to support policy and strategy and the effective operation of processes.'
Processes: the internal processes which the organization employs to achieve its results: 'Excellent organisations design, manage and improve processes in order to fully satisfy, and generate increasing value for, customers and other stakeholders.'

Results
Customer results: the most important outcome is the effect on customers: 'Excellent organisations comprehensively measure and achieve outstanding results with respect to their customers.'
People results: EFQM places great emphasis on the organization's own people: 'Excellent organisations comprehensively measure and achieve outstanding results with respect to their people'.

Continued on next page

Table 12.1 *Continued*

Results

Society results: as discussed in Chapter 5, 'Social and economic impact', the impact of the organization on society is now an accepted issue across all sectors. EFQM states: 'Excellent organisations comprehensively measure and achieve outstanding results with respect to society.'

Key performance results: The importance of linking performance measurement to organizational strategy is emphasized: 'Excellent organisations comprehensively measure and achieve outstanding results with respect to the key element of their policy and strategy.'

Further information on the criteria for the model will be found at www.efqm.org/Default.aspx?tabid=40.

■ Benchmarking and libraries

There is a considerable history of benchmarking in libraries. One of the pioneers of the approach, Stephen Town of Cranfield University, introduced the topic at the first Northumbria International Conference on Performance Measurement in Libraries and Information Services (Town, 1995). Cranfield University Library undertook a study in the late 1990s, funded by the British Library, to try to devise suitable performance indicators which could be used for benchmarking between academic libraries (Blagden and Barton, 1997). This work involved a number of SCONUL libraries and SCONUL's Advisory Committee (now Working Group) on Performance Improvement (ACPI) commissioned a set of pilot benchmarking projects. As a result of this four university libraries (Derby, Huddersfield, Leeds Metropolitan and Staffordshire) agreed to set up a benchmarking club. The work of this consortium of libraries was reported by Creaser (2003) and covered:

* off-campus services
* shelving
* advice desks
* short loan.

Although the main benefit of benchmarking in this way was felt to be the support of internal decision making, additional benefits claimed from this work included:

- networking between groups of staff involved in similar tasks
- exchange of views and generation of new ideas
- staff development
- greater local ownership of processes and tasks
- university recognition – providing considerable 'political' value.

In 2000, SCONUL published a benchmarking manual (Town, 2000), which defined the process in terms of three phases – planning, comparing and acting. These, in turn, can be broken down into seven steps, which are similar to the benchmarking wheel described above:

- *Defining*: what measures are to be used? Who is to be involved?
- *Partnering*: finding other libraries with which it is appropriate to work: usually this involves finding libraries similar in size, position in league tables, subjects covered, age and so on.
- *Agreeing*: setting out the ground rules, including ethical issues such as confidentiality.
- *Measuring*: identifying the critical success factors and the measures that will be used. Identifying whether existing data collection and analysis are adequate to provide the needed information and if not devising new methods and protocols.
- *Collecting*: recording a profile or context, then actually gathering the data together. At this stage staff will visit each other's libraries.
- *Analysing*: processing the data, including normalizing them so as to make comparisons valid. Identifying process and performance differences.
- *Acting*: using the results obtained to pursue purposeful change and setting targets based on what has been learned. The whole process can then be repeated, often turning attention to new areas that are suitable for benchmarking.

The standard user survey developed by SCONUL (see Chapter 3, 'User satisfaction', and Appendix 1, 'Data collection methods') has enabled some benchmarking between libraries to be carried out. Creaser (2005) reported that this enabled valid comparisons to be made between libraries but warned: 'there are a number of areas where care must be taken in order for the analyses to have the greatest value, for example in the choice of comparators. It is also important to ensure that the survey methodology has been applied in a consistent way in all institutions included.' She added: 'Variations in the time period over which the survey was conducted, or the physical medium through which it was administered, are acceptable, however.'

Public libraries have also been heavily involved in benchmarking. Favret (2000) reported that up to the mid-1990s there was relatively little activity that was called benchmarking, but that a considerable number of initiatives in which libraries participated, such as the Charter Mark process, were benchmarking in all but name. CIPFA set up a public libraries benchmarking club in 1999, partly in response to the new government requirement to pursue Best Value (see www.ipfbenchmarking.net/). In its first year the club focused on:

- staffing
- use of space
- stock management
- mobile libraries.

David Fuegi has described the work of the public libraries benchmarking club in the following way:

> The aim of the club is to combine the benefits of networking through groups such as quality circles with a set programme of investigations into processes and methods of service delivery. The research is founded on statistical or process analysis between library authorities. The enquiries lead to an examination of management processes and the effectiveness of policies. Regular exchange of information and a continuous cycle of research topics provides the appropriate forum for all authorities wishing to support their best value initiatives. The emphasis is directed towards how best to add value.
>
> (www.mdrpartners.com/Text Only/projects.htm)

■ Benchmarking in practice

Benchmarking can be relatively simple, using readily available statistical data to highlight issues. For example, Roswitha Poll reported on an analysis of the number of items added to stock per employee in ten German university libraries during 1997, as shown in Table 12.2 (Poll, 2000).

Table 12.2 German university libraries: items added per full-time equivalent staff member

Library no.	Items added	Staff (FTE)	Items per FTE
1	25,983	9.40	2,764
2	36,531	8.75	4,175
3	44,968	18.55	2,424
4	49,613	16.60	2,989
5	27,639	9.40	2,940
6	37,250	12.22	3,048
7	56,596	14.75	3,837
8	37,971	10.50	3,616
9	34,679	4.94	7,020
10	45,753	10.05	4,553
Arithmetic mean			3,737

These data provide a useful example of both the possibilities and the dangers of benchmarking in this way. The individual libraries can view their own achievements against the mean and this should raise questions for them. However, it should *not* lead to the assumption that library 9, which is achieving a throughput of over 7000 items per employee per annum, is 'better' than library 3, which managed under 2500. All kinds of factors could be at play:

- the nature of the material handled by library 3 could be much more complex or, perhaps for reasons of its historical importance, require much more detailed attention than material acquired by library 9
- library 9 may have outsourced part of its operations, so that the processes undertaken by its staff are less onerous and time-consuming than those undertaken by staff at library 3
- the way in which the two libraries calculate the effort expended could be different
- the types of items counted could be different.

This emphasizes that data of this nature can only ever produce *indications* of where further investigation may be worthwhile. If in fact the two libraries appear on the surface to be very similar, these data suggest that it may be worthwhile for managers at library 3 to examine why such differences are apparent, perhaps by looking at the other libraries' processes and then devising ways to exploit what they have learned by redesigning their own processes.

■ Benchmarking and service improvement: the evidence

Recently, Stephen Town and his colleagues have examined examples of benchmarking to try to establish whether in fact it can lead to service improvement. This work used a Quality Maturity Model (QMM), derived from the Software Engineering Institute's Capability Maturity Model (CMM), which postulates that there are five levels at which a library can be placed according to its approach to quality management. These are:

- Level 1 (Initial) 'The quality management process is ad hoc, and occasionally even chaotic. Few processes are defined, and success depends on individual effort and heroics.'
- Level 2 (Repeatable) 'Basic quality management processes are established. The necessary management processes are in place to repeat earlier quality levels.'
- Level 3 (Defined) 'The quality processes are documented and standardised. All work derives from the organisational strategy.'
- Level 4 (Managed) 'Detailed measures of the quality process are collected. The quality process is quantitatively understood and controlled.'
- Level 5 (Optimizing) 'Continuous quality improvement is enabled by quantitative feedback and from piloting innovative ideas.'

(Wilson and Town, 2005)

The conclusions of Wilson and Town's study are interesting and informative. The study 'suggests that benchmarking can have a beneficial long-term effect on library and information service quality. However, it also indicates that this effect may only occur in library and information services that already have a pre-existing quality approach' (Wilson and Town, 2005). This is consistent with the broader experience of organizations in both public and private sectors, and suggests that benchmarking is not a panacea but simply one tool among many which managers can use to help improve performance.

■ Limitations of benchmarking

It has also to be remembered that what can be achieved through benchmarking is limited by the comparability of the data which are gathered, as the above example from Germany illustrated. This is a particular problem with quantitative data and it is all too easy to make false assumptions. A recent investigation by LISU (Greenwood and Creaser, 2006) found that 'there is considerable variation in the methods used to compile figures . . . and many of the figures are not truly comparable between (library) authorities'. The reasons that this occurs include: organizational differences, difficulties in apportioning costs to or from the library within its broader organizational setting and different accounting protocols. For this reason, considerable effort has to be expended to ensure that like is being compared with like.

■ Conclusion

It has been shown in many sectors that benchmarking, the purposeful comparison of processes and data, can yield helpful results in performance improvement. It is critical that such exercises are carefully planned and that the right benchmarking partners are identified. Many different methodologies may be used to collect and analyse data, but comparability is perhaps the most important issue for managers to think about.

To gain maximum value, benchmarking should be thought of as a long-term activity, with cycles of planning, partner identification, data collection, analysis, action and monitoring.

■ Resources

- Various published resources can be used in benchmarking. Indeed, the LISU annual statistical report (see Chapter 6 'Inputs') explicitly states that 'one main objective of this volume is to assist librarians in making comparisons of their performance with others'. The LISU website is at www.lboro.ac.uk/departments/ls/lisu/index.html.
- The *SCONUL Benchmarking Manual*, referred to above, is a loose-leaf publication edited by Stephen Town and available for purchase from SCONUL (see www.sconul.ac.uk/pubs_stats/pubs/publications.html).
- Libraries that use the LibQUAL+™ methodology (see Chapter 3, 'User satisfaction') may use this to provide benchmarking data, although some reservations have been expressed about this kind of usage so care needs to be taken to ensure comparisons are valid.

■ References

Blagden, J. and Barton, J. (1997) Can You Compare One University's Library Performance With Another? *2nd Northumbria International Conference on Performance Measurement in Libraries and Information Services, Longhirst Hall, Northumbria, UK*, Newcastle upon Tyne, Information North.

Creaser, C. (2003) *As Others See Us: benchmarking in practice*, LISU Occasional Papers 33, Loughborough, LISU, www.lboro.ac.uk/departments/ls/lisu/downloads/OP33.pdf.

Creaser, C. (2005) Benchmarking the Standard SCONUL User Survey: report of a pilot study, *SCONUL Focus*, (34), 61–5.

Favret, L. (2000) Benchmarking, Annual Library Plans and Best Value: the implications for public libraries, *Library Management*, **21** (6 and 7), 340–8.

Greenwood, H. and Creaser, C. (2006) *Best Practice in Data Collection: report of a benchmarking exercise for Leicestershire Library Services and Warwickshire Library and Information Service*, Occasional Paper no. 36, Loughborough, LISU, www.lboro.ac.uk/departments/ls/lisu/downloads/op36.pdf.

Handy, C. (1995) *Beyond Certainty: the changing worlds of organisations*, London, Hutchinson.

Poll, R. (2000) Three Years of Operating Ratios for University Libraries, *Performance Measurement and Metrics*, **1** (1), 3–8.

Town, J. S. (1995) *Benchmarking and Performance Measurement*, Northumbria International Conference on Performance Measurement in Libraries and Information Services, Newcastle upon Tyne, Information North.

Town, J. S. (2000) *SCONUL Benchmarking Manual*, London, Standing Conference of National and University Libraries.

Wilson, F. and Town, J. S. (2005) Benchmarking and Library Quality Maturity, *6th Northumbria International Conference on Performance Measurement in Libraries and Information Services, Durham*, http://hdl.handle.net/1826/948.

13
The balanced scorecard

■ Introduction

It will be readily apparent from earlier chapters and especially from the description of benchmarking in the last chapter that the performance of a library can only be assessed by examining a range of measures and indicators so as to achieve a balanced view of its various services and operations. This observation brings us back to the issue first raised in the preface, namely that 'what gets measured gets managed'. The ever present danger of performance measurement is that by focusing attention on particular aspects of service, it will encourage partial and therefore deficient management attention. To achieve a holistic vision and strategy is extremely difficult with social systems such as libraries and information services, where human interactions make measurement and assessment difficult, if not at times impossible. There is always a temptation to make assumptions on the basis of readily available, and thus often quantitative, data rather than on the information that would in fact illuminate the situation, but which is more difficult and more expensive to collect. To try to counter this tendency, management theorists and practitioners have emphasized the need for broad models which are capable of reflecting the complexity of real world organizations acting in complex environments. The *balanced scorecard* is perhaps the best known example, with the widest acceptance. There are a number of other models in use, one of which, the EFQM Excellence Model, was described in Chapter 12, 'Benchmarking'.

■ Defining the balanced scorecard

Devised initially by Robert Kaplan and David Norton in the USA (Kaplan and Norton, 1992, 1996), the idea of the balanced scorecard was to try to create assessments of organizational performance which took into account all the different relevant factors. In many ways, this development was a reaction to the excessive reliance on financial measures – and in particular the financial 'bottom line' – which had dominated industrial and commercial enterprises for many years.

Kaplan and Norton were particularly concerned that financial measures tend to be backwards looking. They may tell us what the business has done in the past, but they do not necessarily tell us where it is going in the future. They also ignore many of the assets of an organization, such as reputation, knowledge, loyal customers and skilled employees. For a library, Poll has argued that the essential issue is to replace the financial focus with a user focus: 'libraries do not strive for maximum gain but for best service' (Poll, 2001) – see also below.

The balanced scorecard approach requires the analysis of an organization from four different perspectives, as shown in Table 13.1.

Table 13.1 Balanced scorecard perspectives

People's learning and growth	The ability to be a learning organization and so sustain the ability to change and improve through employee skills and knowledge.
Business processes	The ability to operate appropriate business processes and to excel at doing so.
Customer perspective	The expectations and experiences of customers, associated with the reputation and image of the organization.
Resources perspective	The ability to harness all resources and use them wisely

These four perspectives are centred around clarity of:

- vision – where the organization is going and what is wishes to be
- values – what it believes to be an appropriate way of acting
- strategy – how it believes it should develop towards its vision.

■ Library implementations of the balanced scorecard

A number of libraries have used the balanced scorecard approach, examples including the University of Virginia in the USA (Self, 2003) and a consortium consisting of the University and Regional Library Münster with the Bavarian State Library Munich and the State and University Library Bremen in Germany (Poll, 2001). It has also been used quite widely by UK libraries across all the sectors. For example, the University of Hull Library Services publishes its balanced scorecard aims, performance measures and targets. In its 2005–6 scorecard plan (www.hull.ac.uk/lib/downloads/balanced_scorecard_0506.pdf) it categorized its scorecard measures in the following way:

1 Open for learning – the customer service perspective:
   • *How well is the library meeting the needs of our users?*
2 Value for money – the financial perspective:
   • *How well are the library's finances managed to achieve our mission?*
3 Working smarter (*sic*) – the internal process perspective:
   • *How do the library's internal processes function to deliver library collections and services efficiently?*
4 Building the e-campus – part of the learning and growth perspective:
   • *How do we develop our people and systems to ensure that goals are met in the future?*
5 Collaboration and reach-out – another part of the learning and growth perspective:
   • *How do we develop our people and systems to ensure that goals are met in the future?*
6 Staffing for the future – again part of the learning and growth perspective:
   • *How do we develop our people and systems to ensure that goals are met in the future?*

This is a good example of the way in which the principles behind the balanced scorecard can be adapted to meet the particular requirements of a specific library. The finance area, for example, is not neglected but it is designed in such a way that it relates to the key financial responsibility, that of achieving value for money for the expenditure of public funds.

A further feature of Hull's implementation is that they associate two targets with each measure. As they explain, 'if we achieve target one, then we are performing at the level we hoped to reach. Achieving target two indicates that we are making progress, but we still have some way to go' (www.hull.ac.uk/lib/using_our_libraries/performance/balanced_scorecard/). For example, they state that target 1 for self-service issues as a percentage of total issues is 50%, but target 2 is 45%. This provides a useful zone within which to manage performance and prioritize resources.

The number of performance indicators used within a balanced scorecard approach varies, although Kaplan and Norton suggest that 20–25 measures is about right (Kaplan and Norton, 1996). Roswitha Poll, in the example referred to above, used 20 indicators, as follows:

- user perspective:
  —market penetration, i.e. the percentage of the population registered as actual users
  —user satisfaction
  —opening hours compared to demand
  —cases of use (issues, in-house use) per member of the population
  —immediate availability i.e. the percentage of immediate loans divided by the total number of loans (including reservations and ILL)
- electronic services:
  —the percentage of the population using electronic library services
  —the percentage of accesses to electronic library services coming from outside the library
- financial perspective:
  —the cost of the library per member of the population
  —the cost of the library per case of use
  —acquisitions expenditure compared to staff costs
  —the percentage of staff costs per library service or product as a proportion of total staff costs
  —the percentage of acquisitions expenditure spent on electronic media
- processes:
  —acquired items per FTE staff year
  —average processing time for acquired items
  —the number of stages involved in providing a product or service (for every library service)
  —the percentage of all staff costs spent on electronic services and the provision of electronic media
- potential:
  —the library budget as a percentage of the institution's budget
  —the percentage of current expenditure devoted to information and communication technologies

——the number of formal training hours per staff member
——the number of short-time illnesses per staff member.

It is perhaps worth noting that at the time this work was carried out electronic services were relatively new and not completely embedded in library services. As has been demonstrated earlier, the integration of performance measurement for electronic services with that for traditional ones is likely to remain problematic for some time, but the balanced scorecard offers a framework for developing integrated measures. Indeed, Town has suggested that the balanced scorecard may provide a useful framework for developing measures for electronic services: 'The recognition of different stakeholder perceptions is key to this approach, and helps to present the right measures to the right audience' (Town, 2004).

However, it needs to be emphasized that the balanced scorecard approach only makes sense as part of a comprehensive strategic planning and monitoring framework. This takes us beyond the scope of this book, although a number of writers have offered models showing how the balanced scorecard can be used within strategic planning (for example, Schneiderman, 2004). Valiris and Chytas (2005) demonstrate the combination of the balanced scorecard approach with multi-criteria decision making (MCDM), 'an approach that takes explicit account of multiple conflicting criteria in decision-making'.

■ Conclusion

The balanced scorecard provides a useful framework for achieving an overall view of library performance, helping to ensure that no area is overlooked and that managers focus their effort where it is most needed. There are some similarities with LibQUAL™ (described in Chapter 3, 'User satisfaction'), which also tries to take a balanced view by examining different areas of service, although that is based on user expectations and perceptions rather than on the managerial view which informs the balanced scorecard.

Many libraries have successfully used the balanced scorecard, or a variant of it, and it has proved of value in different sectors. However, examples of its application to libraries where electronic services are dominant are still needed.

■ Resources

* The Cerritos public library in California has created a useful guide to the application of the balanced scorecard to libraries, at http://cml.ci.cerritos.ca.us/scorecard/.
* An online video presentation on the balanced scorecard has been made available by the US Federal Library and Information Center Committee (FLICC) Federal Library and Information Network (FEDLINK) and is available at http://loc.gov/flicc/video/balance/balancedscore.html.

■ References

Kaplan, R. S. and Norton, D. P. (1992) The Balanced Scorecard: measures that drive performance, *Harvard Business Review*, **70** (1), 71–9.

Kaplan, R. S. and Norton, D. P. (1996) *The Balanced Scorecard: translating strategy into action*, Boston MA, Harvard Business School Press.

Poll, R. (2001) Performance, Processes and Costs: managing service quality with the balanced scorecard, *Library Trends*, **49** (4), 709–17.

Schneiderman, A. M. (2004) *How to Build a Balanced Scorecard*, www.schneiderman.com/Concepts/Scorecard/How_to_Build_a_Balanced_Scorecard/how_to_build_a_BSC_intro.htm.

Self, J. (2003) From Values to Metrics: implementation of the balanced scorecard at a university library, *Performance Measurement and Metrics*, **4** (2), 57–63.

Town, J. S. (2004) E-measures: a comprehensive waste of time? *VINE: The Journal of Information and Knowledge Management Systems*, **34** (4), 190–5.

Valiris, G. and Chytas, P. (2005) Making Decisions Using the Balanced Scorecard and the Simple Multi-attribute Rating Technique, *Performance Measurement and Metrics*, **6** (3), 159–71.

14
Standards

■ Introduction

There are considerable benefits from the development and use of standards in performance measurement, not least reduction in individual effort and the possibility of producing results which are truly comparable. It is not surprising, therefore, that over the years different sectors have developed standards and guidelines as a basis for service, some of which have statutory backing. For example, public libraries in England and Wales have been required by law to offer a 'comprehensive and efficient service' since the Public Libraries Act of 1964, though what is meant by that has in the past been poorly defined. An attempt to resolve this came in the early 2000s with the development of public library standards to try to provide a yardstick for assessing service economy, efficiency and effectiveness (see below). Another example can be found in the health service sector, where a standards-based approach to accreditation was introduced in 2002 by the Health Libraries and Information Confederation (HELICON), which remarked that 'part of the quality improvement process in libraries is the development of standards that can be used to assess and support library and information services in providing cost-effective, client-centred services' (Fowler and Trinder, 2002).

In addition to sectoral standards and guidelines, there is a small number of formal international standards which have been developed by experienced professionals and have received endorsement by the national standards authorities such as BSI and NISO. These are described later in this chapter.

■ Public library service standards

Public library standards were introduced in April 2001 in the UK and subsequently modified in the light of experience and following the publication of the major report, *Framework for the Future*, in February 2003 (Department for Culture, Media and Sport, 2003). In 2006, public libraries were expected to meet standards defined in terms of ten criteria (www.culture.gov.uk/NR/rdonlyres/07070797-AE22-4064-8BAF-FEEE2ABA99F9/0/libstandards_06.pdf):

- the proportion of households living within specified distance of a static library
- aggregate scheduled opening hours per 1000 population for all libraries
- the percentage of static libraries providing access to electronic information resources connected to the internet
- the total number of electronic workstations with access to the internet and the libraries catalogue (available for public use through both static and mobile libraries, and other service outlets) available to users per 10,000 population
- requests
  —percentage of requests for books met within 7 days
  —percentage of requests for books met within 15 days
  —percentage of requests for books met within 30 days
- number of library visits per 1000 population
- the percentage of library users 16 and over who view their library service as:
  —very good
  —good
  —adequate
  —poor
  —very poor
- the percentage of library users under 16 who view their library service as:
  —good
  —adequate
  —bad
- annual items added through purchase per 1000 population
- the time taken to replenish the lending stock on open access or available on loan.

Each of these measures is accompanied by a target. For example, the target for the penultimate measure, 'Annual items added through purchase per 1000 population', is set at 216. In some cases targets are related to the type of library authority. The background to the development of these service standards has been described by Favret (2000).

■ Academic library standards

It is unusual for academic libraries to have to meet mandatory standards of the type which are required of the UK public library sector. However, they are required to play their part in enabling their institutions to meet accreditation requirements, which in some countries is effectively a standards-led approach. This often leads to a tension between implied standards and institutional autonomy, which can drive priorities, and library managers need to be aware of this. In particular, the general shift towards the assessment of teaching in relation to stated learning outcomes has made library-centred standards somewhat irrelevant.

In the USA it is noticeable that the Regional Accrediting Agencies, led by the Council for Higher Education Accreditation (CHEA), have also moved to standards based on student learning outcomes:

> These accrediting bodies believe that outcomes assessment measures institutional effectiveness and that effectiveness can be defined in terms of achieving student learning outcomes and improving educational quality.
>
> (Hernon and Dugan, 2002)

Hernon and Dugan note, however, that there is considerable variation between accrediting agencies on the level of prescription in their standards. Some are highly generalized, while others require, for example, evidence of provision for and successful delivery of information literacy programmes. Thus the Western Association of Schools and Colleges (WASC) specifically asks for such evidence:

> How does the institution ensure that its members develop the critical information literacy skills needed to locate, evaluate and responsibly use information? How does it utilize the special skills of information professionals to support teaching, learning and information technology planning?
>
> (Western Association of Schools and Colleges, 2001, in Hernon and Dugan, 2002)

■ Other sectors

Again, the hard and fast standards approach is unusual in other sectors. Health libraries, as noted above, have developed their own standards under the leadership of HELICON, though these are sometimes referred to as a 'checklist' and the individual standards as 'measurement criteria'. As an example, criterion 3.1.1 states that 'stock and electronic resources are selected and updated in consultation with users and are demonstrably up to date'. An explanatory note states that 'evidence will be required to show that users are involved in the resource selection process. Evidence of the use of guidelines or core lists may be given but these should not be used at the expense of user consultation'. This criterion is mandatory (it is either met or it isn't) while some others are graded (Fowler and Trinder, 2002).

■ International, cross-sectoral standards
ISO 11620

The ISO standard 11620:1998 (Information and documentation: library performance indicators) has been developed by a team of experts in the field, who issued a technical report (ISO/TR 20983) in 2003 with additional performance indicators for electronic library services. It is worth noting that, at the time of writing, the standard that national standards organizations will supply is technically ISO 11620:1998 but will in fact be the 2003 version incorporating Amendment 1 (which is BSI 14691).

ISO 11620 is intended to be applicable to all types of library in all parts of the world and as well as specifying the indicators themselves provides the methodology to be used in collecting and analysing the data. However, it explicitly states that it does not include 'indicators for the evaluation of the impact of libraries either on individuals or on society'.

The standard begins with definitions of terms: a 'user', for example, is simply a 'recipient of library services'. It then sets out the criteria for inclusion of an indicator in the standard: it has to be 'thoroughly tested, validated and (preferably) documented in the literature'. In other words the standard is effectively a drawing together of work which has been undertaken by libraries and research centres over the years, refining and agreeing on common terminology, methodology and usage.

There are five categories of indicator:

- user perception
- public services (by far the largest section)
- technical services
- promotion of services (although at present no indicators have been defined in this area)
- user services.

As an example, indicator B.2.4.2 is headed 'Loans per capita'. The objective of defining this indicator is 'to assess the rate of use of library collections by the population to be served'. It applies to all libraries which have a loan collection and can be used with specific collections, branches, etc. as well as with the library service as a whole. The indicator is defined as: 'the total number of loans in a year divided by the population to be served'.

Both 'loan' and 'population to be served' have been defined in the introductory part of the standard so as to remove any ambiguity. Note that the latter term implies that the correct data relate to both users and non-users – all people who are eligible to use the library's services.

The method to be used is to 'count the total number of loans in a year', although a note instructs that inter-library loans are to be excluded. The indicator itself is then calculated by simply dividing total number of loans in a year by the number of people in the population to be served, and then rounding off to one decimal place.

The standard also provides some commentary on the limitations of the indicators and issues which need to be considered. For the above indicator these would include its sensitivity to alterations in library practice such as changes in loan periods or in loan allocations and the effects of external factors such as literacy levels and in-library study conditions.

ISO 11620 is continuously reviewed by ISO Technical Committee 46 (Information and documentation), Sub-Committee 8 (Statistics and performance evaluations). The sub-committee consists of leading experts in the field, currently chaired by Dr Roswitha Poll of Universitäts- und Landesbibliothek Münster, Germany, with significant input from IFLA.

ISO/TR 20983

A technical report does not have the same standing as an international standard, but is intended to inform the community about current thinking.

Unlike international standards, which must go through a formal voting process and gain approval by at least 75% of the national member bodies that cast a vote, technical reports can be issued by a simple majority vote in the relevant ISO committee. The latter is the status of the current document on performance indicators for electronic library services.

TR 20983:2003 references ISO 11620, in particular by drawing attention to those performance indicators in the standard that apply to both traditional and electronic library services, such as user satisfaction or 'correct answer fill rate', which measures the performance of reference services that could be provided in person or remotely, or both. As in ISO 11620, the technical report draws heavily on work undertaken within the library practitioner and research communities, notably the European Commission funded EQUINOX Project (Brophy et al., 2000), work in the USA by Charles McClure, John Bertot and their colleagues (Bertot et al., 2001) and the ARL e-metrics reports (see www.arl.org/stats/newmeas/emetrics/) – see Chapter 6, 'Inputs'.

As an example, TR 20983 describes one indicator as 'number of documents downloaded per session', defined as 'the number of documents and entries downloaded in part or in whole from each electronic resource, divided by the number of sessions on each service during a specified time period'. Again there are notes on the limitations of the indicator, which could be affected by the levels of skills possessed by the users, whether services are free or have to be paid for and the amount of promotion of the service in which the library has engaged. The report also suggests that it would be unwise to aggregate all the data from every database but that data for similar types (e.g. electronic journals) could be aggregated. The suggested indicator has been adapted from EQUINOX indicator 4 (see page 97) and it is proposed that it could be used alongside another indicator, 'cost per document downloaded'.

ISO 2789

ISO 2789:2003 (Information and documentation. International library statistics) is produced by the same sub-committee of ISO/TC 46 as ISO 11620, Sub-Committee 8. This is important, because many of the definitions used in ISO 2789 underpin the calculation of performance indicators in ISO 11620.

ISO 2789 again begins with terms and definitions, some of which have helpfully updated the previous version of the standard by addressing the requirements for keeping statistics of electronic services. For example, ISO 2789's definitions, which are far more extensive than ISO 11620's, now provide an explanation of what is meant by an 'electronic book' or 'eBook': it is a 'digital document, licensed or not, where searchable text is prevalent, and which can be seen in analogy to a print book (monograph)'. It is worth remembering that, while such definitions may be open to criticism or disagreement, the provision of an internationally defined term is very helpful for many purposes, not only in the measurement of performance.

The standard contains six categories:

- libraries (how the number of libraries in an administrative unit, such as a public library authority, should be counted)
- collection
- library use and users
- access and facilities
- expenditure
- library staff.

An Annex deals with methods of measuring the usage of electronic library services, which are taken to include:

- OPACs
- library websites
- collections of electronic resources, subdivided into databases, electronic serials and digital documents
- mediated delivery of electronic documents
- electronic reference services
- training of users on electronic services
- internet access via the library.

It is suggested that statistics should be collected on the use of electronic services, focusing on two questions: 'how many times have users accessed an electronic library service?' and 'how many documents did they find that they thought relevant?'. It is acknowledged in this part of the standard that the development of suitable measures is an ongoing issue, and that there are particular problems in reconciling statistical data produced by different systems – the discussion of Project COUNTER in Chapter 6, 'Inputs', is directly relevant to this.

In addition to statistical data derived from the library's different systems, ISO 2789 makes suggestions as to data which can be collected through surveys of various types. These might include:

- general surveys which aim to address market penetration
- specific surveys to assess specific forms of use, for example if wishing to assess the ease of use of the OPAC.

This is probably the least satisfactory part of the standard, as it is able only to address some major issues briefly (ease of use would be one) although these need far more extensive treatment in a complex methodological framework. Refer to Chapter 8, 'Outputs', for further discussion of approaches to this particular question.

A useful annex to the standard suggests ways of 'grossing up' data where there is an incomplete set – for example, when attempting to create a regional or national statistical return where one or more libraries have failed to provide data.

■ Conclusion

Standards provide a powerful means of guiding library performance measurement, since they offer authoritative advice on the indicators that can best be used and on the ways data can be collected and analysed to support the derivation of performance indicators. Their application varies widely across different sectors, with public libraries being the major sector where they are mandatory.

Standards are evolving continuously as experience leads to their refinement and new services, or new ways of delivering services, are introduced. Thus, while current versions offer a snapshot of good practice, it is always necessary to adjust to revised editions as they become available.

■ Resources

- Information on standards in different sectors has been compiled by the Information Team at CILIP and is available to members at www.cilip.org. uk/enquiryandsearch/enquiries/professionalinformation.

- Current information on UK public library standards can be obtained from the DCMS website at www.culture.gov.uk/global/publications/archive_2004/library_standards.htm.
- International standards, including electronic versions, are available for purchase from ISO and national agencies, such as BSI and NISO.

■ References

Bertot, J. C. et al. (2001) *Statistics and Performance Measures for Public Library Networked Services*, Chicago IL, American Library Association.

Brophy, P. et al. (2000) *EQUINOX: Library Performance Measurement and Quality Management System: performance indicators for electronic library services*, Dublin, Dublin City University, www.equinox.dcu.ie/reports/pilist.html.

Department for Culture, Media and Sport (2003) *Framework for the Future: libraries, learning and information in the next decade*, London, DCMS.

Favret, L. (2000) Benchmarking, Annual Library Plans and Best Value: the implications for public libraries, *Library Management* **21** (6 and 7), 340–8.

Fowler, C. and Trinder, V. (2002) *Accreditation of Library and Information Services in the Health Sector*, 2nd edn, Health Libraries and Information Confederation, www.nelh.nhs.uk/librarian/Accreditation_Checklist_2nd_Edition_2002.pdf.

Hernon, P. and Dugan, R. E. (2002) *An Action Plan for Outcomes Assessment in Your Library*, Chicago IL, American Library Association.

Western Association of Schools and Colleges (2001) *Handbook of Accreditation*, Alameda CA, WASC, www.wascweb.org/senior/handbook.pdf.

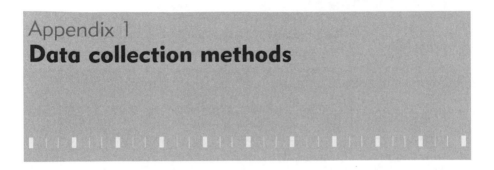

Data collection methods

■ Introduction

This appendix contains descriptions of the main methods used in libraries for collecting data in support of performance measurement. This, together with the succeeding appendices on data analysis and the presentation of results, is intended to offer practical advice to those engaged in designing and carrying out assessments of library services.

Comments in the earlier parts of this book on data collection methods should be read in conjunction with these appendices. In particular, care should be taken to select methods which are appropriate to the question being asked and the differences between quantitative and qualitative methods should be borne in mind. Further, it is important to bear in mind *how* the data will be analysed and presented when selecting methods for data collection. There is no point in gathering sets of data which cannot be analysed, either because the tools are not available or the resource implication is too great.

It is assumed that before deciding on a method to use, and before designing a data collection instrument, an overall evaluation plan will have been put in place. Chapter 1, 'Background', outlines the elements that such a plan should cover.

■ General issues about surveys and other data collection methods

It is appropriate to begin with some general advice about the conduct of surveys and other data collection methods. This is presented in the form of ten golden rules of data collection and applies particularly to methods involving human subjects.

1 Always observe strict ethical standards and in particular never do anything which could subject a data subject to harm, humiliation or embarrassment. Where necessary obtain permission in advance to carry out a survey or other data collection exercise. Allow participants to withdraw at any stage, without demanding a reason.
2 Always explain the exact purpose of any survey and the use to which data gathered will be put.
3 Explain who you are and always provide contact details.
4 Do not assume knowledge on the part of respondents. Explain everything clearly. Keep language simple and unambiguous.
5 Arrange questions in a logical sequence. Ask one question at a time.
6 Avoid leading questions which might suggest what is the 'right' answer.
7 Always run a pilot and make amendments based on what you find out.
8 Analyse all the results. Do not be selective at this stage but allow the data to reveal all that it can.
9 When presenting the results do not make claims which your data do not support.
10 Acknowledge your sources – and your assistants.

With most data collection exercises it is necessary to take a sample from the whole population being studied. Techniques for selecting samples are therefore discussed next.

■ Sampling
Deciding on a sampling method

In most cases it is necessary to take a sample from the population being surveyed rather than contacting everyone, simply because the number of people who would need to be contacted would otherwise be too large to handle. However, there are occasions when a total population survey, sometimes called a *saturation survey*, is both feasible and desirable. For example, a small university may be able to survey all of its staff without too much difficulty and the diversity of such populations may in any case make sampling undesirable. In all cases it is very important to be clear as to the definition of the *population* which is being studied – for example, is it all *registered users* of the library or all *active users* or all *active and potential users*?

In order to draw a sample of the population it is necessary to have a *sampling frame*, which is the source of data from which the sample can be drawn. For example, general population surveys sometimes use the telephone directory as a sampling frame. However, it is fairly obvious that this is not representative of the population as a whole. Telephone directory entries usually refer to households rather than individuals although of course this may be fine for household surveys. However, not everyone has a landline, especially now that many people rely on a mobile or use internet telephony. Furthermore, some people are ex-directory and the entries are inevitably somewhat out of date. It is therefore important to think through the relationship between the sampling frame and the population, so that any possible bias can be considered when the results are being evaluated. Such possible bias must always be highlighted in any conclusions which are published, internally or externally.

There are two major types of sampling: *random*, often called *probability*, *sampling* and *non-random*, or *non-probability*, sampling. These are described below.

Random sampling

In most cases it is desirable to select a random sample from the population. In other words the people surveyed are representative of all the characteristics of the population as a whole. In more technical terms, every member of the population has an equal, non-zero and calculable probability of being included in the survey. It is then possible to calculate the degree of representativeness of the results of the survey.

Ensuring that a sample is random is actually a lot more difficult than it seems at first glance, because bias can be introduced in many different ways. It is important to bear in mind that the critical issue is that the actual respondents to a survey need to be a random sample of the population. Action needs to be taken, therefore, to check that those responding meet the general population characteristics. This can be a real problem for many studies because some sections of the population are often found to be more likely to respond than others. An obvious example would be that if an online questionnaire is employed, it is more likely to be completed by habitual than by occasional computer users! Sending the request to complete it to all users, or to a random sample of users, will not therefore produce results which are necessarily characteristic of the whole population.

These are some of the common ways of selecting a pseudo-random sample:

1 Provide a code for every member of the population, for example by numbering them from 1 to n. Then select random numbers in the same range, taken from random number tables or more likely generated by computer software until the desired sample has been identified. During this operation any duplicates need to be discarded.

2 Select a starting point anywhere within a comprehensive list of members of the population and then choose every nth entry until the required sample has been selected. In this method, called *systematic sampling*, it is crucial that the ordering of the list is unrelated to the significant characteristics of the population.

3 Divide the population into groups according to a specific criterion, such as age or gender, and then randomly select individuals from each group. Known as *stratified random sampling* this approach is important where you know that you want to compare one group within the total population with another. There is a further decision to be taken as to whether, within this method, *proportionate* or *disproportionate* sampling should be used. The former is more common and occurs where the number of people selected from each group is directly related to their numbers in the total population. Thus if there is equal gender balance in the total population, the same number of people would be selected from the male group as from the female group. Sometimes, however, disproportionate sampling is appropriate, as where there is a small group of people that it is essential to have represented. An example might be sampling all library users but ensuring that some from the group of users with disabilities were included.

4 Divide the population into clusters or groups on a basis that does not necessarily represent it as a whole. This approach, known as *cluster sampling*, is often used where there is no sampling frame available or where the cost of proceeding on a purely random basis would be too high – think, for example, of an interview survey where a random sample might produce people with addresses all over the country.

5 First generate a random sample using one of the approaches above but when this sample has been identified, sample again from within it. An example might be to take a random sample of universities from all those in the country, then to select academic departments randomly from within the selected universities; then to select members of staff from within the selected departments.

Non-random sampling

In many studies, especially those which take a qualitative approach, representativeness is not the key issue. Here judgement is used to select respondents who are likely to have the information which is needed. For example, if accessibility of library services is the issue, it makes sense to select a sample of users who have disabilities rather than a random sample of the population as a whole, even though everyone is affected by accessibility issues.

The following are common methods of purposive sampling:

1 Interviewers may be told how many people with specific characteristics to sample. This is known as *quota sampling* and is often used with general population surveys, for instance in a shopping centre. The interviewer is told to interview, say, ten men and ten women and simply stops people as he or she sees fit until enough of each gender have participated. The method may involve selecting people in proportion to their membership of the population as a whole but this is not essential. Where the method does involve selecting on this basis, it is sometimes called *dimensional* sampling.
2 People may be stopped and asked to participate without any attempt to define their characteristics. Known as *convenience*, *accidental*, or even *haphazard* sampling, this could involve simply stopping anyone passing the library entrance until the required number of interviews has been conducted. It is subject to all kinds of bias and must be used with great care.
3 Particularly in social science studies which use grounded theory (see Chapter 2, 'Theoretical considerations'), it is common to use *purposive* sampling. Here the researcher deliberately selects respondents on the basis of their characteristics. For example, observation of a population may lead the researcher to develop a theory about its behaviour, which

is then tested and refined by interviewing carefully selected individuals, known as *key informants*. There is no pretence that this is in any way a random sample.

4 Interviewees may be asked to suggest other people who might be willing to be surveyed. This approach, known as *snowball* sampling, is very useful where it is difficult to identify the most appropriate members of the population to survey. Academic libraries may find the approach useful if they are trying to study the behaviour of inter-institutional groups of researchers, who know each other but who may not be known to the library staff.

Sample size

One of the most difficult questions to resolve when designing a survey can be the appropriate sample size to use. There are a considerable number of factors to consider and there is never an absolutely 'right' sample size. In general terms the larger the sample the more likely it is to be representative of the population as a whole but this is not always a great help when resources and time are limited – as they always are. The most critical consideration is whether the aim is to undertake a quantitative study, producing statistically significant results, or a qualitative analysis.

One way of thinking about sample size is to consider how many participants are needed to ensure that it is unlikely that a small number of 'maverick' individuals could seriously skew the results. For example, if only two people are asked for an opinion and one happens to have deep-seated, extreme views, then the wrong conclusions could easily be reached about the typical attitude among the population. If ten people had been asked, then the extreme view would be more likely to be seen as unrepresentative. A general rule of thumb is to use about 15 respondents per variable. For example, if you are stratifying your sample by gender and by age range (using, say, four different ranges), then about 120 respondents would be needed. The number sampled would then be increased to allow for non-responses.

There are different opinions about this, however. At one end of the spectrum Jakob Nielsen argues that perfectly satisfactory usability testing (admittedly something of a special case) can be carried out with as few as five people (see www.useit.com/alertbox/20000319.html). His argument is that five people will identify 85% of usability problems; 15 people would identify nearly 100%. However, with a limited budget it is better to test with five to start with, then improve the design and re-test with another five and then repeat the process again. Far more insights will have been gained than through a single test with 15 respondents.

At the other end of the spectrum, there are well established statistical procedures for determining sample sizes in different circumstances. Sampling error – the errors introduced by sampling instead of surveying the whole population – is related to standard error (SE), which is dependent on the size of the sample. It is worth noting that population size is relatively unimportant, especially for very large populations, which is why national polling companies can predict voting intentions from samples of at most a few thousand electors out of many millions.

In general the aim is to reach a 95% confidence level. What this means is that there is a 95% probability that the results reported are accurate within x% of what would have been found if the whole population had been surveyed. The value of x, known as the *confidence interval*, is calculated from the sample size and response variation.

Further discussion of sample size calculation is beyond the scope of this book, but various resources to assist the reader are suggested below.

Response rates

For a variety of reasons, it is often found that response rates, especially to questionnaire surveys, are quite low. The crucial question that needs to be asked is whether the respondents are representative of the sample as a whole and, if not, whether this is likely to have introduced bias into the results. Unfortunately, it is often the case that non-respondents are not typical of the whole population. For example, it is often found that non-users of the library are less likely to respond to a library questionnaire than users. One answer to this is to substitute new subjects who have similar characteristics to the non-respondents. For instance, in an interview survey it may be feasible to identify the fact that non-users are under-represented and to select more non-users deliberately until a balance is achieved. In many cases, however, it is either impossible (because the characteristics of non-respondents are unknown) or economically infeasible (because of the costs of repeating the survey with a new group) to replace non-respondents. In such cases it is important that any likely bias is considered in drawing conclusions from the data.

Sources of further information

- Random.org provides a website which both introduces the concepts behind random sampling and offers a source of random numbers. See http://random.org/ and especially http://random.org/essay.html.
- Jerry Dallal's web-based *Little Handbook of Statistical Practice* contains many useful pages on sampling. *Sample Size Calculations* is a particularly good introduction to that topic – see www.tufts.edu/~gdallal/size2.htm.

▪ Customer feedback analysis

All organizations which directly serve customers need to provide a means for those customers to make known their views on the service they have experienced. The mechanisms that can be used to achieve this include:

1 A feedback form on the service website (see http://lis.newport.ac.uk/feedback.htm for a typical example from an academic library).
2 Comment forms or cards available to physical visitors. These can be very simple but should give instructions on where to return the card since it may be taken away from the service point where it was picked up. It is also good practice to ensure that cards can be returned anonymously; providing a box with a slot through which to drop the card is much better than requiring the user to hand the completed card to a member of staff, especially if it turns out that the comment is about that member of staff!
3 Recording of comments and service problems by staff. Although often neglected, a record of the routine enquires which frontline staff have to deal with is invaluable in identifying issues for attention. These can be as simple as noting that frequent enquiries as to the location of the photocopiers indicates a problem with either their siting or the library's signage, or both.
4 Analysis of reference and other enquiries, including those received through chat and other technology-based services. Similar to the above, but these cases can reveal issues to do with the collection, access rights, interoperability of digital services and so on.

Such feedback mechanisms can be seen as part of a more comprehensive approach to customer relationship management (CRM). CRM systems build up personal profiles of users (and sometimes non-users) by collecting together intelligence gathered from many different sources. Although not widely used in libraries, CRM has become commonplace among commercial service organizations, and its use may well spread. Obviously customer feedback then forms a useful source of information on individuals' preferences, likes and dislikes.

It is a mistake to label feedback mechanisms as if they were intended solely for 'complaints' since both positive and negative feedback is to be welcomed. However, because complaints will undoubtedly be received it is good practice to ensure that if customers wish it, they can obtain a meaningful and preferably personal response. Where a number of users have made similar comments, it may be worthwhile disseminating the response either through the library website or in the printed newsletter or bulletin if one exists.

It sometimes appears as if customer feedback mechanisms are put in place but nothing happens as a result of them. It is worth remembering that there is no point in providing these mechanisms unless the data gathered are analysed, reported on and lead to action!

Sources of further information

- There is a set of comment forms used and an analysis of comments received during the University of California Libraries' Collection Management Initiative at www.ucop.edu/cmi/finalreport/index.html. This forms a helpful example of the use of customer feedback through a specific project.
- A useful longitudinal case study of CRM implementation in a non-profit service organization (the Institute of Technology in Oslo), with a good background analysis of the field, can be found in Bendik (2003).

■ Questionnaires

Questionnaires are perhaps the most commonly used data collection instrument. However, their apparent simplicity masks the difficulty of designing and distributing a good questionnaire as there are many pitfalls for the unwary. These include asking leading questions which guide the respondent to the 'right' answer, asking questions which are ambiguous or forgetting to provide space for every possible answer.

The following is a guide to the development of questionnaires. Refer also to the ten golden rules on page 176.

1 Be clear about what you're aiming to find out and limit yourself to what is essential. Remember that people are giving up their own time to complete the questionnaire, and the longer it is the less likely they are to complete it.
2 Decide the distribution method, bearing in mind resources and likely response rates. Options include:
   —online questionnaires (but how will you direct people to them?)
   —postal distribution (which may be expensive, especially as it is good practice to include a post-paid return envelope)
   —personal distribution (for example at the library exit, but then how do you sample non-users and avoid other possible bias?).
3 Design the questionnaire itself:
   a) Provide a heading which succinctly explains which organization the questionnaire is issued by and its purpose

   Blankshire County Library
   User Satisfaction Survey

   b) Explain what you want the respondent to do and why

   Please help us improve library services by taking a few minutes to complete this questionnaire and returning it to us in the enclosed reply-paid envelope. Thank you.

   c) Ask any questions you need answered to enable you to identify the demographic or other groups to which the respondent belongs. Be very careful to include all possibilities. (Note: some researchers prefer to leave this section until last; others feel that these questions, provided they are not intrusive, offer a gentle way in to the substantive questions.)

   What is your age group (please tick one box)?
   18 or under ❑   19–39 ❑   40–59 ❑   60 or over ❑

d) Link each question to the aims in step 1 above, placing them in a logical order.

How satisfied are you with the range of books provided in the Library?

Very satisfied	❏
Fairly satisfied	❏
Neither satisfied nor dissatisfied	❏
Fairly unsatisfied	❏
Very unsatisfied	❏
Don't know or not applicable	❏

e) Provide space for respondents to write their own comments where this is appropriate (open questions). Always include a space like this for any final comments, perhaps on matters you have not previously identified. This ensures that respondents have an opportunity to tell you what *they* want to say.

Are there other ways in which you feel we could improve the library's services?

_____

_____

_____

f) If you may want to interview or otherwise contact individual respondents again, make sure you can identify them and that they have the opportunity to opt in or out of this further stage.

We would like to contact some respondents to follow up the findings of our survey. If you would be willing to be contacted again, please insert your name and daytime telephone number in the space below.

_____

g) Provide a return address (even if you provided a reply-paid envelope, since it may have gone missing!) or other indication of how the questionnaire is to be returned. Even with online surveys there should be some means for respondents to contact you if they wish to do so, perhaps through an e-mail address.

Please return the completed questionnaire in the envelope provided
to:
J. R. Smith, Deputy Librarian, Blankshire County Library, Middle
Street, Witchtown, Blankshire BZ1 6LB

h) Say thank you.

Thank you for completing this questionnaire. Your views will help us to
improve our services.

Using response scales

There is a considerable variety of ways of gathering data in cases where
there is a range of possible answers and you want to guide the respondent
rather than simply allow an open response. The aim may be to ask people
to respond by making a choice along a continuum of agreement/disagree-
ment to propositions, usually from 'totally agree' to 'totally disagree' or
equivalent, or it may be to react to a list of options. Some of the more
common response scales are described below but in each case it is important to allow the respondent to opt out by providing a 'don't know' or
'other' alternative.

Likert scales

The most common type is the *Likert scale* (sometimes called the *summated
rating scale*), although there are many others. They are used to gather information on respondents' attitudes and are thus suitable for assessing
complex issues which cannot be answered by a straightforward yes/no
response. A simple question with a Likert scale is shown in Figure A1.1.

There are differences of opinion whether Likert scales should contain
an odd or even number of points (ignoring the 'don't know/not applicable'
column for the purposes of this argument). With an odd number, as in the
example opposite, there is a central point which may be taken to equate to
neutrality – the respondent neither agrees nor disagrees. If there were an
even number of scale points, for example by dropping the central one, this
would force the respondent to make a choice. Someone who feels fairly
neutral would have to decide whether to go for 'fairly satisfied' or 'fairly dissatisfied'.

	Very satisfied	Fairly satisfied	Neither satisfied nor dissatisfied	Fairly unsatisfied	Very unsatisfied	Don't know or not applicable
How satisfied are you with the photo-copying facilities provided in the Library?						

Figure A1.1 A Likert scale

The questionnaire designer needs to decide whether this is a good or bad thing, but it should be borne in mind that forcing respondents to choose may produce artificial results – what do they do if they are genuinely neutral?

The analysis of responses to Likert scales needs to be carried out with great care. In particular, if the respondents have been asked to indicate whether they are, say, 'very satisfied', 'satisfied', 'neutral', 'dissatisfied' or 'very dissatisfied' with a particular aspect of service, such answers *cannot* be treated as quantitative data. Although analyses which do precisely this are commonly encountered, frequently giving a numerical 'score' to indicate the 'average' response, the inference is spurious. The reason is that there is no way of knowing whether the intervals between the points on the scale are equal in the minds of respondents, so attempts to compare responses in quantitative terms are doomed to failure.

If quantitative analysis is intended, it is much better to provide a true scale (say a line marked with equal intervals from 1 to 10) and ask respondents to indicate where on that scale their response lies. However, even here there are pitfalls and the responses need to be validated in other ways.

Semantic differentials

In these scales pairs of opposites are provided and the respondent is invited to select a numerical value which best expresses their agreement or disagreement. Figure A1.2 on the next page illustrates a simple

What is your opinion of library staff?							
Knowledgeable	6	5	4	3	2	1	0	Ignorant
Approachable	6	5	4	3	2	1	0	Dismissive
Antagonistic	6	5	4	3	2	1	0	Friendly
Sociable	6	5	4	3	2	1	0	Unsociable
Unco-operative	6	5	4	3	2	1	0	Co-operative

Figure A1.2 A semantic differential

semantic differential. Note that it is usual to avoid putting all the 'pleasant' attributes on one side of the scale so as to cancel out any tendency to always mark to one side or the other.

Checklists
One of the simplest devices is to provide a list of points and invite respondents to tick those with which they agree or which best describe their views or activities. Figure A1.3 shows such a checklist.

During the past month, how often did you visit the library website?
(Tick one box only)

a. Never ❏
b. Once or twice ❏
c. 3 to 10 times ❏
d. More than 10 times ❏

Figure A1.3 Use of a checklist

Many examples of questionnaires can be found on library websites and in the published literature. An example of a questionnaire template developed for use by UK academic libraries is shown in Figure A1.4.

Library Satisfaction Survey
Please help us further improve library and information services by taking a few minutes to complete this short questionnaire

Please complete all questions apart from the last Question 14 (any other comments and suggestions), which is optional

Figure A1.4 The SCONUL Library Services survey template (reproduced by permission)

Continued on next page

About You

1. **Which group are you in?**
    Undergraduate ❏
    Postgraduate (Taught Course) ❏
    Postgraduate (Research) ❏
    Academic Staff ❏
    Other Staff ❏
    Other ❏

2. **Are you:**
    Full-Time ❏
    Part-Time ❏
    Not Applicable ❏

3. **Which Faculty/School/Department are you in:**
    A ❏
    B ❏
    C ❏
    D ❏
    Not Applicable ❏

4. **What is your age group:**
    21 years and under ❏
    22–26 years ❏
    27–39 years ❏
    40–49 years ❏
    50 and over ❏

5. **Are you:**
    Female ❏
    Male ❏

6. **What is your ethnic group?**
    Ethnic monitoring helps to ensure that our services are relevant to the needs of all ethnic groups and are provided fairly. We therefore invite you to assist us by answering the following question. This is in accordance with best practice as advised by the Commission for Racial Equality, and our statutory duty under the Race Relations Act 2000.

    Please choose <u>one</u> group to indicate your cultural background.

    Asian or British Asian: Indian ❏
    Asian or British Asian: Pakistani ❏
    Asian or British Asian: Bangladeshi ❏
    Asian or British Asian: Chinese ❏
    Asian or British Asian: Any Other Asian Background ❏

Figure A1.4 *Continued*

Black or Black British: Caribbean ❑
Black or Black British: African ❑
Black or Black British: Any Other Black Background ❑
Mixed: White and Black Caribbean ❑
Mixed: White and Black African ❑
Mixed: White and Asian ❑
Mixed: Any Other Mixed Background ❑
White: British ❑
White: Irish ❑
White: Any Other Background ❑
If you selected 'Any Other . . . Background please complete the box below

Your Use of Library and Information Services

7. **Which branch of the Library do you use most frequently?**
Main Library/Learning Resources Centre ❑
Branch A ❑
Branch B ❑
Branch C ❑
Branch D ❑
Branch E ❑
Not applicable ❑

8. **On average, how frequently do you visit that library?**
Several times a day ❑
Once a day ❑
Several times a week ❑
Once a week ❑
Less than once a week ❑
Less than once a month ❑

9. **On average, how often do you access library and information services via a computer (eg the library catalogue, e-journals, electronic resources like Web of Knowledge, &c)?**
Several times a day ❑
Once a day ❑
Several times a week ❑
Once a week ❑
Less than once a week ❑
Less than once a month ❑

Figure A1.4 *Continued*

10. Please think about the various activities you did the last time you visited the library <u>in person</u>. How successful were you in completing these?

	Very successful	Fairly successful	Neither successful nor unsuccessful	Fairly unsuccessful	Very unsuccessful	Don't know or not applicable
Looked for library materials on the shelves						
Sought help from library staff						
Borrowed library materials						
Used a PC in the library						

11. Please think about the various activities you did the last time you accessed library and information services via a computer. How successful were you in completing these?

	Very successful	Fairly successful	Neither successful nor unsuccessful	Fairly unsuccessful	Very unsuccessful	Don't know or not applicable
Used the library catalogue						
Made a reservation on the library system						
Renewed a loan on the library system						
Used an electronic journal						
Used an electronic resource (e.g. Web of Knowledge)						

Figure A1.4 *Continued*

12.   We'd like you to rate your satisfaction with the following library services, along with how important you think they are:

	Very satisfied	Fairly satisfied	Neither satisfied nor dissatisfied	Fairly dissatisfied	Very dissatisfied	Don't know or not applicable	Very important	Fairly important	Neither important nor unimportant	Fairly unimportant	Very unimportant	Don't know or not applicable
Range of books												
Course books and essential texts												
Range of e-books												
Range of print journals												
Range of electronic journals												
Photocopying												
Printing												
Study facilities (study desks, etc.)												
Provision of PCs												
Reliability of PCs												
Library catalogue												
Library website (other than library catalogue)												
Range of electronic resources (e.g. Web of Knowledge.)												
Opening hours												
Library environment (noise, heating, ambience, etc.)												
Helpfulness of the library staff												
Expertise of the library staff												

13.   Please indicate how much you agree or disagree with the following statement:

	Strongly agree	Slightly agree	Neither agree nor disagree	Slightly disagree	Strongly disagree	Don't know or not applicable
Overall, the library provides a good service to me						

Figure A1.4 *Continued*

---

14.   Any other comments or suggestions?

Note: *If you have a specific question to which you'd like a response, please provide your e-mail address*

_____

_____

_____

_____

_____

Submit survey

Thank you for completing this questionnaire
The results will be used to make further improvements to
our library and information services

Figure A1.4 *Continued*

Sources of further information

- It is sometimes helpful to make use of a structured package which assists in the design, distribution and analysis of questionnaires. A widely used example among libraries and information services is Libra from Priority Research Ltd (www.priority-research.com/). The LibQUAL+™ instruments were described in Chapter 3, 'User satisfaction', and are available to subscribing libraries at www.libqual.org/.
- There are a number of websites which provide tools to create online questionnaires, including:
  —Free Online Surveys (http://freeonlinesurveys.com/) – what it says on the tin! However the price you pay is advertisements – subscribe if you don't want them littering your survey
  —Zoomerang (http://info.zoomerang.com/) – a subscription service although small questionnaires can be created without charge.

▪ Interviews

In essence an interview is rather like a questionnaire administered in person, through a dialogue. Because two people are interacting, there is much more scope for following up interesting answers and encouraging interviewees to explain what they mean. Unlike in a questionnaire survey it is also harder for interviewees, once they have agreed to participate, to disengage. The *focus group interview* is a special case which is dealt with separately below.

There are many different types of interview and many ways of categorizing them. For any given situation it is important to select those features which are most appropriate to the case. The following descriptions cover the most commonly encountered features.

Types of interview
Structured interviews

In essence structured interviews are questionnaires read by the interviewer, who also notes down the replies. There is no scope for divergence from the set questions, although in some circumstances the interviewer will be given some scripted prompts. However, in order to avoid influencing the respondents, the interviewer must try to keep the conditions exactly the same between interviews. So, for example, the same kind of environment should be used, questions should be asked in the same tone of voice, and so on. Usually the interviewer will try to appear neutral. The aim is to achieve uniformity between respondents, minimizing any external effects. This is particularly important where the subject matter is emotive.

Semi-structured interviews

Where the interviewer is allowed widespread use of prompts and may rephrase questions or explain what a question means in case of doubt, the term *semi-structured interview* is used. If a question seems inappropriate to a particular respondent it may be omitted and the interviewer may add in additional questions for clarification, especially if the responses take an unexpected direction. Thus there is a clear structure which is being followed but significant flexibility is allowed. It is critical that the interviewer makes a careful note of the questions which were actually asked in each instance.

Unstructured interviews

In the case of *unstructured interviews* the event is much more like a conversation between two people, where the direction depends on what is said and interesting avenues are explored without there necessarily being any prior idea of which questions will be asked. In practice, the entirely unstructured interview is impractical, since the point of the procedure is to gather information on a particular subject. The conduct of unstructured interviews requires considerable skill and experience and usually considerable piloting with feedback from a third party. Both semi-structured and unstructured interviews are widely used in qualitative research, where the interviewer is trying to establish not just what happens but why.

Standardized interviews

Questions used in interviewing may invite an open response or may take the form of a tick-list of options. In the latter case they are known as *standardized interviews*.

Group interviews

In some circumstances it may be desirable to carry out a *group interview*, where the interviewer gathers a group of people together and questions them. Note that this is not the same as a *focus group interview* (see page 200). An example of this technique might be where a library has run a class on, say, information skills and questions are then asked of the class as a whole. Either verbal answers can be given or each member of the class can write down their own answers, perhaps on a pre-printed form. The latter is, of course, close to a questionnaire approach.

Panel interviews

In longitudinal studies it is often useful to be able to re-interview people over significant periods of time to find out how their views and experiences have changed. The *panel interview*, which can be conducted either as individual interviews or with a group, involves the selection of a set of interviewees who are willing to be approached more than once. It is of course important to establish this willingness at the outset. A mechanism to replace panel members who drop out, for whatever reason, is also necessary.

Narrative interviews

The idea behind the *narrative interview* is to listen to the experience of the interviewee through the medium of storytelling. Thus the interviewer's role is primarily to provide prompts to enable the interviewee to select and tell relevant life stories. Refer to Chapter 2, 'Theoretical considerations', for background information on narrative-based approaches. The analysis of narrative interviews can be particularly challenging since they must be kept with their context.

Conducting interviews
Using different media

Although traditionally interviews were almost always conducted face-to-face, other forms are now widespread. The telephone interview has become established as a favourite form for market research companies and is useful where the study sample is geographically widespread and personal contact is infeasible. A more recent development is the computer interview, where the interviewee interacts with a computer to respond to questions. This has proved especially helpful in traumatic circumstances such as rape counselling, although great care needs to be taken with this approach since such respondents also need human support. There is some evidence that groups familiar with technology, such as teenagers, are more forthcoming in computer interviews than person-to-person.

Whatever the medium to be used, it is important that interviewers are properly trained since their abilities and performance are crucial to the success of the method. There are many desirable characteristics for interviewers, but perhaps the most vital are to display a pleasant and receptive manner which inspires confidence and to be a good listener. This latter point is critical, since the most common fault among inexperienced interviewers is to talk too much and not listen enough!

The interview schedule

It is slightly confusing that the set of questions to be used in an interview is referred to as the *interview schedule* although this has nothing to do with timetabling the interviews, which is a separate issue. With unstructured and semi-structured interviews the term *interview guide* is sometimes used, to emphasize that the conversation may diverge from the pre-planned questions.

Many of the points about questions covered in the description of questionnaires above apply also to interview schedules, and of course the ten golden rules apply. In particular:

- Start with easy questions so as to gain the interviewee's confidence. This is one reason that many interviews begin with demographic information, but be careful about asking for sensitive information (such as age) early on – this is better left to the end, and prefixed with 'do you mind if I ask . . . ?'
- Questions should be short and to the point, using clear, non-technical language (do not, for example, refer to 'circulation' when you mean 'book issues'). Because the questions will be read out, it is useful to practise them orally to ensure that the language and expressions used sound natural in spoken form.
- Avoid leading questions (e.g. 'do you agree that library staff are helpful?').
- Ask one question at a time (e.g. do not ask 'do you use the library regularly or do you find it difficult to get here?').
- Avoid hypothetical questions unless this is a deliberate part of your technique (as it would be, for example, if you were using contingent valuation to assess economic impact, as described in Chapter 5, 'Social and economic impact').
- Ensure there is a logical flow to the questions, so that the conversation can proceed naturally. It is a good idea to tell the interviewee what you are going to ask about as you start each new theme that you wish to cover.

The interview itself

Where you are able to control the environment, do everything you can to make the interviewee feel at ease. Ensure, as far as possible, that there will be no interruptions.

It is good practice to provide the interviewee with your contact details at the start, to gain consent to recording the interview (see below) and to explain how confidentiality and anonymity will be handled. The interviewee should be assured that they can withdraw from the interview at any time. It is not usual to agree to supply a transcript of the interview, although in some circumstances (such as with very senior and/or famous people) that may be requested. There are also occasions when it can be helpful to get the interviewee to check their responses later – they may want to clarify what they have said when they reflect on it.

Interviewers must remain neutral throughout the interview, no matter what the provocation and should try to avoid being drawn into giving their own opinions, as can happen when interviewees say things like, 'Oh, they're hopeless – don't you agree?' All responses should be given a full hearing, even if they seem irrelevant – they can always be discarded later!

It is important to stick to the allotted time but to allow a short period for the interviewee to add anything they want to at the end of the session. Interviews should always finish with thanks to the interviewee for their time and their help, stressing that the study is important and that the interviewee's replies have been helpful.

Recording the interview

A variety of different methods can be used to record interview responses. With a structured interview, using mainly closed questions, it would be usual to fill in responses on a paper form, using a new form for each interviewee. Handwriting responses becomes more difficult and more prone to error where open questions are used and can be distracting for the interviewee. For this reason it is usually much better to record the interview with the interviewee's permission and then to transcribe the recording later. Miniature solid-state data recorders are ideal for this purpose, although they must be tested *in situ* and care taken to ensure that the battery is sufficiently charged for the length of the interview. However, even where recording is used it is essential to make brief handwritten notes. These will help the interpretation of the recording and form a safety net in case the recording fails.

It is also possible to record interviews directly onto a laptop or other computer. Computer Assisted Personal Interviewing (CAPI) and Computer Assisted Telephone Interviewing (CATI) are methods where the questions are read from and replies recorded immediately on the computer. With true computer interviewing, the responses are of course saved automatically on a database.

Transcribing interview recordings

Where the interview has been recorded, the recording should be checked immediately at the end of the session. It is also helpful to make any additional notes on the interview, such as on any problems experienced, at that stage.

Depending on the purpose of the interview a number of different approaches to transcription may be taken. For research studies where perhaps the evidence is to form part of a published paper, a more rigorous approach would be taken than a practitioner study focused on illuminating use of a particular service. For the former a full transcription might be necessary, but this is a very time-consuming process – roughly five to six hours are needed to transcribe a one hour interview. Using human transcribers is therefore very expensive. An alternative way to proceed is to use speech-to-text software such as Dragon Naturally Speaking. Although in theory this could be used in the interview, in practice the software needs training with each voice and this is rarely practical.

For practical purposes, therefore, partial transcription (sometimes called *semi-transcription*) may be used where only selected parts of the audio file are transcribed. The problem is that these parts may then take on unmerited significance or be quoted out of context, so the researcher must take great care to avoid these potential problems.

Not only does the transcription have to be made but it must be checked carefully. It is all too easy for the statement:

> . . . **we have no problems with using the library** . . .

to be transcribed as

> . . . **we have, you know, problems with using the library** . . .

The actual analysis of interview data is discussed in Appendix 2, 'The analysis of data'.

Sources of further information

- The East Midlands Oral History Archive (EMOHA) has produced a number of information sheets on interviewing, among which 'How can I be safe while interviewing?' has important pointers for anyone

thinking of conducting interviews away from their place of work and especially if interviewing individuals in their homes (www.le.ac.uk/emoha/training/no6.pdf).
- An example of an interview schedule, associated questionnaire and transcribed data is included in the VITAL (Value and Impact of IT Access in Libraries) Project Workbook, available as a Word document at www.cerlim.ac.uk/projects/vital/workbook.doc.
- A popular transcription software tool called Transcriber can be downloaded free of charge at http://trans.sourceforge.net/en/presentation.php.

■ Focus group interviews

It is worth emphasizing that focus groups are a kind of interview. Many of the principles which underlie good interview techniques also apply to focus groups but because a number of people are being brought together there are other issues concerned with group interaction. Focus groups are not group interviews – where the group is asked questions and all members are expected to respond to the questions posed by the interviewer (see above) – but rely on participant interaction for their dynamic.

It is this interaction that gives focus groups their power. One person may make a comment and this sparks off a reaction in another. Soon a discussion or conversation is in progress. The skilled focus group facilitator steers this interaction with a light touch – enough to ensure that the participants keep to the broad points being explored but not enough so that their contributions are being led. In this way, the focus group technique enables attitudes, beliefs and feelings as well as facts to be identified, and gives an opportunity for participants to reflect on their own behaviour and experiences.

Focus groups can have a number of purposes:

- identifying key issues of concern to users
- testing out possible future scenarios for services
- illuminating responses from broader surveys, especially questionnaires
- gathering feedback on tentative conclusions from other studies.

Of course, the point of the activity is to collect data. This should be obvious but it's easy to forget, in the emphasis on ensuring a group can interact well, that they are only being brought together to generate data which can be used in measuring performance. The following are suggested as key steps in organizing and running a focus group.

1 Secure participation of six to ten people with the required common characteristics. It is not a good idea to try and run a focus group with people with a wide variety of different characteristics which you want to explore. For example, if you need to find out the opinions of people of different ages, it is better to run a series of separate groups with each age range, rather than one mixed group. When you have gathered the data you might then run a mixed group to see if any of your tentative conclusions spark off debate.

2 Plan a session no longer than 1.5 hours. Beyond that time people become tired and may tend to lose concentration or interest.

3 Appoint both a facilitator and a note taker. This is critical. The facilitator cannot also take notes on the discussion.

4 Record the discussion. Test the equipment beforehand and make sure batteries are fresh. Get permission from all participants for the recording.

5 Have five or six prepared questions on the theme you want to pursue. It is as well to pilot these either within your own team or through an individual interview.

6 Ensure the environment – the room and other facilities you will be using – is suitable. Chairs should be comfortable, the room should be quiet and free from distractions or interruptions and refreshments should be provided, preferably at the start. Large name tags, which can be read without squinting, should be provided if people don't know each other. Above all, make sure everyone feels safe psychologically throughout the interview – this is part of the facilitator's responsibility.

7 At the agreed time welcome people and ensure they are comfortably seated. Explain the purpose of the exercise and set out the ground rules at the start including such issues as confidentiality and anonymizing of quotations. Confirm consent to recording the interview.

8 During the session, the facilitator must ensure that everyone can and does participate and that no one dominates the discussion, which should be allowed to develop but not to wander!

9 The facilitator should close the interview carefully: first by reflecting back key points and if possible obtaining consensus, and thus

obtaining confirmation that this has been understood; then, finally, by thanking everyone for their time and participation.

10 It is worth noting what people say after the close of the formal session. Hopefully it won't happen but it is not unknown for a participant to muse informally, 'Of course, what I really think is . . .'!

11 Immediately after participants have left, the recording should be checked. Whether or not the recording has worked properly, the facilitator and the notetaker should make their own summaries of the conversation independently.

After the interview the recording may be transcribed (see the section on interviews above) and the two sets of notes should be checked against it.

Sources of further information

- One of the problems for facilitators is helping the discussion along without directing it. There is a useful section on *non-directive probes* in Silverman (2006) – see www.mnav.com/bensurf.htm#probes.
- A useful web page entitled Basics of Conducting Focus Groups will be found at www.managementhelp.org/evaluatn/focusgrp.htm.
- The eVALUEd Toolkit contains sample focus group questions for library staff at www.evalued.uce.ac.uk/tools_archive/useandusers/perceptions/Perceptions of EIS-library staff.doc.
- Chapter 8 of Hernon and Altman (1988) is devoted to focus groups.
- Online focus groups are becoming more common. Rezabek (2000) has written a paper discussing their advantages and disadvantages, and providing examples.

■ Diary studies

It can be very useful to ask people to keep a diary of their interactions with a service over a period of time, thus providing longitudinal data coupled with contemporaneous accounts of those interactions. Sometimes the diary may be unstructured – it is a record of interactions with the service in the respondent's own words using their own headings. Sometimes the diary may be structured, so that it becomes very much like a longitudinally completed questionnaire.

An attraction of diaries is that superficially they appear to require less effort on the part of the investigator. You simply recruit diarists and set them off, receiving all the data back at a later date. This is misleading, however. The work needed to set up a diary study is considerable and factors that need to be considered include:

1 The capabilities of the diarists. Do they have the, usually written, skills needed to make a comprehensible and comprehensive record of the encounters? Diary methods are not suitable for people who do not have reasonably good literacy skills. Care must be taken to ensure that this does not bias the sample.
2 The training needed to ensure that diarists understand precisely what is expected of them.
3 The difficulty of ensuring that diarists are neutral in their approach, precisely because they need to be so well briefed in advance. This can easily turn them into sympathetic advocates, or at the very least change their behaviour in terms of frequency and length of interaction with the service.
4 How long to run the diary study. It needs to be long enough to capture 'typical' data but not so long that diarists become bored and give up.
5 How the data will be analysed once they are collected. This may dictate the form that the diary takes. For example, diaries can be free-form, allowing the diarist to record observations in a completely unstructured way, or they may contain headings or other structure. The former can be very difficult to analyse.
6 Ethical issues, such as those of confidentiality (see Chapter 1, 'Background').
7 The need to maintain regular contact with the diarists, to ensure that the process is proceeding smoothly and to answer any queries.

It is also usually necessary to interview diarists to obtain background information and to clarify what they have recorded. This may imply 'before' and 'after' interviews, adding to the resource requirement of this method.

There are many different formats which can be used for diaries. They could simply be blank sheets of paper which participants are asked to write on but it is usually better to offer something a little more formal. For example, an A5 booklet can be used, with instructions printed on the inside cover so that diarists can remind themselves of what you want from time to time. The inside back cover could even contain a model entry, although this needs to be done carefully so as not to over-influence participants. If you are interested in specific activities it is sometimes useful to print descriptors on each page, or the pages may be subdivided into sections within which observations can be recorded.

It is not always easy to judge the quality of data derived from diary studies, since they are open to a number of different types of error. As noted above respondent conditioning can occur, since the very act of keeping the diary may affect behaviour. The information recorded may be incomplete, since all diary entries will be partial and it is left to the diarist to judge what it is important to record. There is a well documented 'first day' effect whereby entries are more informative at the start of the study than later and in the case of expenditure surveys always appear to show that people spend more on the first day they keep a diary than subsequently! Depending on when entries are recorded, there may be errors from incorrect recall, as when a diarist fills in the diary at the end of each day but may recall only some of the relevant events, or recall them inaccurately.

A number of diary-like studies can be undertaken using new communications technologies. For example, it is possible to get participants to record their diary entries using voicemail, or a blog can be set up for each participant. These approaches can be very attractive to some participants but may be off-putting to others. Again the possibility of bias in the sample must be considered.

Sources of further information
- The eVALUEd Toolkit contains a template for a student diary concerned with the use of electronic resources. See www.evalued.uce.ac.uk/tools_archive/impact/impact/i_1_Student_diary.doc.
- Librarians and researchers have frequently used diaries to explore information-seeking behaviour. Thórsteinsdóttir (2001) and Hyldegård (2004) provide examples.
- A good overview of and guide to using diaries for research is provided by Alaszewski (2006).

■ Observation
There are many different ways of using observation in evaluations but they can be broadly categorized as:

- *Participant*, overt or obtrusive observation, where the observer is part of the group. The issue here tends to be that participation affects behaviour and it would be unethical not to reveal the purpose of participation. However, the former problem can be obviated by using recall of past events through the *critical incident technique*.
- *Non-participant*, covert or unobtrusive observation, where the observer is outside the group being observed and does not come into direct contact with it. This type of observation may be important to ensure that the evaluation does not affect behaviour but it is always difficult to judge *why* people are behaving as they are, rather than just *what* they are doing.

Both approaches have been used quite extensively in libraries, particularly in examining front of house and electronic services. The following brief notes suggest some of the most important issues to consider.

Participant observation

It is important in these cases to be very well prepared with clear issues to be explored. A typical scenario would be the testing of a new web interface, where a group of people might be gathered together to try it out while being observed. Here the participants are well aware of the nature of the exercise, so they are likely to ask questions and make comments. The best strategy here is to respond with new prompts. So if asked, 'what does this icon represent?' by a participant, the observer might reply, 'what do you think it means?' or 'how would you check it out if you were on your own?'.

The critical incident technique involves asking people, such as staff or users, who have participated in the service under analysis to recall specific incidents which they have experienced and which have been significant in terms of outcomes and impacts. The technique can make use of interviews or can be undertaken by asking participants to write down their account of the incidents. Usually, each participant will be asked to recall more than one incident, including both positive and negative examples. The resulting data can be analysed using content analysis techniques (see Appendix 2, 'The analysis of data').

Non-participant observation

The essence here is to watch what is happening and then make notes about it, avoiding any actions which might affect the behaviour of those being observed. In some circumstances it is necessary to use prompts. For example, if you wanted to observe the operation of the circulation desk, one strategy would be to take some books and have them issued to you! It would be feasible to use some prompts while doing this, provided they are of a kind which would normally be asked by a user.

Mystery shopping

A particular type of observation, which is used very widely in service industries, is called *mystery shopping*. The term 'shopping' is used simply because retail was the first sector to use the technique, but for some reason *mystery customer* has never come into common usage. The mystery shopper is an individual, acting as a customer, who observes and reports on the service received. It is important that anyone acting as a mystery shopper should be independent, objective and critical. The general requirements for using this method are that:

• the mystery shopper remains anonymous throughout the exercise
• the individual is well trained in advance and uses a predetermined checklist; obviously the checklist must remain hidden from the service staff and for this reason it may be completed after the event
• the mystery shopper makes every effort to act as would any ordinary customer
• the completed checklist is usually supplemented by any general observations
• judgements should be based on multiple observations.

Mystery shopping has been criticized on a number of grounds:

• It is ethically questionable, since staff are being assessed without being aware of it. The counter argument is that customers are doing the same every day – the mystery shopping exercise is merely revealing this to management.
• It only provides information on processes, not on their outcomes and impacts.

- Because the checklist has to be completed after the event, the mystery shopper's memory of what happened is recorded, not the actual event.
- It is very difficult to repeat the test frequently enough to be sure that what has been observed is representative of typical service delivery. As a result action may be taken on atypical events.

In response to the ethical issue, some commentators have stressed that mystery shopping should never be used as a means of assessing individuals.

An example of the use of mystery shopping in libraries is contained in the LISU Report, *As Others See Us* (Creaser, 2003), and examples in academic libraries are provided by Jones and Woodman (2005) and Murray (2005). Beards (2006) has published an account of the use of mystery shopping by public libraries in London. More generally, an analogous technique has been used quite widely to test library's reference services by asking 'typical' questions and marking the responses on grounds of accuracy, utility or user satisfaction, although Richardson (2002) has questioned this approach on the grounds that the questions asked in most of these studies are not typical of the real world.

Sources of further information
- A detailed guide to the critical incident technique is provided by Twelker (2003).
- For libraries, observation checklists may best be linked to professional and procedural standards. For example, the ALA has published *Guidelines for Behavioral Performance of Reference and Information Service Providers* (www.ala.org/ala/rusa/rusaprotools/referenceguide/guidelinesbehavioral. htm), which would form a specific set of checkpoints for observation of these services.
- Cooper and Urquhart (2005) have discussed the ethical dilemmas of providing a professional service and undertaking research-oriented observation at the same time.
- The use of *mystery students* in higher education is discussed by Douglas and Douglas (2006).

■ Peer review

The idea behind peer review is that one of the best ways to make judgements about the quality of a product or service is to ask a qualified expert to assess it. The method is widely used in assessing academic papers prior to publication, when the author's peers are asked to provide an opinion about a paper's suitability, using a range of carefully specified criteria. In this context peer review is often referred to as 'refereeing'. The method is also commonly used in assessing grant applications for research, development or other funding.

Peer review can in fact be used much more widely and it is not uncommon for libraries to invite experts to help them assess their performance in particular areas. Sometimes this is formalized within quality assurance processes, as with UK academic institutions' teaching quality assessments where experts will review the library's role and contribution. The original, intensive series of visits to institutions to examine all aspects of teaching provision has now been superseded by a 'light touch' regime, although this still involves considerable work by institutions. The bedrock of this quality assurance system is peer review.

A more informal type of peer review is exemplified by the longstanding programme of library buildings visits which members of SCONUL undertake. These emphasize that the role is one of learning from what others have achieved – see Edwards (2005) for a recent report on these visits.

An interesting example of peer review used more widely in the policy arena is in the European Union's Programme to Combat Social Exclusion (http://ec.europa.eu/employment_social/social_inclusion/peer_en.htm). This involves a policy in one country (for example Sure Start in the UK during 2006) being examined by experts from others (in this case France, Germany, Hungary, Latvia, Lithuania, Malta and Poland) to see what lessons can be learned.

Successful use of peer review depends on:

- the identification of peers who are willing and able to take a full part in the process
- establishing exact criteria on which judgements are to be made
- transparency: ensuring that the process contains no hidden agendas or other surprises
- mechanisms to ensure fairness, for example by ensuring there are no conflicts of interest

- careful design of the whole process to ensure it is as economic as possible
- structured reporting; ideally all reports should be open to all involved, where necessary having been anonymized.

Sources of further information

- SCONUL produced an *aide memoire* for peer reviewers carrying out assessments of learning resources. See www.sconul.ac.uk/ activities/quality_ass/papers/Aide_MemoireFeb2003.pdf.
- Many journals publish their peer review criteria and procedures, which can offer a useful example of the process. See, for example, those of the Royal Society at www.pubs.royalsoc.ac.uk/index.cfm?page=1035.

■ Delphi technique

The Delphi technique is a method which is used to obtain consensus among a group, usually of experienced stakeholders. It is frequently used in forecasting trends, where it is important to take into account a wide range of opinions but equally important to reach a common view on which to plan. It has been defined as 'a technique that elicits, refines, and draws upon the collective opinion and expertise of a panel of experts' (Gupta and Clarke (1996) in Howze and Dalrymple (2004)).

The essence of the Delphi technique lies in the establishment of a range of views on a particular topic, then the gathering of opposing or subtly different analyses and finally the reaching of a considered overall synthesis to which the majority assent. A facilitator is appointed to manage the process and a panel of expert participants identified.

As with any technique, it is important that the object of the exercise is defined precisely at the start. This then enables precise questions to be formulated, which are then sent to participants. The latter should not only be experts in the field, but need to be willing to give a significant amount of time to the exercise, since the essence of the Delphi technique lies in iteration and full participation. When responses to the questions are received, they are collated and then fed back to participants in the form of statements, though without identifying who has said what. Each participant then reviews these statements and provides further opinions and views. The process continues until a consensus starts to emerge, with the facilitator phrasing statements to highlight both commonalities and points of difference.

An advantage of the Delphi technique is that participants are anonymous and the effects of group dynamics, where one participant might be influenced by another to omit, say, a controversial view, are avoided. A disadvantage is that consensus can all too easily turn out to be the lowest common denominator, and innovative – perhaps unpopular – ideas can be swamped. Nevertheless, it has been used effectively in strategic planning in libraries. An example, addressing the issue of 'the library as place' in a time of rapid technological change, is described by Ludwig and Starr (2005) who conclude:

> Our experts clearly expect librarians to take on a wide variety of new roles, from informationists and educators to archivists and knowledge managers. They expect libraries to fill empty spaces left by shrinking print collections with new services ranging from classroom spaces to visualization laboratories to consumer health collections.

Sources of further information

- A sample set of questionnaires for a Delphi study can be found at www.medsch.wisc.edu/adminmed/2001/orgbehav/delphi.pdf. These show how the initial collection of ideas moves through the assessment of strengths and weaknesses into a process of voting and quantification of the results.
- It is sometimes useful to carry out Delphi studies face-to-face. Dick (2000) has written a useful paper on this approach.

■ Environmental scanning

The idea behind environmental scanning is to observe what is happening in the library's external environment and the trends which appear to be emerging as a way of identifying both the effects of current services and the likely pressures for change. In essence it is concerned with checking how the performance of the library measures up to the broader operational environment and how well it is positioned to change in response to likely external stimuli. Renfro and Morrison (1984) describe it as identifying 'important emerging issues that may constitute either obstacles or opportunities. This process helps institutions allocate their resources in a way that anticipates or responds to changes in the external environment.'

Although there are many ways of carrying out an environmental scan, one useful approach is to categorize significant factors into:

- demographic and social issues
- legal requirements
- political requirements
- economic issues
- technological change.

The methods used to gather data may include:

- analysis of documentary evidence; this may be purely manual or may involve identification of key terms and frequencies
- analysis of statistical data showing trends
- review of publications which relate to the broader environment, including websites
- interviews with experts and leading figures, such as politicians and senior managers.

The external environmental scan will then need to be related to the internal profile (see page 90), augmented as necessary with specific detail on inputs, processes and outputs.

Critics of environmental scanning point to several pitfalls and disadvantages:

- It is difficult to organize in a way that will produce effective results in the long term.
- Individual beliefs often over-influence the reporting of trends.
- Relevance is extremely difficult to assess and if wrongly estimated can lead to major loss of resources.
- Managers are not always willing to discuss the results and incorporate them in their planning because they are usually based on ephemeral and incomplete data.

Both environmental scanning and the Delphi technique are focused on the future – they offer ways of systematically assessing and predicting trends that will be of importance to the organization, thus enabling current service performance to be considered against likely future requirements.

Sources of further information

• For some years the ACRL has undertaken an annual environmental scan. Although the results are only available to members, a description of the process can be found at www.ala.org/ala/acrl/acrlpubs/crlnews/backissues2003/may3/newsfield.htm.
• OCLC also undertakes periodic environmental scans. For an example see www.oclc.org/reports/escan/default.htm.

■ Experiments

It is worth noting that one way of assessing performance is to experiment with new systems or new ways of doing things. Although experimentation may more usually be associated with scientific research, in fact libraries have long used it as a way of assessing the potential of a service. For example, many new technology-based services are launched as experimental services, often designated as a β (beta) version. In effect this means that a close-to-final version is made available for users to try out, usually accompanied by warnings that some glitches remain. This is a favourite release route for many major corporations such as Google and Microsoft and can be adopted by libraries. Incidentally, the form of testing sometimes wryly referred to as γ (gamma) testing, whereby a product full of bugs is released on the unsuspecting public, is not recommended!

From a performance measurement perspective the critical issue is to ensure that the experiment is monitored, the results assessed and the new service modified in the light of this learning. For this reason β versions are sometimes released only to a selected group of users, on the understanding that they will provide feedback as a *quid pro quo* for early access. Whether this approach, or a more open one, is taken it is important to try to observe the principles of sampling referred to earlier in this appendix. For example, there is little point in getting only experienced users to try out a service which is then going to be launched on the general public.

It is also possible to use experiments to assess the impact of library services more directly. For example, Hernon and Dugan (2002) suggest that students might be taught the use of Boolean logic to help them reduce the number of hits retrieved per search. Subsequent analysis of statistical information from datasets used by those students could then be examined to see whether the objective has been achieved and whether any behavioural changes are persistent. Ethical considerations would, however, preclude the use of a control group which remained untaught.

A particular issue with experiments is that they should be undertaken with a specific purpose in mind. For example, a β release might be used as a way for checking usability, or to try to identify remaining bugs in software, or as a way of checking that the system is fully interoperable with other products. It is not usually a good idea to try to fulfil too many different purposes with a single experiment.

Experimentation is not limited to technology-based services. A library might, for example, experiment with new publicity materials, with a new form of guiding, with different ways of arranging bookstock or with any other aspect of service. However, it is important always to make clear to users when a service is experimental, since the launch may raise expectations which it will be hard to fulfil long-term.

Sources of further information

- The testing of computer software is a complex business, but basic guidelines can be found in the online *Test Management Guide* (www. ruleworks.co.uk/testguide/index.htm).

■ Additional resources on data collection

The following toolkits may be helpful when designing your data collection exercise:

- the MLA guide called *Know Your Community: a best practice guide for public libraries*, available at www.mla.gov.uk/resources/assets//C/Consultation_toolkit_IPF_2nd_edition_9191.pdf, which summarizes the different ways in which customer surveys can be conducted
- the eVALUEd Toolkit: www.evalued.uce.ac.uk/
- the EFX Toolkit: www.cerlim.ac.uk/projects/efx/toolkit/index.html
- the *Little Handbook of Statistical Practice*: www.tufts.edu/~gdallal/ LHSP.HTM

- the Improve Your Library evaluation resources provided by teachernet: www.teachernet.gov.uk/teachingandlearning/resourcematerials/ schoollibraries/.

■ References

Alaszewski, A. (2006) *Using Diaries for Social Research*, London, Sage.

Beards, S. (2006) Mystery Shopping: improving enquiry techniques, *Library + Information Update*, **5** (4), 38–9.

Bendik, B. (2003) The Implementation Puzzle of CRM Systems in Knowledge-based Organizations, *Information Resources Management Journal*, **16** (4), 33–45.

Cooper, J. and Urquhart, C. (2005) The Information Needs and Information-seeking Behaviours of Home-care Workers and Clients Receiving Home Care, *Health Information and Libraries Journal*, **22** (2), 107–16.

Creaser, C. (2003) *As Others See Us: benchmarking in practice*, LISU Occasional Papers 33, Loughborough, LISU, Library and Information Statistics Unit, Loughborough University, www.lboro.ac.uk/departments/ls/lisu/downloads/OP33.pdf.

Dick, B. (2000) *Delphi Face to Face*, www.uq.net.au/action_research/arp/delphi.html.

Douglas, A. and Douglas, J. (2006) Campus Spies? Using mystery students to evaluate university performance, *Educational Research*, **48** (1), 111–19.

Edwards, J. A. (2005) SCONUL Buildings Visit 2005, *SCONUL Focus*, (36), 75–7.

Gupta, U. G. and Clarke, R. E. (1996) Theory and Applications of the Delphi Technique: a bibliography 1975–1994, *Technological Forecasting and Social Change*, **53** (2), 185–211.

Hernon, P. and Altman, E. (1988) *Assessing Service Quality: satisfying the expectations of library customers*, Chicago IL, American Library Association.

Hernon, P. and Dugan, R. E. (2002) *An Action Plan for Outcomes Assessment in Your Library*, Chicago IL, American Library Association.

Howze, P. C. and Dalrymple, C. (2004) Consensus Without all the Meetings: using the Delphi method to determine course content for library instruction, *Reference Services Review*, **32** (2), 174–84.

Hyldegård, J. (2004) Collaborative Information Behaviour: exploring Kuhlthau's information search process model in a group-based educational setting, *Information Processing and Management*, **42** (1), 276–98.

Jones, P. and Woodman, J. (2005) How Do Others See Us? Mystery visiting as a tool for service evaluation, *SCONUL Focus*, (34), 51–3.

Ludwig, L. and Starr, S. (2005) Library as Place: results of a Delphi study, *Journal of the Medical Library Association*, **93** (3), 315–26, www.pubmedcentral.nih.gov/articlerender.fcgi?artid=1175798.

Murray, S. (2005) Mystery Shoppers in Liverpool, *SCONUL Focus*, (36), 25–7.

Renfro, W. and Morrison, J. (1984) Detecting Signals of Change: the environmental scanning process, *The Futurist*, **48** (4), 49–53.

Rezabek, R. J. (2000) Online Focus Groups: electronic discussions for research, *Forum: Qualitative Social Research*, **1** (1), www.qualitative-research.net/fqs-texte/1-00/1-00rezabek-e.htm .

Richardson, J. V. (2002) Reference is Better than We Thought, *Library Journal*, (127), 41–2.

Silverman, G. (2006) How to Get Beneath the Surface in Focus Groups, www.mnav.com/bensurf.htm.

Thórsteinsdóttir, G. (2001) Information-seeking Behaviour of Distance Learning Students, *Information Research*, **6** (2), http://InformationR.net/ir/6-2/ws7.html.

Twelker, P. A. (2003) *The Critical Incident Technique: a manual for its planning and implementation*, http://wvvw.tiu.edu/psychology/Twelker/critical_incident_technique.htm.

Appendix 2
The analysis of data

■ Introduction

Having spent time and resources collecting data, it is clearly important that they be analysed thoroughly and properly. A lot will depend on the type of data collected – especially on whether they are quantitative or qualitative – and on the purpose for which they have been collected. For example, a survey of existing users in a small branch library on a specific topic might merit only manual analysis and a very straightforward report. At the other extreme a national study, possibly including comparisons between different libraries or even across sectors, will probably require detailed and complex analysis. In the latter case it might well be necessary to employ a trained statistician or other professional.

However, in each case the aim is the same. It is sometimes expressed as three stages (Miles and Huberman, 1994), especially when some of the data being analysed are qualitative in nature:

- *data reduction*, by gathering data together, coding them and expressing them in comparable ways so as to create datasets from which meaning can be extracted
- *data display*, which takes the datasets and presents them in ways that make their meaning clear, for example in lists or charts or graphs; note that this is still part of data analysis – presentation for reporting purposes is covered in Appendix 3, 'The presentation of results'
- *drawing conclusions*, which finds the patterns and themes that emerge from the data; this stage also looks for exceptions and contradictions.

In this appendix the aim is simply to present the rudiments of data analysis as might be applied within a single library conducting its own studies. However, it should be stressed that it is very easy to analyse data wrongly, and advice should always be sought by anyone who does not have the expertise and experience gained through training and practice. Even the calculation of averages is not as straightforward as it may seem!

■ Quantitative data

Most studies produce at least some quantitative data even if they only relate to the numbers of people surveyed or the numbers of items analysed. In very small studies it may be feasible to analyse these data by hand, using a calculator, but it is usually better to make use of suitable computer software. The simplest to use are spreadsheets, such as Microsoft Excel or OpenOffice Calc, which enable a table of data to be created. Quite complex calculations can be performed, although it may be sufficient to use the software to produce totals and various kinds of average (see below). Similarly it is possible to use a general-purpose database package such as Microsoft Access or OpenOffice Base to manipulate the data. A step up from using a spreadsheet or database would be to utilize one of the specialist data analysis packages, of which SPSS (Statistical Package for the Social Sciences) is by far the most common.

It is important when analysing quantitative data to be clear as to the type of data which are bring analysed. There is a basic distinction between nominal data, ordinal data, interval data and continuous data, as discussed below.

- *Nominal* data is where the values can be coded, but where those codes cannot themselves be manipulated to produce results. For example, female staff could be coded '0', while male staff were coded '1'. In other words nominal data allow only for qualitative classification.
- *Ordinal* data is where the values can be put in some kind of order. For instance, users might rate their satisfaction with the library's services on a scale where '0' means 'very dissatisfied', '1' means 'fairly dissatisfied, '2' means 'neither satisfied nor dissatisfied', '3' means 'fairly satisfied' and '4' means 'very satisfied'. It is easy to place the results in order – '4' always means more satisfied than '3'. However, as was noted in Appendix 1, 'Data collection methods', it is not possible to assume

that the intervals between these values is equal, so we certainly cannot say that the difference between '2' and '3' is the same as the difference between '3' and '4'.

- *Interval* data can be represented according to an *interval scale* and are found where the distance between adjacent points is always the same. However, the zero point is arbitrary. So, time periods can be measured according to an interval scale: the time between 1965 and 1974 is the same as that between 1975 and 1984 (ignoring any effects of leap years). However, the year 0 CE is not particularly meaningful – it certainly doesn't mark the beginning of time.
- *Continuous* data can take on any value within determined limits. For example, the cost of a book could be anything between £0.01 and, say, £100,000.

Calculating averages and standard deviations

The most common analysis carried out on quantitative data is the calculation of averages. However, the term 'average' can mean a number of different things, and the type of average used will depend on the type of data (see above) and the aim of the analysis:

- The most common average and what is usually meant when the term 'average' is used on its own is the *arithmetic mean*. This is the sum of all the measurements divided by the total number of measurements.
- The *median* is the central point of a distribution. Half of the individual measurements are above the median and half below.
- The *mode* is the value which occurs most frequently.

It is often useful to calculate the *standard deviation* from the arithmetic mean to show how dispersed the data are or, looking at it the other way, how tightly they are clustered around the mean. For example, this might show that most library users visit the library a similar number of times, with a few exceptions, or it could show that there is very wide variation in the number of visits. The arithmetic mean could be the same but the standard deviation would show up the difference.

Significance tests

The key question that needs to be asked when quantitative data have been analysed is, 'is this result statistically significant?'. The idea behind this question is to test the likelihood of a key threat to the validity of any results that are produced, namely that the effect being reported came about purely by chance. Unless a whole population or very large sample has been taken, it is almost impossible to *guarantee* that the result obtained was not simply a matter of chance. For example, if a coin is tossed ten times, most people will acknowledge that there is a possibility that it will land tails ten times, even though the probability is low. But there is also a chance, albeit with much lower probability, that it will land tails 100 times or even 1000 times in a row. The statistical significance test is intended to tell us how likely it is that instead of a real phenomenon, what we are seeing is a chance result.

It is beyond the scope of this book to discuss the many different significance tests in detail. The selection of appropriate tests is a complex issue but one of the most common tests can be used as an example of some of the key considerations.

The χ^2 test is a *non-parametric* test used to check *goodness of fit* and *independence*:

- *Non-parametric* means that it does not assume knowledge of the underlying distribution of the population being studied. For example, it is not necessary to know what the mean value is for the population as a whole.
- *Goodness of fit* tests how well the observed values fit the values that were expected according to the *null hypothesis*, which is the hypothesis that is being tested. For example, the null hypothesis might be that a new library service makes no difference to the library's users.
- *Independence* tests whether there is any association between what are believed to be independent variables. If the variables are truly independent then we can say that knowledge of one tells us nothing about the other. For example we might establish that knowledge of the gender of library users tells us nothing about the books they are likely to borrow, or we might, through the χ^2 test, establish that there is a high probability that these variables *are* related.

The actual calculation of χ^2 is quite complex because it is necessary to calculate *degrees of freedom* and to verify whether various conditions are fulfilled. A table of χ^2 values can then be checked to discover p, the probability that the result came about by chance. The convention is that if p is equal to or less than 0.05, then the results are statistically significant. However, this is an arbitrary cut-off point and the decision on significance should be taken by considering all the factors.

Many of the averages, other characteristics and tests of significance can be carried out automatically by packages like SPSS. However, it is vital that they are not used without a clear understanding of their appropriateness and meaning.

■ Qualitative data

The general idea with the analysis of qualitative data is to try to establish connections between data elements, so as to extract themes and exceptions to those themes. For example, we might be trying to establish what the general opinion of users is about the library's book selection criteria. We might also try to identify exceptions to the general opinions expressed. Because the raw data are usually in the form of text (or audio) the term *content analysis* is often used: it is defined as 'any technique for making inferences by objectively and systematically identifying specified characteristics of messages' (Holsti, 1969). Bear in mind the three-step process described in the introduction to this appendix.

- *Data reduction*. The first step is to become familiar with the data. For example, interview transcripts should be listened to or read through several times. At that point a start can be made on coding. Specific themes can be identified and the transcripts marked up or tagged to show occurrences. A particular passage may of course have more than one tag.
- *Data display*. This involves grouping data together and organizing them in such a way that connections can be identified and tested.
- *Drawing conclusions*, which in essence means taking the tentative conclusions from the ways in which the data have been displayed and checking them for consistency and validity.

One of the critical factors which will need to be taken into account is the nature of the data collected. For example, unstructured data, such as an interview transcript, may need a different approach from structured data such as a series of textual answers to items in a questionnaire. It is also worth remembering that data entry and data reduction are both valuable in beginning to understand the content and for this reason some analysts prefer to undertake this work themselves rather than leave it to an assistant.

As with quantitative data analysis, it is perfectly possible to analyse small amounts of qualitative data by manual means, or to use general purpose software packages such as Microsoft Word or OpenOffice Writer. Indeed, where there is a limited amount of data to analyse, it can sometimes be more efficient to annotate a printout with coloured highlighter pens or even to copy data onto Post-It notes which can then be arranged and re-arranged in themes (as above).

However, with larger datasets and where more sophisticated analysis is needed, it is better to make use of a software package designed for the purpose. This class of software is known as computer assisted qualitative data analysis software (CAQDAS). The leading packages are Atlas.ti and Nudist. The former is generally regarded as more sophisticated and has a hypertext structure with an intuitive user interface. The latter is sometimes regarded as rather more advanced in the way it handles coding. In many ways, however, the choice is a matter of personal preferences and experience. They both do the same job. In brief, they help the researcher to link together *data* and *concepts* through *coding*. The codes can be thought of as labels which are applied to pieces of text or other media. They enable similarities in the data to be identified, even where different words may have been used. In this way commonalities are identified and themes are established.

The process of analysing qualitative data involves a series of steps:

1 Immersion in the data in order to start to comprehend them. Above all, this stage enables the researcher to become familiar with the data and to start to see themes that may emerge.
2 Synthesis of themes by identifying quotations and tagging them in a meaningful way. In essence this is a process of finding the common threads. Note that this is a process of *inductive*, rather than *deductive*, reasoning. The aim is to find statements which are likely to be true from the evidence gathered.
3 Paying attention to 'outliers' – data which seem to tell a different story – sometimes called *negative case analysis*. This helps the study to embrace

the concept of variability, rather than trying to find 'one size fits all' explanations.

4 This leads into a stage of theorizing, developing explanations for the observed phenomena. At this point is it is important to be open to alternative explanations. One way to check these out is to go back to respondents and ask them if they find your explanations convincing.

5 In the context of performance measurement, there may be no need to go further than this but in the classical application of grounded theory and related approaches (see Chapter 2, 'Theoretical considerations') there would then be a stage of refining the emergent theory and examining how well it fits into the broader context. In performance measurement terms this might be accomplished by comparing the findings with those of previous, related studies.

It is important to maintain links to the context of each quotation that is extracted, as these are vital when the data and conclusions are presented (see Appendix 3, 'The presentation of results').

■ Sources of further information

- There are many introductions to data analysis available, including Rowntree (2000). Among the best online resources is Gerard Dellal's *Little Handbook of Statistical Practice* (www.StatisticalPractice.com) and the *Electronic Statistics Textbook* (www.statsoft.com/textbook/stathome. html). If you would like to try out the calculation of the χ^2 test, there is an online resource which does this for you at http://faculty.vassar.edu/ lowry/csfit.html.

- Training courses on a variety of software packages are readily available from local colleges or other training providers, although for the more complex software, especially for qualitative data analysis, it may be best to contact a local university.

- Spreadsheets and databases are covered by a wide variety of books and manuals, including Schmuller (2005) and Alexander and Zey (2006). SPSS is a complex tool and is best not used without prior training; however, Pallant (2005) provides a useful overview.

- Atlas.ti is again better used by those who have first attended a suitable training course. There is a helpful support website at www.atlasti.de/, including a downloadable demonstration. An example of its use in a library context can be found in Guidry (2002).

■ References

Alexander, M. and Zey, R. (2006) *Microsoft Access Data Analysis: unleashing the analytical power of Access*, Chichester, Wiley.

Guidry, J. A. (2002) LibQUAL^{TM} Spring 2001 Comments: a qualitative analysis using Atlas.ti, *Performance Measurement and Metrics*, **3** (2), 100–7.

Holsti, O. R. (1969) *Content Analysis for the Social Sciences and Humanities*, Reading MA, Addison-Wesley.

Miles, M. B. and Huberman, A. M. (1994) *Qualitative Data Analysis: an expanded source book*, London, Sage Publications.

Pallant, J. (2005) *SPSS Survival Manual: a step by step guide to data analysis using SPSS for Windows* (version 12), Maidenhead, Open University Press.

Rowntree, D. (2000) *Statistics Without Tears: an introduction for non-mathematicians*, London, Penguin.

Schmuller, J. (2005) *Statistical Analysis with Excel for Dummies*, Hoboken NJ, Wiley.

The presentation of results

■ Introduction

It is sometimes tempting to breathe a sigh of relief when the data collection is finished and the analysis is complete. The results are to hand, so what else needs to be done? In fact the next stage is one of the most crucial – the presentation of results to the intended audience in a manner which is both clear and unambiguous and which highlights critical issues. Hopefully, the purpose of the exercise will have been decided before the data collection itself was designed, so that the intention behind the whole activity will be clear. However, it is worth reiterating at this stage that performance measurement can be carried out for a wide range of reasons including:

- advocacy and public relations, or even self-justification
- accountability over the short or long term
- management of services with a view to change and improvement
- reallocation of resources between services, including innovation.

■ Deciding on the message

The most critical part of presentation is deciding on what the key message should be. Of course there may be more than one but it is worth bearing in mind that as the number increases the impact diminishes! A useful rule of thumb is that, except for extensive evaluations, it should be possible to write an executive summary (see also below) which is no more than one page in length. A reader with limited time will be able to absorb the main messages in this way, using the body of the report to explore detailed findings and the logical argument.

Regular reports may have a standard format or house style, so that there is no need to devise a new one each time, although such formats will of course need to be reviewed from time to time.

■ Deciding on the audiences

With an internal study, the audience may be obvious – the managers who commissioned it. However even here it is worth considering whether there are other audiences who need to, or have a right to, know about your findings. For example, a study of library circulation will also be of interest to staff who work on the issue desk.

With many studies there are multiple audiences: library management and institutional management would be a typical example. Here it is worth considering the production of alternative presentations, simply because matters which library managers will take for granted, may not be so obvious to those running a local authority or a university.

■ Forms of presentation

Although most performance measurement activities will result in some form of written report, there are alternatives and it may be necessary to present the report using other media. Typically these might include an oral presentation to a group of managers, perhaps using PowerPoint slides, or a web-based presentation.

■ Structuring the presentation

The classic structure for a written report has a lot to commend it. It consists of:

- a *title page*, giving a meaningful description, the author's name and affiliation and the date of the study
- an *executive summary*, which tells the reader very briefly what has been investigated, what has been discovered and what conclusions, including recommendations, have been reached
- an *introduction*, which sets out the location of the study, its background, its aims and objectives and the methods you have used; you may also

wish to refer to key literature, but this should be kept very short – you are not writing an essay or a thesis!

- your *results* – what the data you have collected and analysed are telling you
- your *conclusions*, derived from your results; a cardinal error is to write conclusions which on examination turn out to be based on presuppositions rather than the actual evidence to hand; include here a short section on the limitations of your study
- your *recommendations*; these should not just state what needs to be done but should suggest who should do it and within what timescale; you may also wish to recommend that there should be a further study, or a review, after a specified time has elapsed
- *appendices* can be used to present the actual data collected and any other material which is important to the study but not critical to the flow of the report; these may be made available separately in order to keep the size of the report within bounds, possibly via a website.

■ Presenting quantitative data

There is a danger with quantitative data that they can very easily be presented to appear to mean rather more than in fact they do. Indeed there is now a documented 'Lake Wobegon Effect', where every instance (that could be every library) turns out to be better than the norm. This is a reference to Garrison Keillor's mythical hometown where 'all the children are above average'!

Tables

Quantitative data are usually summarized in a table. The simplest type is the straightforward *frequency table*, which can be used to present categorical, nominal, ordinal and continuous data, the last type provided it has been grouped (as in Table A3.1 opposite, which shows the age distribution of respondents to a survey).

An additional column might be added to such a table to show the percentage of values falling in each group (row).

Table A3.1 A frequency table

Mark, %	Frequency
0–20	0
21–40	2
41–60	6
61–80	12
81–100	4

Table A3.2 Frequency table with percentages added

Mark, %	Frequency	Percentage
0–20	0	0.0
21–40	2	8.3
41–60	6	25.0
61–80	12	50.0
81–100	4	16.7
Total	24	100

Bar charts

Data from a frequency table can be plotted in a wide variety of ways. Perhaps the most familiar is the *bar chart*, in which the length and thus the area of the bars indicates frequency. In the example in Figure A3.1 on the next page, the display is of the satisfaction of users with the library's inter-library loan service. Note that the bar chart is similar to a histogram (see below) but that the data categories are not computable, e.g. it is not possible to say that they are of equal extent, as you could if they were, for example, ranges of the age of respondents.

A bar chart is a good way of showing data in categories where the aim is to highlight differences. Because the height of the bars is proportional to frequency it is easy to see at a glance both categories with high values and those with low, or zero, values. Bar charts usually have a gap between the bars, which can be drawn horizontally or vertically.

Pie charts

A pie chart is an alternative, where the area of the 'slice' indicates frequency. See Figure A3.2 on the next page.

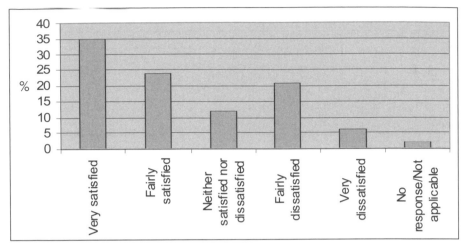

Figure A3.1 A bar chart

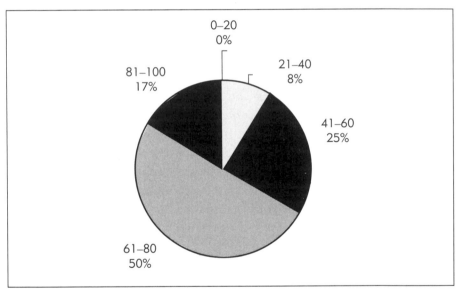

Figure A3.2 A pie chart

Pareto charts

A *Pareto chart* looks superficially like a bar chart but differs in that the data are presented in order by their frequency. For example, suppose a survey is undertaken to find the reasons that books supposedly available cannot be found on the shelves. The categories are the reasons, which might include:

- books mis-shelved
- books missing from stock
- catalogue record error
- system error.

Figure A3.3 shows the Pareto chart constructed from such data. The left hand vertical axis shows the number of occurrences while the right hand vertical axis shows percentages. The line is used to indicate cumulative percentages.

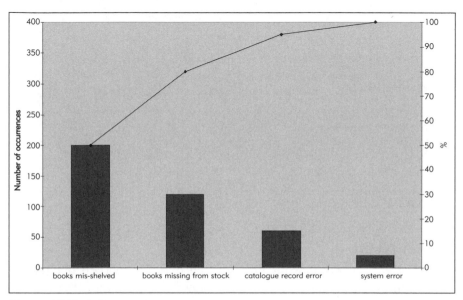

Figure A3.3 A Pareto chart

Pareto charts are useful for highlighting the most significant issues and for showing what percentages of problems could be resolved by solving the first *x* of these issues. In this example, if the problems associated with mis-shelving and with books which are missing from stock could be resolved, then 80% of the occurrences of failure at the shelves could be avoided.

Histograms

A *histogram* is used to depict distribution. It is like a bar chart (see above) but used to depict frequency data, with the *x* axis showing non-overlapping intervals of the dataset. The data in Table A3.2 could be used to draw a histogram either using the actual values or the percentages – the shape of the histogram would of course be identical. Figure A3.4 shows the former.

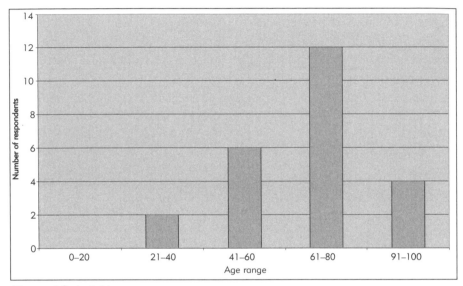

Figure A3.4 A histogram

Scatter plots

A *scatter plot* is a way of showing relationships between two sets of data and is often used to depict correlation. Suppose, for example, that we are interested in the relationship between the size of libraries' budgets and the number of books they issue. We might produce a plot of the kind shown in Figure A3.5 opposite, which appears to show that there is indeed a relationship between budget size and loans. Not all libraries display the same relationship and this in itself might be cause for comment.

Radar charts

Radar charts are another way of depicting data useful where the critical issue is to depict visually comparisons between several aspects of a situation. They are frequently used to show the results of a gap analysis and have been used for this purpose in the LibQUAL™ methodology, described in Chapter 3, 'User satisfaction' (see page 46).

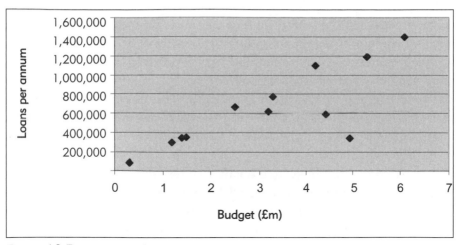

Figure A3.5 A scatter plot

Other ways of depicting quantitative data

There is a huge variety of other ways of presenting data so as to convey their meaning. With the ready availability of software like Microsoft Excel and OpenOffice Calc, it is now very easy to produce three dimensional charts and graphs, to explode pie charts and so on. Animated presentations can be created in PowerPoint or Impress and can then, if desired, be exported into another document. With a little training, it is not difficult to create Flash presentations to include in a web page. In fact these techniques are now so accessible that there is a danger that the presentation can overshadow the content!

■ Presenting qualitative data

Most qualitative data are presented in the form of text, although frequently there will be supporting quantitative data, for example on demographics. As discussed in Appendix 2, 'The analysis of data', the organization of this data will usually be according to themes, revealed through the use of tagging during analysis. Very often there is a huge amount of data, which makes selection for presentation difficult. However, by keeping in mind the audience for the report it is possible to select the most appropriate examples to illustrate the theories and findings that have emerged. Where the data being presented include quotations or descriptions of behaviour, perhaps in the words of interviewees, a consideration will be to find the most compelling examples but without compromising the integrity of the study.

For a qualitative study to be valid it is imperative that the interpretation and presentation is systematic and that it is fully grounded in the data which have been collected. Because this is so crucial, it is also important that the process used to interpret the data is made clear. This may be summarized in the text and, with a full report, would appear in greater detail in an appendix.

Presentation of findings from qualitative research will often be accompanied by comparison with the available published literature, or at least with parallel studies. These will be interwoven in such a way that the reader can see the juxtaposition of conclusions from the study being reported, the data examples chosen to illustrate those findings and relevant material from other sources. However, this can lead to a temptation to indulge in general discussions; the key is to remain close to the data which have been collected in the study being reported.

In order to enable the reader to follow the argument, it is particularly important with qualitative studies that there is a clear, logical progression from one concept or finding to the next in the results section of your report. Each topic should be introduced, evidenced and discussed and then a link created to the next. At the end all the findings should be drawn together in some way.

Where evidence is presented in the form of quotations it is important to identify where the quotation comes from, while maintaining anonymity and confidentiality. This may be achieved by stating the type of respondent (e.g. student, teacher, administrator, librarian). In some cases it may be appropriate to give a letter code to identify individuals. As an example, the following quotation is derived from the final report of the Non-Visual Access to the Digital Library: the use of digital library interfaces by blind and visually impaired people (NoVA) Project (www.cerlim.ac.uk/projects/nova/nova_final_report.pdf) where users with visual impairments and those in a control group were interviewed about their experiences of using websites. It illustrates one method of attributing comments:

> It tells me that there is a text-only version. I tend to steer clear of them because they are often not as up to date as the graphical version
>
> (visually impaired user D).

It is worth emphasizing that quotations should normally be presented as they were recorded, without correcting grammar. Exceptions may be made to clarify the meaning but these should always be placed in square brackets.

A final issue in presenting qualitative results is that of minimizing researcher bias. Since everyone interprets the world in their own way (see Chapter 2, 'Theoretical considerations') there is a real danger that the selectivity necessary to present evidence in a meaningful way will lead to partial reporting. One way to avoid this is to use *peer debriefing*, which in essence means sharing data and interim analyses with colleagues. Another possibility is to use extensive quotations, which provide the reader with opportunities to cross-check the conclusions being drawn. Triangulation of methods (see Chapter 1, 'Background') is a further counter to researcher bias.

■ Resources

- Standard spreadsheet, presentation and other readily available packages contain some sophisticated tools for presenting data. Most spreadsheet packages, for example, will automatically generate a range of different types of chart.
- *The Little Handbook of Statistical Practice* has a helpful section entitled 'Look at the data!' at www.tufts.edu/~gdallal/plots.htm.
- The Economics and Social Research Council (ESRC) has developed a Communications Toolkit (www.esrc.ac.uk/ESRCInfoCentre/Support/Communications_Toolkit/), which includes sections such as a step-by-step guide to developing a communications strategy and 'Creating a communications culture internally'. Although intended for holders of research grants, there is useful advice that can be applied more generally.

Index

Evaluating the Impact of your Library
Sharon Markless and David Streatfield

Having a full understanding of impact is the key to library service development. Focusing on impact should help in thinking creatively about the service, making the case for resources, enabling sound development planning and enhancing job satisfaction.

It can be difficult to get a grip on the rather slippery concept of service impact, but the authors have developed an effective answer. Their rigorously tested evidence-based approach helps LIS managers to work through a structured process of impact evaluation linked directly to their own objectives and priorities.

The core chapters of the book take managers through this process model for impact assessment, backed by tools and examples to equip them with all that they need to address their own service impact questions. Chapters cover:

- the demand for evidence
- getting to grips with impact
- the research base of this work
- setting objectives, success criteria and impact indicators
- activities and process indicators
- thinking about, gathering and interpreting evidence
- setting targets and development planning
- moving forward.

This book is an essential tool for practising library and information service managers and policy makers in the field. It is equally relevant to public, education, health and special libraries and information services, and is also of value to higher education professionals and students.

2006; 192pp; hardback; ISBN 978-1-85604-488-2; £39.95

Developing Strategic Marketing Plans that Really Work
A toolkit for public libraries

Terry Kendrick

Many government and other reports stress the need to get public libraries back into the lives of potential users. However, it quickly becomes apparent to public librarians that marketing is far more than simply creating a set of leaflets. What they need is a simple, practical guide to an integrated marketing planning process, from initial goals to implementation of marketing strategies.

This highly practical and down-to-earth book, with free, downloadable templates and forms on the web, will de-mystify the marketing planning process and set it in the context of modern public library services. Through a series of easy-to-implement process steps the reader will see not just what is possible but what is likely to work quickly, and deliver real impact on performance indicators, in a public library context. The book is structured as follows:

- ambition as the basis for marketing planning
- making sense of the market for public library services
- creating segment-specific value propositions for users and non-users
- priorities: making sound choices
- clear objectives and winning strategies
- attention-grabbing marketing communications
- implementation and quick progress.

The text is fully international in scope and is written for those practitioners at all levels of library management who recognize the importance of marketing planning in shaping and positively influencing the direction of public library services.

2006; 240pp; paperback; ISBN 978-1-85604-548-3; £34.95

Managing Change
A how-to-do-it manual for librarians

Susan Carol Curzon

. . . required reading . . . ONLINE

Managing Change may become a constant companion.
CANADIAN LIBRARY JOURNAL

Guiding staff and organizations through turbulent times – budget cuts, personnel shortages, new technologies, reorganization and consolidation – is an absolutely necessary skill for today's library managers. Susan Curzon, one of Library Journal's Librarians of the Year, has completely revised her classic change manual.

This guide outlines the step-by-step processes and detailed instructions necessary for conceptualizing the issues; planning; preparing; decision-making; controlling resistance; and implementing changes. Practical guidance for dealing with technology's impact on libraries, applying the latest research in change management, and developing new strategies for coping with change are included.

An all new 'Teaching Tools' section – featuring sample scenarios; questions and discussion points; coaching prompts; motivational tips; and more – helps managers share the knowledge with their staff and colleagues. With a foreword by Michael Gorman, this updated essential guide will help you not only cope – but thrive – in our constantly changing library environment.

2006; 144pp; paperback; ISBN 978-1-85604-601-5; £39.95